Praise for *Toxic Beauty*

"Most American women have no clue that the 'rugged individual' model held up for emulation includes placing the responsibility for one's health and safety squarely on the consumer's shoulder! When it come to cosmetics, each woman is on her own in judging safety of products with no meaningful information from the producer and no aid from government watch-dogs. The research, if done at all, can be withheld by the company. Dr. Samuel Epstein is the first to speak out on this 'Toxic Beauty' product hazard, and to give women some guidelines for meaningful protective action. It is a 'must-read' for all those who care about public health!"

—DR. ROSALIE BERTELL

"*Toxic Beauty* is the most important book of the decade. As a medical doctor, Sam Epstein clearly understands the causes of diseases such as cancer, diabetes, and other inflammatory diseases through the exposure to petrochemical and synthetic toxins found in everyday consumer products. This book is a transparent truth of the consumer industry. It is a must-read for everyone."

—HORST M. RECHELBACHER, founder of Aveda

"If you are a woman *Toxic Beauty* is a guide that is crucial for your library. It is loaded with practical tools and resources to help you navigate the surprising and shockingly toxic secrets of the personal care products industry, and help you preserve your good health while maintaining or improving your beauty."

—DR. MERCOLA, founder of Mercola.com, most visited
natural health site in the world

Other Books by Samuel S. Epstein, MD

The Mutagenicity of Pesticides (1971)

Drugs of Abuse: Their Genetic and Other Chronic Nonpsychiatric Hazards (1971)

The Legislation of Product Safety: Consumer Health and Product Hazards (1974)

The Politics of Cancer (1978)

Hazardous Wastes in America (1982)

Cancer in Britain: The Politics of Prevention (1983)

The Safe Shopper's Bible (1995)

The Breast Cancer Prevention Program (1998)

The Politics of Cancer, Revisited (1998)

Unreasonable Risk: How to Avoid Cancer and Other Toxic Effects from Cosmetics and Personal Care Products: The Neways Story (2001; Second Edition, 2005)

GOT (genetically engineered) MILK! The Monsanto rBGH/BST Milk Wars Handbook (2001)

The Stop Cancer Before It Starts Campaign: How to Win the Losing War Against Cancer (2003)

Cancer-Gate: How to Win the Losing Cancer War (2005)

Shopper Beware: How to Avoid Cancer and Other Toxic Effects from Cosmetics and Personal Care Products (Japan, 2006)

What's In Your Milk? (2006)

Other Books by Randall Fitzgerald

The Hundred Year Lie: How Food and Medicine are Destroying Your Health (2006)

TOXIC BEAUTY

How Cosmetics and Personal-Care Products Endanger Your Health . . . And What You Can Do About It

SAMUEL S. EPSTEIN, MD
WITH RANDALL FITZGERALD

BENBELLA BOOKS, INC.
Dallas, TX

BENBELLA

BenBella Books, Inc.
6440 N. Central Expressway, Suite 503
Dallas, TX 75206
www.benbellabooks.com
Send feedback to feedback@benbellabooks.com

Printed in the United States of America
10 9 8 7 6 5 4 3 2 1

Library of Congress Cataloging-in-Publication Data is available for this title.
ISBN 978-1933771-62-5

Proofreading by Stacia Seaman and Jennifer Canzoneri
Cover design by Laura Watkins
Text design and composition by PerfecType, Nashville, TN
Index by Shoshana Hurwitz
Printed by Bang Printing

Distributed by Perseus Distribution
perseusdistribution.com

To place orders through Perseus Distribution:
Tel: 800-343-4499
Fax: 800-351-5073
E-mail: orderentry@perseusbooks.com

Significant discounts for bulk sales are available. Please contact
Robyn White at robyn@benbellabooks.com or (214) 750-3600.

To my wondrous wife Catherine, who has made all things possible.

CONTENTS

FOREWORD

To varying degrees, the American public, as well as that of other nations, is exposed to carcinogenic and other toxic pollutants in air, water, and the workplace. At least minimally, these exposures are all subject to explicit federal regulation.

Nevertheless, the entire American public remains exposed to carcinogenic and other toxic ingredients in consumer products—household, food, cosmetics, and personal care. While today's consumers increasingly want to make informed shopping decisions, nearly all are still doing so in the dark. They receive highly misleading information from the industries involved, while the Food and Drug Administration (FDA), the supposedly responsible regulatory agency, remains recklessly silent.

Of particular concern are cosmetics and personal-care products. These are regulated under the 1938 FDA Federal Food, Drug, and Cosmetic Act, which requires that all ingredients in these products must be labeled on their containers. The Act also gives the FDA authority to protect consumers from dangerous products, including requiring that their labels must bear a clear warning statement to prevent any health hazard. However, seven decades after the Act was passed, the FDA still takes the reckless position that the industry is responsible and accountable for the safety of its products. Accordingly, the FDA fails to regulate the industry, let alone warn the public of the dangers of its products. It's no wonder that, at the 1997 hearings on the FDA Reform Bill, Senator Edward Kennedy warned that, "The cosmetics industry has borrowed a page from the playbook of the tobacco industry by putting profits ahead of public health."

In reader-friendly language and with meticulous scientific documentation, Dr. Epstein details the wide range of toxic ingredients in currently marketed cosmetics and personal-care products along with those ingredients' effects. The ingredients fall into five categories, and are listed in five tables: frank carcinogens, hidden carcinogens (carcinogens that contaminate other ingredients, or ingredients that are precursors of carcinogens), endocrine disruptors (ingredients that are hormonally toxic, particularly to women and their fetuses), penetrating agents (ingredients that pass through the skin), and allergens. Other tables list the toxic ingredients in a wide range of common products.

Fortunately, *Toxic Beauty* is not a gloom and doom book. Also listed are safe alternative products, including those that are certified organic. Concerned and responsible shoppers can readily download the book's five tables on toxic ingredients from the author's Cancer Prevention Coalition Web site, www.preventcancer.com, or from NaturalNews.com. They can then use these tables while shopping to avoid buying products with toxic ingredients.

Dr. Epstein is well recognized as a leading international expert and crusader on avoidable causes of cancer and other life-threatening diseases. I have known him well for more than two decades, and have endorsed his critical initiatives in protecting our health and lives.

The importance of the information in this book cannot be overstated. *Toxic Beauty* is a must-read for all concerned citizens.

Quentin D. Young, M.D.
Chairman, Health and Medicine Policy Research Group, Chicago
Past President, American Public Health Association

INTRODUCTION
Why You're at Risk

If you're a woman reading this book, you have a one in eight chance of getting breast cancer during your lifetime. You probably already know someone from your family, or from your circle of friends and acquaintances, who has battled this disease and lost, if not her life, then pieces of her body. The psychological toll alone from breast cancer and chemotherapy can be devastating, and anything designed to help relieve the pain, the suffering, and the self-image concerns would normally seem a godsend.

When it comes to our health and the knowledge we need to influence it, even the best of intentions can go awry and exact the cruelest consequences. When the "Look Good . . . Feel Better" program began in 1989, it had the noble-sounding goal of teaching breast cancer patients techniques to help restore their appearance and self-image during and following their treatment. Established by the Cosmetic, Toiletry, and Fragrance Association (the U.S. trade association later renamed the Personal Care Products Council), along with the National Cosmetology Association, the program gives away more than 1 million cosmetics and personal-care products each year to about 30,000 breast cancer patients. Further adding to the program's aura of legitimacy, it is administered nationwide by the non-profit American Cancer Society (ACS), which trains volunteers and acts as the scientific authority endorsing the program and its products.

The products donated by the twenty-two participating major cosmetic companies, including eye and cheek colors, lipsticks, moisture lotions, and other make-ups, surely assist these women in restoring their self-image and rebuilding their social and professional lives. What could possibly be wrong with such a compassionate program, you might ask, especially since it has a seal of approval from the ACS?

Here is where the story takes an unexpected turn. In 2005, acting out of curiosity and longstanding concerns about the ACS and the companies involved in the program, I reviewed the ingredients in Look Good kit products and discovered that ten of the twelve products contained toxic ingredients. Estée Lauder's LightSource Transforming Moisture Lotion, Chanel's Sheer Lipstick, and Merle Norman Eye Color, for instance, all contain ingredients incriminated as carcinogenic, contaminated with carcinogens, or demonstrated to be precursors of carcinogens.

A carcinogen, for those of you who have read or heard the word, but are uncertain of its meaning, is a chemical shown in standard tests by recognized scientific authorities, the National Toxicology Program, or by the International Agency for Research on Cancer, to cause cancer in mice, rats, or directly in humans.

The Look Good products also contain ingredients, notably paraben preservatives, one of which has been incriminated as a probable cause of breast cancer, that disrupt the normal hormone processes of the body. Warnings by the ACS over the years have cautioned breast cancer patients who are undergoing chemotherapy not to use hormonal creams because hormone-disruptive chemicals can delay recovery or even trigger a recurrence of cancer. But here is a program scientifically endorsed and promoted by the ACS that distributes cosmetics to breast cancer patients which contain hormone-disruptive ingredients.

How can one possibly explain or excuse the "Look Good" program? The answer to that question has a lot to do with why we have been losing the war against cancer ever since it was declared by President Nixon in 1971. Spending on the cancer war by the taxpayer-funded National Cancer Institute has always been predominantly directed to diagnosis and to treatment, virtually excluding support for prevention and informing the public of avoidable causes of cancer. These misplaced priorities have contributed to a state of mind within the broader "cancer establishment" and the public at large that makes programs like "Look Good . . . Feel Better" deeply flawed.

To understand that state of mind, consider the conflict of interest that arises as a result of where the ACS gets its substantial funding, apart from public donations. The major cosmetics and personal-care companies that distribute complimentary products through the "Look Good" program are also big donors to ACS, each contributing a minimum of $100,000. These "Excalibur Donors," as the ACS calls them, also include petrochemical, power plant, and hazardous waste industries, whose environmental pollutants have also been incriminated as major causes of breast and other cancers.

Caveat Emptor Means Buyer Beware

Many people in the German-speaking countries of Austria, Germany, and parts of Switzerland can look at a product label and say, "I would never buy this product because it contains these toxic ingredients." They educate themselves about what they use and display a sensitivity to what is safe, in contrast to most U.S. consumers, who remain uninformed. Even the majority of U.S. toxicologists are poorly informed about the toxic ingredients in everyday consumer products. This lack of awareness among North Americans is one of the reasons why I felt the strong need to write this book.

U.S. consumers generally assume that if any cosmetic or personal-care product posed a danger to health, the U.S. Food and Drug Administration (FDA) would warn us. This faith and trust is woefully misplaced. A tragic example occurred in April 2007, when a seventeen-year-old cross-country runner at Notre Dame Academy on Staten Island, New York, died after absorbing high levels of a chemical ingredient from sports creams she had applied to her skin. The track star's mother still could not believe a skin cream could kill and was quoted as telling reporters, "I did not think an over-the-counter product could be unsafe."

Even though the 1938 Federal Food, Drug, and Cosmetic Act explicitly directs the FDA to require that "The label of cosmetic products shall bear a warning statement . . . to prevent a health hazard that may be associated with a product," the FDA still marches to the beat of industry drummers' assurances of safety. Most people would be surprised to learn that the 1938 Act *does not* require cosmetics or personal-care products and their ingredients to be approved as safe before they are marketed and sold to consumers. FDA oversight begins only after consumers have become guinea pigs in the marketplace—which often means *after* some of those consumers have become public health statistics.

Virtually everybody takes for granted that our everyday personal-care products and cosmetics are harmless and tested for safety. We also believe that the deodorants, shampoos, soaps, perfumes, lipsticks, and dozens of other common products in our lives are conveniences we should be entitled to enjoy without fear of any dangerous consequences. *Toxic Beauty* reveals a shocking truth—most of these products carry invisible price tags, with hidden costs to our health and to our lives.

Nearly one out of every two men and more than one out of every three women will get cancer in their lifetime. The cosmetics and personal-care product industries bear significant responsibility for this health crisis. Every day at least three personal-care products are applied to the skin of infants and children. Men use an average of ten, and women use six or more cosmetics and an average of thirteen personal-care products. Some products are used several times a day, such as fragranced soaps. If you add up all of the individual ingredients in each of these products, you discover that you expose yourself to dozens of toxins daily.

More than 10,500 personal-care and cosmetic products are sold in North America, yet few have ever been assessed for their impact on human health. The prevailing attitude of the industry and its individual companies—and the FDA—is that these products and their ingredients are innocent until proven guilty. So how is guilt established? When sufficient numbers of people sicken or die. But even that cruel standard fails to reveal the full dimensions of our health challenge because the harm from these chemicals often occurs over extended periods of time and involves exposures to multiple toxic ingredients. There is no practical scientific way by which their toxic effects can be differentiated from the effects of exposure to other toxic industrial chemicals. The cosmetic and personal-care product industries use this uncertainty to create a smokescreen from behind which they claim that the concentrations of toxic ingredients in their products are too tiny and insignificant to cause harm.

To illustrate the dimensions of what we confront, consider the fact that at least 3,000 mostly synthetic chemicals are used in the U.S. by the fragrance industry alone. At least 900 of them have been identified as having some degree of toxicity by the National Institute of Occupational Safety and Health. This is the main reason why this book spotlights labeling practices that mask and distort the identity of ingredients that could harm us. By hiding behind trade secrecy laws, manufacturers keep all of us ignorant about what really lurks inside their products, enabling them to cut corners, if not ignore safety altogether, to maximize their profits.

Some of the ingredients in these products become unwelcome squatters in our body fat and organs. More than 10,000 U.S. citizens of all ages and walks of life have had their blood tested over the past decade by the U.S. Centers for Disease Control and Prevention in attempts to determine the extent of the "body burden" of synthetic chemicals that we all absorb during the course of "normal" living. By even conservative estimates, we carry trace amounts of hundreds of these chemicals in our bodies at any one time. Many of these chemicals come from our daily contact with toxic ingredients in cosmetics and personal-care products.

Another group of toxic ingredients found in cosmetics and personal-care products, allergens, produce reactions on the skin and can sometimes become severe. As these ingredients have proliferated in products, sensitivity to these ingredients has spread within the general population. In the nearly thirty countries comprising the European Union, warning labels are required on perfumes and fragrances that contain twenty-six known allergens, while in the U.S. no such requirement exists. Even when U.S. companies label their products as "fragrance-free" or "hypoallergenic," you cannot be sure this is the case: these terms are often misleading or meaningless because manufacturers are not required to test or prove these claims.

Cosmetics and personal-care products today constitute our single largest but generally unrecognized class of avoidable exposure to toxic ingredients and their health dangers. These products are so potentially dangerous because:

Our skin is highly permeable. Less than one-tenth of an inch thick, skin is a porous membrane that is highly sensitive to toxic chemicals. What we put on our skin affects our health just as much as, if not more than, what we put in our mouths.

Penetration enhancers make skin even more permeable. There is an entire category of chemicals used in many cosmetics and personal-care products, called "penetration enhancers," that are designed to make other ingredients penetrate the skin more readily and deeply. A new penetration enhancer, minute atom-sized ingredients known as nanoparticles, is now being increasingly added to some of these products, notably sunblocks. These penetrating agents force anti-wrinkle cream, moisturizers, and other ingredients deep into the skin, where they can reach the bloodstream and, through it, the entire body, with unpredictable toxic effects.

Toxic ingredients applied to skin bypass liver enzymes. To varying degrees, all carcinogens and other toxic ingredients in personal-care and beauty products are absorbed through your skin, directly into your blood, and then circulate all over your body. These ingredients bypass the detoxifying enzymes in your liver that protect you from toxins in food. That means the harmful chemicals that you apply to your skin are much more toxic, and pose greater cancer and other risks, than if you *ate them*. To quote from Horst Rechelbacher, past president of Aveda and now CEO of Intelligent Nutrients, "Don't put anything on your skin that you wouldn't put in your mouth."

Toxic ingredients produce cumulative effects. Your multiple everyday exposures to carcinogens and other toxics from multiple cosmetics and personal-care products pose unpredictable additional dangers to health. Some ingredients interact on your skin or in your body, adding to each other's toxic effects. Other ingredients, when they interact, multiply their toxic effects, causing damage far beyond what any one toxin would have done on its own.

Exposure to toxic ingredients is prolonged. When you spray or roll deodorant under your arms, splash or rub perfume on yourself, or apply any other personal-care and beauty products, their ingredients can persist on your skin for extended periods, resulting in prolonged opportunity for absorption. Also, your exposure to these products started early, even in the womb, when your mother applied products to her body, absorbed many of them, and passed some on to you through the placenta.

Some elements of my message about the health impacts of our exposure to industrial chemicals has seeped into the popular press. Cancer researcher Devra Davis, Ph.D., writing in a February 2007 issue of *Newsweek* magazine, offered this warning: "We're beginning to realize that the sum total of a person's exposure to all the little amounts of cancerous agents in the environment may be just as harmful as big doses of a few well-known carcinogens. Our chances of getting cancer reflect the full gamut of carcinogens we're exposed to each day—in air, water and food pollution and in cancerous ingredients or contaminants in household cleaners, clothing, furniture, and the dozens of personal-care products many of us use daily."

You will learn in this book how preventable exposures to toxic ingredients in cosmetics and personal-care products take place daily in your home, as well as during every trip to your beauty or nail salon. You will also find out about safe alternatives, particularly organic, to most toxic ingredients, and what you can do to protect yourself, your family, and your friends.

This book will expose numerous self-serving industry myths. Prominent among them are the growing claims about anti-aging products. Over the past decade, our culture's preoccupation with appearing youthful has inspired the industry to produce a line of products known as cosmeceuticals. Existing in a gray area between cosmetics and drugs, cosmeceuticals are now the fastest growing sector of the cosmetic industry and yet one of the least scrutinized. In these pages you will learn the disturbing truth about these products: that the great majority of them have highly questionable, if any, benefits, and many can be toxic.

Another myth revolves around how the chemical industry and its cosmetics and personal-care companies try to reassure us that, so long as carcinogenic ingredients or contaminant amounts remain below their arbitrarily defined "thresholds," or safe limits, they create no toxic effects. The poison is only in the dose, they tell us, and claim (falsely) that the doses to which we are exposed are too low to be harmful. This mantra is misleading salesmanship rather than basic science. There is an overwhelming scientific consensus that there is no basis for assigning safe limits or thresholds for carcinogens. Self-interested attempts to argue or prove the contrary amount to a reckless abuse of consumer trust, and the health consequences of this abuse will be felt for generations to come.

An Information Deficit Exists

Cosmetics remain a huge and immensely profitable business, with annual sales of about $50 billion in the U.S. alone, and $2 billion spent on advertising. While there are hundreds of companies involved in this ever-growing business, most brands and products are controlled by just a few global giants, notably Estée Lauder, Max Factor, Procter & Gamble, Revlon, and L'Oreal, and their subsidiary companies.

Over a decade ago, during U.S. Senate committee hearings, Sen. Edward Kennedy of Massachusetts warned the public that "The cosmetics industry has borrowed a page from the playbook of the tobacco industry by putting profits ahead of public health." As information in this book will demonstrate, the truth of that statement has since been more than adequately confirmed.

When we try to be conscientious in our buying choices, we face a series of virtually insurmountable obstacles to the exercise of common sense. It is not only trade secrecy that thwarts us in our attempts at self-education; there is also the confusion inherent in ingredient identification. While the U.S. and all other nations require the labeling of the ingredients in cosmetics and personal-care products, at best this is often uninformative. Labels present such an alphabet soup of complex chemical names that most of us need a toxicology dictionary to read them. But without guidance as to which ingredients are safe or harmful, such dictionaries will remain useless and consumers will continue to flounder blindly in uncertainty. This book is intended to help provide that guidance by demystifying the complicated ingredient names and the frequently misleading product labels they appear on. Consumers should have an absolute right to know—and understand—what carcinogens and other ingredients and contaminants are in their cosmetics and personal-care products.

Cosmetics and personal-care products remain unregulated by the FDA. There are no requirements for the safety testing of ingredients, or for label warnings identifying those ingredients known to pose cancer risk, hormonal danger, or allergenic and other toxic effects. Making matters worse, for decades the FDA has taken no regulatory action against products containing known toxic ingredients, such as seizure, recall, or requirement of "black box" warning labels. Taking advantage of the FDA's regulatory abdication, the cosmetics industry continues to market products containing toxic ingredients to unsuspecting consumers by boasting that if their products were unsafe, the FDA would alert us.

In recognition of these serious dangers and the virtual absence of information about them, the 1995 *The Safe Shopper's Bible,* which I co-authored, reviewed some 4,000 U.S. consumer products. These included cosmetics and personal-care products, household products, and food. The book provided detailed, reader-friendly listings of ingredients that posed risks of cancer, allergy, and other toxic effects. It also provided information on safe alternative products, generally sold by small non-mainstream companies. The book was designed to encourage consumers to vote with their shopping dollars and, in the absence of needed regulation, tilt the marketplace in favor of safe alternative companies and products. Despite legal threats from unfavorably rated companies, the book was published and became a bestseller. Subsequently, I was and remain inundated with requests for further information from the public, news media, and also from a few companies whose products had been unfavorably rated and who have responsively sought safe alternatives. *Toxic Beauty* builds and expands on *The Safe Shopper's Bible* to provide consumers with the most up-to-date and comprehensive information available on the range of unrecognized risks to health from exposure to toxic ingredients through cosmetics and personal-care products.

Safe Alternatives Have Emerged

Fortunately for all of us, and for future generations, a quiet revolution in our thinking and our approach toward toxins is now underway. This sea change in attitudes holds the promise of transforming our roles as consumers, while giving us the power to influence both the marketplace and the institutions that mold public policy concerning what is safe for us to consume.

This trend toward voluntary and economy-driven corporate consumerism and environmentalism takes many forms and has already proven superior to a reliance on ideological or legislative attempts to reduce toxin use. Consumers are banding together to punish chemically reckless companies by boycotting their products. Simultaneously they are rewarding the growing number of conscientious companies that market safe products based on readily available safe synthetic or organic ingredients. From 2002 to 2004, the number of new organic cosmetics and personal-care products more than doubled, from 350 to 840. Also, some supermarket and other chains began to develop their own organic product lines, to lower costs and entice more low-income customers. This book will show you how organic products are not only safer, but have become as effective as mainstream products containing toxic ingredients.

Given that we are exposed to hundreds of chemical pollutants every day in air, water, and food, you may wonder why we should focus on cosmetics and personal-care products. The answer is that, in contrast to pollutants in air and water, over which we have little or no control, we can exercise considerable control over what we put on our skin through personal choice. The toxins in cosmetics and personal-care products are not only the single most avoidable category of threats to our health, they are also the category with the widest range of emerging alternative safe products.

Risk prevention and safe alternatives to toxic chemicals are inter-connected themes throughout these pages. Faced with the reckless indifference of the FDA, along with that of other arms of government, it is up to each of us to take the initiative in protecting our own health. In that spirit, it is our intent and our hope that this book will be a useful self-defense manual for protecting you and your family.

PART ONE

How Our Products Got Toxic

1 | History's Beauty Industry Influences

"What's past is prologue," as William Shakespeare wrote, which is one reason why the history of cosmetics and personal-care products may hold clues to how and why they became the collection of concealed chemical dangers we know today.

Credit often goes to the last pharaoh of ancient Egypt, Cleopatra, for inspiring the creation of a cosmetics industry—and with it, a standard of beauty—that continues to affect our lives 2,000 years later. During her reign from 51 to 30 B.C., her choices of body adornments made a fashion statement that influenced Egyptians, Greeks, and Romans alike. A Greek-speaking direct descendant of the Macedonian general who served under Alexander the Great, Cleopatra ruled over the tastes of the ancient world by drawing upon both Greek and Egyptian traditions of using minerals and other natural compounds to tint the face and fingernails. Her eye shadowing with kohl (a mixture of soot, burnt almonds, and malachite), which she also used to darken both her lashes and brows, and the way she tinted her nails by staining them with a flowering plant called henna, were said to be works of art.

These beauty practices may well have started several thousand years before Cleopatra, however, as an outgrowth of religious ceremonies. It is even thought that perfumery evolved from the burning of resins and gums as incense for ceremonial use. Certain types of cosmetics, or combinations of colors that denoted social class, could only be worn by members of the ruling elite, with violators subject to execution. A parallel tradition arose in China, where the wealthy wore nail polish fashioned from beeswax, gelatin, gum arabic, and egg whites, and only the nobility were allowed to paint their nails gold and silver, which signified the wealth of precious metals.

By 500 B.C., Greek women were applying lead and chalk powder to their faces and crushed mulberries as rouge. Roman women later adopted these practices and added the use of red lipstick made from ochre clays. "A woman without paint is like food without salt," wrote the Roman playwright Plautus (254–184 B.C.), expressing an attitude that prevailed among both sexes, that cosmetics were essential to a woman's sex appeal. But by the first century A.D., Roman poet and satirist Juvenal reflected a different perspective: "This coated face which is covered with so many drugs and where unfortunate husbands press their lips, is it a face or a sore?" He was acknowledging what many had come to suspect—that cosmetics containing toxic mercury compounds, and facial powders containing lead, posed a danger to the health of both the male admirers doing the kissing and those women being kissed.

Attitudes about cosmetics did not undergo another shift until one thousand years later, when the physician and cosmetologist Abu al-Qasim al-Zahrawi, a Spanish Moor also known by the name Abulcasis, wrote a thirty-volume medical practices encyclopedia in which one chapter was devoted solely to cosmetics. He believed that cosmetics constituted a legitimate branch of medicine, which he called the Medicine of Beauty—a concept that has been adopted by the twentieth century cosmetics industry with the advent of claimed anti-aging products.

The commercial perfume industry got its first official blessing in 1190 A.D. when Henry VI, who ruled both England and parts of France, issued patent letters to perfume sellers in Paris. Four centuries later another English monarch, Queen Elizabeth I, made the practice of wearing white lead paint facial make-up popular in the early years of her reign, but the fashion fell out of favor with many of her subjects during the black plague; rumors spread that cosmetics might pose a threat to health because they blocked "body vapors" from naturally circulating. (These concerns, warranted or not, might well constitute the first-ever consumer health alert.) During the subsequent reign of Charles II, however, the nobility and upper classes returned to the heavy use of make-up, including red rouge and lipstick, in the belief that it made them look younger and healthier. One concession to safety: zinc oxide began to replace lead as a facial powder.

Early eighteenth-century Italy saw facial powder at the center of the biggest scandal ever to befall a cosmetics manufacturer. A woman named Signora Toffana, who was well known in upper-class social circles, created a face powder that contained lead and arsenic and sold it to the wives of noblemen and the wealthy. The more affectionate the husband was with pecks on his wife's cheeks, the faster he died from the toxic powder. An estimated 600 husbands died this way, and Toffana was executed as an accomplice in their deaths.

During the reign of Britain's Queen Victoria in the late nineteenth century, cosmetics once again fell into disfavor in that country. The queen considered facial make-up to be vulgar and improper for ladies, and acceptable to wear only if you were an actor or a prostitute. Being simple and plain—which is to say, Victorian—went on to impact much of the English-speaking world's conception of beauty for many years.

The early twentieth century's spirit of discovery and innovation helped to jump-start renewed interest in matters of body care. During the two decades prior to the First World War, an unprecedented number of creations were unveiled that would transform the formulations of cosmetics, and create a personal-care products industry:

- A deodorant invented in Philadelphia and marketed as "Mum" was followed by other deodorants and antiperspirants containing aluminum chloride as the active ingredient.
- The first synthetic hair dye, called "Aureole," was created in the lab of a French chemist.
- Another chemist, in New York, formulated a synthetic mascara and named the product Maybelline, after his sister Mabel.
- In Baltimore, a pharmacist created a skin cream called Dr. Bunting's Sunburn Remedy, later known as Noxzema.

A marriage between celebrity status and public perceptions about the desirability of using cosmetics took firm root in the late nineteenth century with the spreading popularity of photography, and then later with the advent of motion pictures. Women who had previously shunned adorning their faces with cosmetics began to request their application when they sat for portraits in photography studios. It was in this period of the 1880s that internationally known British stage actress Lillie Langtry provided one of the first celebrity endorsements of cosmetics. She used make-up both during her performances and in her normal life off-stage, setting an example that inspired countless women to begin painting their own faces.

A New Cleopatra

Playing the movie role of Cleopatra in 1917, silent film star Theda Bara, Hollywood's first sex symbol, caused a sensation by wearing layers of cosmetics applied by Helena Rubinstein, the cosmetic industrialist responsible for introducing mascara and colored facial powders to mainstream consumers. Theda Bara started another fashion trend by painting her toenails, which newspapers and magazines breathlessly reported to be a milestone in the annals of beauty innovation.

Hollywood films and their glamorous players became the engine generating much of the consumer demand for wider choices in cosmetics and personal-care products. Polish immigrant Max Factor, known as the father of modern make-up, specialized in developing products for movie actors, and later introduced these creations to the general public with the marketing pitch that "every girl could look like a movie star" if she just used his cosmetics. Swedish actress Greta Garbo further refined the use of cosmetics until she had "completely altered the face of the fashionable woman," according to the history book *The Glass of Fashion,* describing that period.

By 1929 a bevy of Hollywood actresses had generated still another new fashion trend—skin tanning, using specially formulated self-tanning liquids and powders. It wasn't until 1936 that a chemist, Eugene Schueller, founder of L'Oreal, invented the first sunscreen. Another eight years would pass before Florida pharmacist Benjamin Green created the first mass-marketed suntan lotion, which came to be known as Coppertone.

During the Roaring Twenties chemists further expanded the cosmetics industry with their laboratory discoveries:

- A group of chemical preservatives called parabens were inserted into products for their anti-microbial effects, and within a few years parabens became the most widely used preservatives in cosmetics and personal-care products.
- An odorless and colorless group of chemical compounds called phthalates were added to cosmetics and personal-care products for the first time to increase their flexibility and to stabilize fragrances.

Fragrances were historically treated as luxury items for use only on special occasions, but by the twentieth century were being used by many women daily. Up until 1921, when Chanel No. 5 was introduced to consumers, perfume fragrances had mostly been derived from natural ingredients and essential oils. Chanel revolutionized the fragrance industry with the introduction of aldehydes and other synthetics, which gave fragrances greater consistency and stability at lower cost. Synthetics captured the imagination of manufacturers, and their advantages helped blind the industry to any consideration of the unknown impact these synthetic ingredients would have on health. Beginning in the 1970s, synthetic scents, usually associated only with perfumes, had been integrated into so many cosmetics and personal-care products that they were a part of normal daily experience.

As Synthetics Multiplied, So Did Health Problems

As use of synthetic chemicals grew, the impacts on human health became impossible to ignore. A skin cream called Koremlu, sold through department stores, contained thallium acetate, which was also used as a rodent poison. Reports began surfacing from hospitals and physicians in 1930 that users of one cream were developing paralysis, abdominal pain, blindness, and other severe symptoms. Only after injured consumers filed lawsuits against the manufacturer was the cream removed from the market in 1932, though in some areas of the U.S. the product continued to be sold for another year.

Exposés began to appear in the media showing how widespread the dangers to health and safety had become. A book called *American Chamber of Horrors* revealed how the rush to create new chemical concoctions for cosmetics had maimed and even killed women. But the book caused barely a ripple in the demand for these beauty enhancers.

One particularly egregious case of unsafe chemicals in cosmetic products involved dozens of women going blind in 1933 as a result of using Lash Lure, a synthetic aniline dye marketed as an eyelash and eyebrow colorant. Aniline comes from coal tar and is also used in hair dyes. Even after blindness and at least one death were documented as resulting from use of the product, it remained on the market for five more years because the U.S. Food and Drug Administration neglected to warn the public and had no regulatory authority to remove dangerous cosmetic products from store shelves.

Authority for such action finally came in 1938, from new regulations called the Food, Drug, and Cosmetic Act—but that authority was limited. The act defined a cosmetic as "an article intended to be rubbed, poured, sprinkled, sprayed on, introduced into, or otherwise applied to the human body for cleansing, beautifying, promoting attractiveness, or altering the appearance." Under the act, cosmetics manufacturers were still not required to evaluate the safety of ingredients prior to the marketing and sale of products. And only after a cosmetic had injured or killed enough people for the pattern of risk to be brought to the FDA's attention would the FDA then have the authority to remove that product from the market. Two kinds of products were excluded from the 1938 law—all soaps, and coal tar dyes, such as the one responsible for the Lash Lure injuries. The law simply required that a label be placed on coal tar dye products warning that "blindness may result from the use of this product."

"During the boom years of the 1950s and 1960s," writes Teresa Riordan in her book *Inventing Beauty: A History of the Innovations that*

Have Made Us Beautiful, "industry was transmuting oil into a motherlode of new wonder synthetics. Researchers broke down natural petroleum into its constituent parts and put them back together in sophisticated new combinations."

During this period of rapid innovation, the following events took place that would set the stage for many of the trends now affecting our lives:

- In 1958, nearly 200 chemicals in foods were declared safe by the FDA, not based on any laboratory testing, but because they had already been in common use in consumer products. This category is called Generally Recognized As Safe.
- In 1966, the U.S. Congress passed the Fair Packaging and Labeling Act, requiring that all consumer products be honestly labeled, which since then has been frequently ignored.
- In 1972, possibly harmful levels of lead were found in three major brands of toothpaste. The FDA took no action because it received assurances from manufacturers that the leaded tubes believed to be the source of the contamination would be phased out of use.
- In 1977, the FDA banned the use of six carcinogenic color additives from cosmetics: Yellow #1, Blue #6, and Reds #10, 11, 12, and 13, which were used in lipsticks. Though the six additives were banned, they were not removed from the marketplace by the FDA or manufacturers, which meant that products containing the color additives continued to be sold for years afterward until existing supplies were depleted.
- In 1986, the National Academy of Sciences, in a report to the U.S. House Committee on Science and Technology, singled out fragrance ingredients as a category of nervous system toxins that should be studied for their impact on human health. Little attention within either government or industry was paid to this warning.

Rather than wait for ingredients in consumer products to cause harm to public health, as remains the tradition in the U.S., many

European policymakers in the early 1990s began pushing for the establishment of a legal "precautionary principle" based on the idea that harm to consumer health should not need to be established with "full scientific certainty" before corrective action is taken. Manufacturers would have to prove their product ingredients were safe to use *before* marketing them to consumers.

Under this precautionary principle, the European Union countries in 2000 banned two phthalates—DBP and DEHP—from all cosmetics and personal-care products sold in all of its member nations, because these ingredients were suspected of being a threat to health. In that same year, two scientists at the U.S. Centers for Disease Control and Prevention developed a method of detecting phthalates in human body fluids that enabled researchers to measure the "body burden" of these chemicals for the first time. Subsequent CDC blood testing of 289 average Americans found DBP, the most toxic of the phthalates, in every person tested.

A lab analysis in 2002 of 72 products, ranging from perfume fragrances to hair sprays, deodorants, and body lotions, found that three-quarters of them contained unlabeled phthalates, according to Health Care Without Harm and the Environmental Working Group. Two years later the Environmental Working Group tested umbilical cord blood from newborns and detected 287 synthetic chemicals, including 180 chemicals that are known to cause cancer in humans or animals, demonstrating that mothers are passing their body burdens of synthetic chemicals directly into their unborn children during gestation, with unpredictable consequences for their children's health later in life.

All of this history, taken together, illustrates how and why we in the U.S. are so vulnerable to exposure to toxic ingredients in products whose safety most people have taken for granted. As you will discover in greater detail in the following pages, the government that should be protecting us either has misplaced priorities, or has been asleep on the job.

2 | The Chemical Threat to Your Health

Before we talk about why most American consumers remain in the dark about the health threat posed by cosmetics and personal-care products, we need to talk a little bit about what that threat is, and how we know it's a threat.

Your Skin Is a Carrier, Not a Barrier

Often called our "miracle garment" because it is so strong yet soft, skin is the body's largest organ; the average adult is covered by about 10 square feet of it. Averaging less than one-tenth of an inch in thickness, a square inch of it holds about twenty blood vessels, 650 sweat glands, and 1,000 nerve endings.

Your skin is enough of a barrier to keep fluids within your body (except for its controlled release of perspiration through sweat glands), but it also readily absorbs many things with which it comes into contact. When your skin wrinkles after being immersed in water, for example, it does so because it has expanded from absorbing some of that water.

Carcinogens in cosmetics and personal-care products pose greater cancer risks than food contaminated with carcinogenic pesticides and other industrial carcinogens because chemicals taken in by the mouth are absorbed by the intestines and pass into venous blood, which is then taken to the liver. Once inside this organ, carcinogens can be detoxified to varying degrees by enzymes before they reach the rest of the body. Carcinogens absorbed through the skin, in striking contrast, bypass the liver and enter blood circulation—and body organs—without this protection.

Even more disturbingly, there is evidence that the permeability of skin to carcinogens may be greater than that of even the intestines, the part of the body designed for nutritional particle absorption. In evidence presented at 1978 Congressional hearings, the absorption of carcinogen nitrosodiethanolamine (NDELA), was shown to be over 100 times greater when exposure occurred on the skin than through the mouth. (This is particularly important as consumption of the closely related carcinogen diethylnitrosamine in nitrite-preserved bacon has been associated with up to four- and sevenfold increased risk of childhood brain cancer and leukemia respectively.[1])

As difficult as it might be to believe, mainstream manufacturers and regulatory authorities appear unaware of the high permeability of skin, or else simply choose to ignore this as a critical concern. (One Canadian manufacturer even labeled its cocoa butter product as "Fast Absorbing." The product contained three carcinogens, diazolidinyl urea, TEA, and polysorbate—ingredients you don't want absorbing at any speed.)

Conventional cosmetics and personal-care products contain many frank and hidden carcinogens, making them the most important and still unrecognized class of avoidable carcinogen exposure for the overwhelming majority of consumers in major industrialized nations. The reason for these unique risks can be explained by both individual and interactive factors.

Exposure to carcinogenic ingredients in different products through the skin is lifelong, even preceding birth as a result of maternal skin absorption at the earliest stages of pregnancy. Exposure is also frequently prolonged; many commonly used products are intended to remain on the skin rather than be washed off immediately, providing increased opportunity for absorption. But products don't necessarily need to remain in contact with skin for long periods of time. A 1989 study showed that 13 percent of the carcinogenic preservative butylated hydroxyanisole (BHA) and 50 percent of the carcinogenic pesticide DDT are absorbed through human skin quite rapidly.[2]

What We Know and How We Know It

So we know products applied to the skin can be, and are, absorbed. What kind of evidence de we have on the carcinogenicity of ingredients in cosmetics and personal-care products, and just how reliable is this evidence?

The data we use in this book has been compiled from numerous sources. These include World Health Organization International Agency for Cancer Research monographs; U.S. National Toxicology Program (NTP) reports, based on rodent tests, of some 600 chemicals; and NTP's infrequent *Annual Reports on Carcinogens* (initiated in 1978, with twelve reports published by 2006). These summarize evidence on a range of carcinogens identified through animal tests or human studies.

Additional sources of information on carcinogenic ingredients include the 1980 *Science Action Coalition's Consumer's Guide to Cosmetics*; my own books, including the 1974 *Legislation of Consumer Product Safety* and the 1995 *The Safe Shopper's Bible*; the 1998 *The Breast Cancer Prevention Program*; the 2005 *Unreasonable Risk of Cosmetics and Personal Care Products*; and the non-profit Cancer Prevention Coalition press releases and citizen petitions, an association of which I am the current chairman. Finally, evidence on the carcinogenicity of relatively few ingredients and contaminants is admitted, though usually trivialized or dismissed, in the industry's own Cosmetic Ingredient Review Compendium, published annually by the Personal Care Products Council.

I'll be talking largely about carcinogens rather than other toxins, especially when it comes to particular ingredients. This is because cancer data is the hardest (which is to say, the most convincing) of all health data collected over the past thirty years. Other categories we have good health data on are allergens and hormone-disruptive chemicals. This information is based on two kinds of evidence: evidence from laboratory studies on animals, and evidence from epidemiological studies (studies on humans). In the majority of cases where chemicals that cause cancer in humans were identified by epidemiological studies, animal studies first predicted their toxicity. So we know that mice and rats, the standard test animals, are effective in enabling us to predict which chemicals will be carcinogenic to humans.

There is an overwhelming consensus, in fact, in the informed independent scientific literature—confirmed by expert bodies, including the International Agency for Research on Cancer (IARC)—that positive results in well-designed animal tests create the strong presumption of human cancer risk.[3] It's a consensus that is also reflected in a wide range of U.S. and international legislative and regulatory precedents.

About 800 industrial chemicals in current use have been shown to be carcinogenic in standard rodent tests. The results of most of these positive tests were initially dismissed or challenged by the industry concerned, and in some cases these results are still being challenged, to protect the profitability of products. The industry claims that the products' effects on human beings are the best proof of safety. But doing epidemiological studies on individual carcinogenic ingredients in cosmetics and personal-care products is a largely impossible task to perform.

Epidemiological studies depend on the ability to identify population groups exposed to a particular carcinogen or carcinogens, and then to compare their cancer rates with those in unexposed groups. For instance, large-scale epidemiological studies involving millions of people have been conducted on the effects of tobacco use, based on the comparison of lung cancer rates in people who smoke from one to four packs of cigarettes daily for varying periods of time to lung cancer rates in non-smokers. Smaller-scale studies have been conducted on cancer rates in workers exposed to carcinogenic products or processes in a range of industries, based on comparisons to unexposed workers in the same or other industries, or to unexposed groups in the general population.

Doing epidemiological studies on individual carcinogenic ingredients in cosmetics and personal-care products is so difficult because the vast majority of people are exposed, in varying degrees, to the same products and chemicals. In two notable cases, however, such studies have been successfully performed. Epidemiological studies demonstrated excess risks of ovarian cancer in pre-menopausal women who frequently dusted their genital areas with talc or used talc-dusted tampons. Other studies showed the excess risks of a wide range of cancers in women who used black or dark brown permanent or semi-permanent hair dyes for prolonged periods.

Unlike air pollution and water pollution, where it is difficult to get a handle on the sources of our exposure to individual carcinogens, what we put on our bodies in the form of cosmetics and personal-care products is something that we can control. But there is no way of isolating individual ingredients' effects so as to identify their impacts on health.

Tests for carcinogenicity must be conducted on the products' individual ingredients and contaminants rather than on the products themselves. The effects of carcinogenic ingredients in a single product are too small to detect reliably, let alone be effectively matched to individual ingredients. So it's important to note that when you see labels proclaiming "Not Tested on Animals," these claims relate to the whole product and generally involve irritation or allergy tests in rabbits or guinea pigs rather than toxicity tests on individual ingredients.

The majority of cosmetics and personal-care products manufactured and sold by mainstream companies are veritable witches' brews of carcinogenic ingredients and contaminants. For instance, many baby soaps, baby shampoos, and bubble baths hide a carcinogenic contaminant called 1,4-dioxane in a range of ingredients known as ethoxylates. This contaminant is not intentionally added to these products, but is rather created, as many contaminants are, during the manufacturing processes.

Because we do have clear evidence for the identity of chemicals that induce carcinogenic effects in rodents, and are thus likely to be carcinogenic in humans, our inability to do these kinds of tests is less important. We don't actually need any more studies or scientific data to feel confident about these chemicals' effects. We have reached the point where doing more studies becomes a superb excuse for inaction or delay on the part of industry, when they should be dealing with the problems that have already been identified.

The Vulnerability of Children

By over a decade ago, some thirty U.S. and international studies had confirmed the high incidence of cancers in children whose parents were exposed to a variety of chemical carcinogens in the workplace during pregnancy. Also, an increased incidence of brain cancer and leukemia has been reported in children whose mothers were exposed to nitrosamine carcinogens in nitrite-preserved meats during pregnancy. As opportunities for carcinogen exposure have increased since 1978, we've seen a striking 29 percent increase in the overall incidence of childhood cancers.[4]

Infants and young children, therefore, appear particularly susceptible to carcinogens, a fact that has been fully recognized for well over two decades. This susceptibility reflects their limited ability to detoxify chemical carcinogens due to their immature liver enzymes, as well as the much higher speed at which their cells are dividing. Rapid cell division means a greater probability that exposure to carcinogens will cause genetic mutations in cells and initiate the development of cancer. The effects of this may not appear until much later in life; a 1989 report by the Natural Resources Defense Council concluded that a high percentage of preschool children are likely to develop cancer in later life as a result of consumption of fruits and vegetables commonly contaminated by some eight carcinogenic pesticides.[5]

Despite a widespread recognition of this greater cancer risk to children, common cosmetics and personal-care products, even those aimed at children, still contain toxic ingredients. The often stunning ignorance about this fact was revealingly illustrated in 1994 when *Child Magazine* selected a book titled *Raising Children Toxic Free*, by Drs. Needleman and Landrigan, as "One of the Ten Best Parenting Books of the Year." Although these authors are leading pediatricians and experts on toxic chemicals, they showed no awareness of the toxic and carcinogenic risks of personal-care products, except for in a brief reference to lead in hair dyes.

In 2002, my co-author of the *Safe Shopper's Bible,* David Steinman, purchased two dozen products for babies and sent them to a laboratory to have them tested for the presence of two carcinogens, 1,4-dioxane and ethylene oxide. They were detected in eighteen of the baby products, though, as contaminents, they were not listed on any of the product labels. That means mothers who use multiple products on their children, such as shampoos, soaps, and bubble baths, are potentially exposing their babies to multiple doses of these carcinogens every day. A subsequent study by the Environmental Working Group concluded that at least one-quarter of all personal-care products sold in the U.S. are contaminated with dioxane.[6] With odds like these, the risk of exposure, to our children and ourselves, is gravely high.

Types of Carcinogens

There are two major classes of carcinogenic ingredients. The first is "frank" carcinogens, a category that includes more than forty substances. The second is "hidden" carcinogens, a category that includes approximately thirty substances. The ingredients in this category either can break down to release carcinogens, are carcinogen precursors (precede the emergence of another) or appear as contaminants in a range of ingredients. Carcinogens that can induce genetic damage are also known as "genotoxic."

While frank carcinogens appear on product labels, their complex chemical names convey little or no meaningful information to unsuspecting consumers. Still, at least they are listed; "hidden" carcinogens, as the name suggests, aren't listed at all. Instead, they "hide" in other ingredients (or in combinations of ingredients). For instance, lanolin, which is derived from sheep's wool and is used on babies' skin and the nipples of nursing mothers, is commonly contaminated by DDT-like carcinogenic pesticides.

The presence of hidden carcinogens is unrecognized even by most chemists, toxicologists, and cancer prevention experts, let alone consumers. Hidden carcinogenic ingredients you should be aware of fall into three major groups:

1. **Contaminants:** Carcinogenic ingredients found hiding in otherwise non-carcinogenic ingredients.
2. **Formaldehyde Releasers:** Non-carcinogenic ingredients that break down in the product itself, or on the skin, to release the frank carcinogen formaldehyde.
3. **Nitrosamine Precursors:** Non-carcinogenic ingredients that react with nitrites in the product or on the skin to form potent carcinogens known as nitrosamines. Nitrites appear in personal-care products in one of three ways: 1) nitrites are added to the product as anti-corrosive agents; 2) nitrites are released by the degradation of other chemicals, often when the product is exposed to air; or 3) nitrites turn up as contaminants in the raw materials that make up the product.

Some ingredients cross between categories. Diethanolamine (DEA) is both a frank and hidden carcinogen. By the mid-1970s, it was discovered that DEA, used by metal workers as a detergent or surfactant in cutting fluids, reacted with nitrite preservatives to form the potent carcinogen nitrosodiethanolamine (NDELA) in a process known as nitrosation. A similar interaction occurs between closely related DEA and triethanolamide (TEA) derivatives and nitrites, and it was subsequently recognized that DEA, commonly used in cosmetics and personal-care products, also interacts with nitrite preservatives or contaminants in *any* product, or with nitrogen oxides in the air, to form NDELA on the skin.[6] In 1997 studies showed that DEA is also a frank carcinogen: painting mouse skin with DEA, or its fatty acid derivatives, induces liver and kidney cancers.[7,8]

A Roadmap of Chemical Dangers

The following tables cover the common categories of toxins found in cosmetics and personal-care products. Some of these will be familiar from reading this chapter; others we'll discuss in more detail later on. Chemicals listed in these tables will be referenced throughout the remainder of this book, particularly in Part Two: Identifying Product Dangers.

These charts are also available for download on the Cancer Prevention Coalition Web site (www.preventcancer.com) and from Natural News (www.NaturalNews.com/Toxic Beauty.html).

Table 1: Frank Carcinogens

These chemicals have themselves been shown in laboratory testing of mammals to cause cancer. There are more than forty ingredients in this category that show up in cosmetics and personal-care products.

Acesulfame
Acrylamide
Aspartame (NutraSweet)
Auramine
Bisphenol-A (BPA)
Butadiene
Butyl benzyl phthalate
Butylated hydroxyanisole (BHA)
Chromium trioxide
Coal tar dyes
  • D&C
  • Green 5
  • Orange 17
  • Red 3, 4, 8, 9, 17, 19, 33
  • FD&C
  • Blue 2
  • Green 3
  • Red 4, 40
  • Yellow 6
Cobalt chloride
Cyclamates
Diaminophenol
Diethanolamine (DEA)

DEA cocamide condensate
DEA oleamide condensate
DEA sodium lauryl sulfate
Diethylhexyl phthalate (DEHP)
Dioctyl adipate
Disperse blue 1
Disperse yellow 3
Formaldehyde
Glutaral
Hydroquinone
Lead
Limonene
Metheneamine
Methylene chloride
Mineral oils
Nitrofurazone
Phenylenediamines (following oxidation)
Pyrocatechol
Saccharin (Sweet'N Low)
Silica (crystalline)
Talc (powder)
Titanium dioxide (powder)

Table 2: Hidden Carcinogens

These chemicals a) frequently appear as contaminants in other ingredients; or b) may not cause cancer themselves, but can become carcinogenic or create carcinogenic byproducts under certain conditions, such as when they interact with other chemicals in a product. More than three dozen hidden carcinogens can be found in cosmetics and personal-care products.

CONTAMINANTS	
Ingredient	**Contaminated With**
Acrylate and methacrylate polymers	Ethylhexyl acrylate
Amorphous silicates	Crystalline silica
Alcohol ethoxylates • Laureths • Oleths • Polyethylene glycol (PEG) • Polysorbates	Ethylene oxide, 1,4-dioxane
Butane	Butadiene
Coal tar dyes	Arsenic, lead
Condensates and quaterniums	DEA
Glyoxal and polyoxymethylene urea	Formaldehyde
Lanolin	Organochlorine pesticides, PCBs, ceteareths
Petroleum	Polycyclic aromatic hydrocarbons
Phenol ethoxylates • Nonoxynols • Octoxynols	Ethylene oxide, 1,4-dioxane
Polyacrylamide and polyquaternium	Acrylamide

FORMALDEHYDE RELEASERS

Diazolidinyl urea
DMDM-hydantoin
Imidazolidinyl urea
Metheneamine
Polyoxyethylene
Polyoxymethylene
Quaterniums
Sodium hydroxymethylglycinate

NITROSAMINE PRECURSORS

Brononitrodioxane (nitrite donor)
Bronopol (nitrite donor)
Cocamidopropyl betaine
DEA and fatty acid condensates
DEA sodium lauryl sulfate
Diethanolamine (DEA)
Morpholine
Padimate-O
Quaterniums
Sarcosine
Triethanolamine (TEA)

Table 3: Hormone Disrupters

These chemicals imitate the effects of natural hormones produced by the human body's endocrine system. The endocrine glands—the adrenal glands, pancreas, thyroid gland, pituitary gland, ovaries, and testicles—produce hormones essential to human growth, development, and metabolism. The body mistakes these synthetic chemicals for its own hormones and natural processes are disrupted. About thirty of these disruptive chemicals can be found in cosmetics and personal-care products.

PRESERVATIVES

Parabens
- Benzylparaben
- Butylparaben
- Ethylparaben
- Methylparaben
- Propylparaben

Resorcinol
Triclocarban
Triclosan

DETERGENTS (SURFACTANTS)

Disodium ethylenediamine tetra-acetic acid (Disodium EDTA)
Ethylenediamine tetra-acetic acid (EDTA)
Phenol ethoxylates
- Nonoxynols
- Octoxynols

SOLVENTS (PLASTICIZERS)

Bisphenol A (BPA)
Butylbenzene phthalate (BBP)
Dibutyl phthalate (DBP)
Diethyl phthalate (DEP)
Diethylhexyl phthalate, or dioctyl phthalate (DEHP)
Dimethyl phthalate (DMP)
Nonylphenol (NP)

LAVENDER & TEA TREE OIL

METALLOESTROGENS

Aluminum
Cadmium
Copper
Lead
Tin

SUNSCREENS

4-Methyl-benzylidine camphor (4-MBC)
Benzophenone-3 (BP3), or Oxybenzone
Butylmethoxydibenzoylmethane (BMDM), or Avobenzone (Parsol)
Homosalate (HMS)
Octyl-dimethyl-paba (OD-PABA)
Octyl-methoxycinnamate (OMC), or Octinoxate

Table 4: Penetration Enhancers

These chemicals improve the body's absorption of other ingredients, which can be dangerous if those other ingredients include toxins from the previous three tables. There are approximately thirty-five penetration enhancers that can commonly be found in cosmetics and personal-care products.

GENTLE DETERGENTS

Diethanolamine (DEA)
Monoethanolamine
Triethanolamine (TEA)

HARSH DETERGENTS

Bisabolol
Disodium ethylenediamine tetra-acetic acid (Disodium EDTA)
Ethylenediamine tetra-acetic acid (EDTA)
Glyceryl laurate
Sodium lauryl sarcosinate
Sodium lauryl sulfate

HYDROXY ACIDS

Alpha Acids
Alpha-hydroxy acid
Alpha-hydroxycaprylic acid
Alpha-hydroxyethanoic acid
Alpha-hydroxyoctanoic acid
Glycolic acid
Glycolic acid and ammonium glycolate
Glycomer in cross-linked fatty acids and alpha nutrium
Hydroxycaprylic acid
L-alpha-hydroxy acid
Lactic acid
Mixed fruit acid
Palmitic acid
Poly-alpha-hydroxy acid
Sugar cane extract

    Tri-alpha-hydroxy acid
    Triple fruit acid
Beta Acids
    Beta-hydroxybutanoic acid
    Salicylic acid
    Trethocanic acid
    Tropic acid
Alpha and Beta Acids
    Citric acid
    Malic acid

SUNSCREENS

Benzophenone-3 (Bp-3), or Oxybenzone
Octyl-methoxycinnamate

NANOPARTICLES

Table 5: Common Allergens

These chemicals cause an allergic reaction in many humans. There are about fifty allergenic ingredients in perfumes and fragrances (see Table 7) in addition to these commonly found in cosmetics and personal-care products.

IN HAIR PRODUCTS	
Shampoos	Formaldehyde, fragrances, lanolin, solvents, surfactants
Hair dyes	p-Phenylenediamine (ppd), p-toluenediamine
Waving solutions	Ammonium thioglycolate, glyceryl thioglycolate
IN NAIL PRODUCTS	
Artificial nails	Methyl methacrylate
Nail base coats	Phenol formaldehyde resin
Nail varnishes	Resins (aryl sulfonamide, formaldehyde, methyl methacrylate)
Nail hardeners	Formaldehyde
IN COSMETICS	
Lipsticks	Castor oil, colophony, pigments (e.g., eosin, azo dyes, carmine), perfumes, preservatives, propyl gallate
Eyebrow pencils	Pigments
Eye shadows	Colophony, preservatives (e.g., parabens, triclosan), pigments
Mascaras	Colophony, preservatives (e.g., triclosan, parabens), pigments
IN OTHER PRODUCTS	
Deodorants	Fragrances (e.g., cinnamic salicylate, jasmine, methyl anisate, balsam of Peru)

Shaving products	Propylene glycol
Depilatories	Thioglycolate
Toners	Arnica, coumarin, lanolin, oak moss
Face creams	Benzyl alcohol, lanolin, cetyl alcohol, parabens, propylene glycol, stearic acid
Sunscreens	Benzophenone-3 (oxybenzone), benzyl salicylate, coumarin, para-aminobenzoic acid (PABA)

COLORANTS

2,5-Toluene diamine	FD&C Red 2
3,4-Toluene diamine	FD&C Blue 2
Acid Blue 9	FD&C Yellow 6
Acid Orange 3	Henna
Acid Yellow 6	p-Phenylenediamine (ppd)
Acid Yellow 10	Red 22
Acid Yellow 17	Red 2G
Acid Yellow 23	Resorcinol

PRESERVATIVES

Benzalkonium chloride	Imidazolidinyl urea
Butylated hydroxyanisole	Metheneamine
Diazolidinyl urea	Methyldibromoglutaronitrile
DMDM hydantoin	Parabens
Ethylenediamine	Quaternium-15
Ethyl methacrylate	Thimerosal
Formaldehyde	

See also: Table 7, for common allergens in perfumes and fragrances.

3 | Losing the Winnable Cancer War

Y ou have probably seen newspaper headlines that periodically try to reassure us that the tide of battle has turned, and that we are winning the war against cancer. One story from *The New York Times* in 2005 received much attention by claiming that "cancer statistics do not indicate a cancer epidemic," and that "rates of cancer have been steadily dropping for 50 years."[1]

If only that newspaper account had been something other than wishful thinking! Even a casual reading of data provided by the National Cancer Institute paints a wholly different picture. As detailed in its "Cancer Statistics Review, 1975–2005," while there has been a major decrease in the incidence of lung cancer (due to the reduction in smoking among men and, to a lesser extent, women), other categories of cancers reveal alarming increases over the past three decades:

- Thyroid cancer has increased by 116 percent.
- Acute childhood leukemia has increased by 82 percent.
- Non-Hodgkin's lymphoma has increased by 79 percent.
- Acute adult lymphocytic leukemia has increased by 67 percent.
- Testes cancer has increased by 60 percent.

- Childhood brain cancer has increased by 39 percent.
- Post-menopausal breast cancer has increased by 22 percent.

We're losing the winnable war against cancer. Nearly one in every two men and more than one in every three women will be struck by cancer in their lifetime. That amounts to about 1.3 million people annually in the U.S., a population equal to that of Phoenix, Arizona. Another 550,000 die of cancer each year, a casualty toll comparable to the entire population of Denver, Colorado. Cancer has now literally become a disease of "mass destruction."

As a health columnist for *Rachel's Health News* commented a few years ago in describing the distorted lens through which the National Cancer Institute and the American Cancer Society, known as the "cancer establishment," view cancer success: "As more people are kept alive each year with their breasts or testicles removed, the cancer establishment chalks up another 'victory'—and no doubt the victims are glad to be alive—but we should acknowledge that there's something very wrong with calling this a victory. Slash and burn seems more like a dreadful defeat."[2]

The modern cancer epidemic cannot be explained away as a consequence of our increasing longevity, since incidence and mortality statistics are adjusted by a process known as "age-standardization" to take these trends into account. Nor can the epidemic be largely attributed to faulty personal lifestyle factors. Although smoking is clearly the single most important cause of cancer, as seen in the drop in lung cancer rates as smoking has decreased over the past few decades, the incidence of a wide range of cancers not related to smoking is increasing at disproportionately greater rates.

A 1990 survey of major industrialized nations, including the U.S., Britain and other European nations, and Japan, has shown that cancers not related to smoking are responsible for about 75 percent of the overall increased incidence of cancer since 1950.[3] The survey concluded that "In all the countries studied, mortality rates increased in persons over age 54 from cancer at some specific sites not related to cigarette smoking, including multiple myeloma, cancers of the breast, brain, and other central nervous system sites, and for all cancers except lung and stomach." Contrary to general impressions, the ability to successfully treat most cancers, with the notable exceptions of thyroid and testicular cancers, has not substantially improved for decades.[4]

Neither can the role of high-fat diets be incriminated as a major cause of cancer, in sharp contrast to its clear role in heart disease. Breast cancer rates in Mediterranean countries are relatively low despite diets that contain up to 40 percent olive oil fat. Furthermore, epidemiological studies over the past two decades have consistently failed to establish any causal relationship between breast cancer and the consumption of fat per se, though meat and dairy fats heavily contaminated with carcinogenic pesticides and industrial pollutants do appear to play a role.

Finally, these increasing cancer rates also cannot be attributed to genetic factors. At most, genetics can be directly implicated as a cause in less than 10 percent of all cancers. Two studies published in the *New England Journal of Medicine*, in 1988 and 2000, illustrate the critical importance of environmental factors in cancer rates. In the first, adopted children whose adoptive parents died from cancer had a fivefold increased risk of developing the disease themselves, clearly implicating environmental exposures. In the second study, which compared 9,000 identical twins in Sweden, Denmark, and Finland, the authors reached this firm conclusion: "The overwhelming contribution to the causation of cancer in the population of twins that we studied was the environment."[5] In contrast, a strong body of scientific evidence demonstrates that, apart from carcinogenic ingredients in consumer products, the predominant cause of the modern cancer epidemic is directly related to petrochemical and nuclear industry technologies and their environmental pollutants.

The explosive growth of industrial technologies since the 1940s has, to varying degrees in different nations, outstripped the development of legislative and regulatory controls. About 800 of the estimated 80,000 industrial chemicals in current U.S. use have been shown to be carcinogenic, based on National Toxicology Program tests and evaluation by the International Agency for Research on Cancer (IARC). Our total environment—the air we breathe, the water we drink and bathe in, the places we work, the prescription drugs we take, and the consumer products we buy, including food, household products, and especially cosmetics and personal-care products—has become pervasively contaminated with a multitude of industrial carcinogens. As a consequence, the public-at-large continues to be unknowingly exposed to a wide range of avoidable carcinogens.

In addition to carcinogenic effects, these exposures can induce allergenic, reproductive, genetic, neurological, and immunological effects. Unfortunately, we have no systematic data on their incidence and related mortality trends as is the case with cancer. However, cancer does represent a quantifiable way of measuring the range of adverse public health and environmental impacts that result from runaway industrial technologies. This means that a reduction in cancer rates will also, most likely, be paralleled by a reduction in the incidence of other chronic environmentally induced diseases.

The Folly of "Damage Control"

Cancer statistics reflect the fact that the policies of the federal National Cancer Institute (NCI), funded by tax payers, and the non-profit American Cancer Society (ACS), funded by public and also a wide range of industry donations, are fixated on damage control. They spend most of their budgets on diagnosis, treatment, and treatment-related research rather than on prevention research and action. Despite more than $50 billion in expenditures of taxpayer money by the NCI since President Nixon first declared war on cancer in 1971, less than 2 percent of its budget has gone to cancer prevention. Not surprisingly, overall mortality rates have remained virtually unchanged.

Over the past decades, we have seen the NCI and ACS, hand in hand, issue numerous breathless assurances, eagerly trumpeted by the uncritical news media, that breakthroughs in the war against cancer and in cancer treatment were imminent. In the early years of the "war," the NCI and ACS promised a cure in time for the nation's 1976 bicentennial. Then, in 1984, and again in 1986, the

NCI declared that cancer mortality would be cut in half by the year 2000. Both agencies announced in 1998 that the nation "had turned the corner" in the cancer war and that precipitous drops in mortality would soon occur. None of these predictions have even come true— or even close to it.

The FDA, NCI, and ACS spend millions of dollars on public relations in attempts to reassure the public they are doing a good job, despite their lack of progress. The reason they've failed to make any headway against cancer is this very fixation on damage control over cancer prevention[6]. These and other concerns relating to fiscal malpractice led the *Chronicle of Philanthropy,* the authoritative U.S. charity watchdog, to charge that the ACS is "more interested in accumulating wealth than saving lives."[7]

ACS allocations for prevention, primarily tobacco cessation programs and low-fat diets, are only about 0.1 percent of its budget of about $1 billion annually. NCI's budgetary allocation for prevention of occupational cancer (cancer due to exposure to chemical carcinogens in the workplace), the most avoidable of all cancers and conservatively estimated to be responsible for about 10 percent of all U.S. cancer deaths in adults and children, is about 1 percent.[8] The budget for research on and outreach to African Americans and other ethnic minorities, with their disproportionately high cancer rates, is also about 1 percent of NCI's budget; allocations for all primary prevention activities are well under 5 percent of its total budget.

Further undermining the goal of reducing the incidence of cancer, the NCI's definition of what constitutes prevention is so narrowly defined that it trivializes the major avoidable causes of cancer posed by contaminants in our air, water, workplaces, and consumer products. Instead, the NCI largely blames faulty lifestyle habits, particularly inactivity, lack of exercise, obesity, and faulty diet.

The U.S. cancer establishment's professional mindset and politically misshapen priorities are compounded by disturbing conflicts of interest, particularly for the ACS, because of its relationships with the cancer drug industry, as well as with the petrochemical and other polluting industries. As a previous director of the NCI, Dr. Samuel Broder, admitted, the NCI has become "what amounts to a governmental pharmaceutical company."[6] That mindset has contributed over the last four decades to the NCI's tendency to trumpet most every new "miracle" or "magic bullet" cancer drug as the latest evidence that the "tide is turning" in the cancer war.

To make matters worse, the U.S. cancer establishment has failed to provide Congress, federal regulatory agencies (particularly the Food and Drug Administration [FDA], Environmental Protection Agency [EPA], and Occupational Safety and Health Administration [OSHA]), and even more importantly, the public, with well-documented scientific information on how to avoid causes of cancer, other than pointing to lifestyle faults. That information exists, but remains buried in government and industry files and in scientific literature that is virtually inaccessible to, or not made available to, the general public. That is the major reason why legislative and regulatory action has not yet been taken to reduce or ban these avoidable cancer causes, and why the public continues to be denied its fundamental right to know of such information.

The cancer establishments worldwide still rely on questionable data and biased claims from publicly funded institutional apologists for the status quo and academics working for the very industries they should be exposing. A blatant example was Britain's late Sir Richard Doll, a leading expert on the avoidable causes of cancer in his early career. However, for subsequent decades Doll was employed as a closet industry consultant. He trivialized escalating ratios of cancer, explaining them away by blaming the victims and their lifestyles. This was coupled with his "guesstimates" that pollution and industrial products account for only 3 percent of cancer mortality.[9] Doll was also virtually unique in his insistence that leaded petroleum, low-level radiation, diesel exhaust, radiation from atom bomb tests, and environmental pollutants didn't pose any significant cancer risk. This gross misrepresentation no doubt reflected his professional involvement with a wide range of asbestos, petrochemical, and other industries. It should, however, be noted that in 2002, shortly before his death, Doll finally admitted that most cancers, other than those related to smoking and hormones, "are induced by exposure to chemicals, often environmental."[10]

The worldwide cancer establishments share major responsibility for losing the winnable war against cancer, a fact that is all the more serious in view of the strong influence that U.S. cancer establishment policies continue to exert on other nations worldwide. The mainstream media also share major responsibility, breathlessly and uncritically greeting every new claim of "magic bullet" cancer cures as new triumphs in the war on cancer and reacting to well-documented scientific evidence on the avoidable causes of cancer with limited or critical treatment.

Cancer Risks from Smoking Versus Personal-Care Product Use

Let's return for a moment to smoking and its relation to cancer risk, to help us better understand the pervasiveness and severity of the health threat posed by toxic chemicals in our cosmetics and personal-care products. Smoking in the U.S. and most major industrialized nations, outside of Asia, has been increasingly restricted to lower socioeconomic groups. The use of cosmetics and personal-care products, in contrast, spans all income and racial groups. Moreover, smoking is uncommon prior to adolescence (though children may be exposed to secondhand smoke), whereas direct exposure to personal-care products begins in infancy and even in the embryo, when sensitivity to carcinogens is most acute.

Another key difference is that smoking, at least before addiction kicks in, is a voluntary act—smokers know that smoking is dangerous and choose to assume the risk anyway. This risk is even emphasized by explicit cigarette warning labels. However, there is no such warning at all for the worldwide users of cosmetics and personal-care products.

Evidence for the carcinogenicity of cigarette smoke is largely and persuasively based on epidemiological studies comparing lung cancer and other cancer rates in non-smokers and smokers. While the chemistry of cigarette smoke and of cosmetics and personal-care products is very different, several of the same carcinogens have been identified in both, including formaldehyde, nitrosodiethanolamine, arsenic, DDT, and Endrin.

The strong epidemiological evidence on the risks of smoking is based on comparisons of cancer rates in large population groups that smoke different amounts of cigarettes daily, over different periods of time, with those in groups that have never smoked. Such comparisons are not feasible for most cosmetics and personal-care products because their use is virtually universal in the U.S. and most other industrialized nations. There are only two notable exceptions—instances in which it was possible to define exposed and non-exposed population groups. As documented in a November 17, 1994, Cancer Prevention Coalition Citizen's Petition to the FDA and an accompanying press release, "Dusting With Cancer," major risks of ovarian cancer have been identified in women who use talc-dusted tampons. As well, higher rates of multiple myeloma, non-Hodgkin's lymphoma, leukemia, and bladder cancers have been identified in women who regularly use black or dark brown permanent or semi-permanent hair dyes.

While smoking tobacco is the single most important cause of cancer, causes of cancer not related to smoking still account for about 75 percent of the increased incidence of cancer in the U.S. and other major industrialized nations since the 1950s.[11] It's very likely cosmetics and personal-care products are a significant part of that. Yet, there are striking differences between smoking and cosmetics and personal-care products when it comes to regulation: whereas cigarettes are heavily regulated, including via warning labels, cosmetics and personal-care products remain virtually unregulated.

The following facts should be unarguable:

• The incidence of cancer in the U.S., Canada, Britain, Japan, and other major industrialized nations has escalated to epidemic proportions over recent decades.
• Consumers are unknowingly exposed to carcinogenic ingredients and contaminants through mainstream industry cosmetics and personal-care products, along with food and household products.

- Cosmetics and personal-care products—usually applied to large areas of the skin daily—are, to varying degrees, contaminated with dozens of carcinogens.

For nearly four decades we have been losing the winnable war on cancer because we have relied on the highly biased cancer establishment, which is overwhelmingly focused on damage control—diagnosis and treatment—and gives prevention only the most minimal priority. The cancer epidemic can still be arrested and reversed, but we must develop new strategies that make prevention a more urgent goal than damage control. An essential first step in this process is for consumers to educate themselves about how they can undertake their own cancer prevention strategies, with particular regard to cosmetics and personal-care products, using the information in this book. And as we see in the next chapter, that depends on reestablishing our unarguable right to know the identity of hidden dangers in all products.

4 | You Lost Your "Right to Know"

> "The cosmetics industry has borrowed a page from the playbook of the tobacco industry by putting profits ahead of public health."
>
> —Senator Edward Kennedy, September 10, 1997, at Senate hearings on the FDA Reform Bill

Senator Kennedy's warning actually *understates* the recklessness of the cosmetics industry in its failure to provide warning labels on its products, the way the tobacco industry does. In fact, the cosmetics industry has not only borrowed a page from the tobacco industry's playbook, it has written a whole new play that takes reckless advantage of the FDA's neglect to violate consumers' "right to know."

More than three decades ago, consumer advocate Ralph Nader made one of the first public declarations about how thoroughly the cosmetics safety deck is stacked in favor of manufacturers and against the buying public. "The FDA claims to see great advantages in voluntary [industry] actions—flexibility, speed, and low costs to the FDA," Nader wrote in a chapter about cosmetics safety for the 1974 book *Consumer Health and Product Hazards*, published by MIT Press (a book I co-edited). "However, there are also many negative factors. For successful voluntary action, a basic consensus must exist between industry and the FDA. This will usually reflect, in major part, the industry judgment of the seriousness of the issue. Thus, a company will not usually accept any proposed voluntary action that runs counter to what it judges to be its real interests. The public and consumer interest is not a dominant factor in arriving at this consensus. Further, a corollary of a heavy dependence on voluntary procedures is a very close relationship between the regulators and the regulated." In other words, we cannot depend on the industry to take voluntary action unless it is in the industry's own best interest to do so.

The legislative framework for regulating cosmetics and personal-care products, whether manufactured in the U.S. or imported, is based on the 1938 Federal Food, Drug, and Cosmetic Act, and its United States Code amendments. Other regulations are found in the Code of Federal Regulations, and in the Fair Packaging and Labeling (FP&L) Act.[1]

The 1938 FDA Regulations (21 CFR Sec. 740/10) explicitly stipulate: "Each ingredient used in a cosmetic product and each finished cosmetic product shall be adequately substantiated for safety prior to marketing. Any such ingredient or product whose safety is not adequately substantiated prior to marketing is misbranded unless it contains the following conspicuous statement on the principal display panel: WARNING. THE SAFETY OF THIS PRODUCT HAS NOT BEEN DETERMINED."

Also, despite this stipulation, the act does not specifically require pre-market testing of product ingredients. Manufacturers are not required to provide proof of the safety of any personal-care or cosmetic ingredient, let alone its effectiveness, to the government or anyone else. Safety is the responsibility of manufacturers; the FDA allows them to use their own judgment about whether a product is safe or not, in effect putting them on the "honor system."

As should be clear from the evidence presented in this book, the FDA's presumption that industry will exercise responsibility is naïve at best and negligent at worst. The wording of the act may not require manufacturers to provide the government with evidence of their products' safety, but it certainly gives the FDA full authority, if it so chooses, to protect consumers from dangerous products by insisting that products containing dangerous ingredients be labeled with appropriate warning statements. Such a warning "shall appear on the label prominently and conspicuously as compared to other words, statements, or devices and in bold type on contrasting background to render it likely to be read and understood by the ordinary individual under customary conditions of purchase and use, but in no case may the letters and/or numbers be less than 1/16 inch in height, unless an exemption pursuant to paragraph (b) of this section is established." The FDA may also require the labels of products that contain ingredients of which the safety has not been substantiated to include the words, "Warning. The safety of this product has not been determined" (as specified by the regulation quoted above).

However, the FDA has rarely exercised these options since its founding, no matter how dangerous the product and its ingredients have been shown to be. The very few exceptions are the following nine prohibited ingredients in the 1938 Food, Drug, and Cosmetic Act:

- Complexes containing zirconium, as ingredients in aerosol products, as they can induce granulomas in the lung.
- Hexachlorophene, because of its neurotoxicity. However, this ingredient may still be used in the absence of "an alternative (effective) preservative."
- Mercury compounds, because of their neurotoxicity.
- Chlorofluorocarbon propellants, although they may still be exported. (The reason is not stated.)
- Bithionol, as it can cause photosensitivity.
- Halogenated salicylanilides, as they can induce photosensitivity.
- Chloroform, "because of its animal carcinogenicity and likely hazard to human health."
- Vinyl chloride, as an ingredient in aerosol products, because of its carcinogenic effects.

- Methylene chloride, "because of its animal carcinogenicity and likely hazard to human health."

In 1979, the FDA expressed concerns about significant nitrosamine contamination "in a variety of cosmetic products." The Agency asked "for voluntary industry action," and left open the possibility of taking regulatory steps. Although the requested voluntary action was not forthcoming, the Agency still has not used its regulatory authority.

As mentioned, it has been well known since 1978 that ethoxylate detergents are contaminated with 1,4-dioxane at levels as high as 100 parts per million.[2] In 1985, the FDA requested that manufacturers limit the level of dioxane in cosmetic products to less than 10 parts per million. A decade later, levels in some products were found to range up to 80 parts per million[3], but the FDA still took no regulatory action against dioxane-contaminated detergents. A further example of the FDA's regulatory recklessness is its continued failure to require labeling of alpha-hydroxy acid "skin peelers," even though the Agency admitted in 1992 that these chemicals pose a serious risk to health.

As for the industry and its record of voluntary actions and compliance, it should be noted that manufacturers have only voluntarily discontinued the use of three ingredients that are known to be toxic:

- Methylcoumarin (6-MC), as it can induce photosensitivity.
- Musk ambrette, because of its neurotoxicity ability to induce photosensitivity.
- Acetylethyltetramethyltetraline (AETT), because of its serious neurotoxicity, in addition to its discoloration of internal organs.

If and when manufacturers do conduct safety testing of ingredients used in their products, the results become privileged information and there is no requirement that they be made public. Because safety testing is strictly voluntary, not even the FDA has access to this information, nor does the Agency even know that studies have been conducted. Under the law, for all intents and purposes, consumers have no right to know whether the cosmetics and personal-care products they use are safe or not.

Again, Ralph Nader made these very points in his chapter in *Consumer Health and Product Hazards*:

> The best safety and toxicity data are those which are subject to independent peer review and published in the open literature. However, the cosmetics industry still regards such data as important commercial information, and tries to keep them a trade secret. Since industry pays for the testing, the suspicion always exists that 'he who pays the piper, calls the tune.' Adverse test data can be suppressed or deemphasized, and test protocols can be shaped to favor the desired results. . . . The law does not provide for the safety of a cosmetic to be properly established by a full range of toxicological tests conducted prior to marketing. The burden of proof of lack of safety of the marketed product continues to lie on the FDA, which suffers under the additional disadvantage of not being able to demand sufficient information to determine what is in a cosmetic in the first place.

This pattern of woeful consumer neglect by the FDA regarding cosmetics has never wavered regardless of which political party controlled the U.S. Congress or White House. Opportunities for reforms that would benefit consumers have come and gone. One came in 1978, during the presidency of Jimmy Carter, when the General Accounting Office (GAO), the investigative arm of Congress, reported that about 100 ingredients in cosmetic products were "suspected carcinogens" based on a list compiled by the National Institute of Occupational Safety and Health in its Registry of Toxic Effects of Chemical Substances. At least twenty-four other ingredients were suspected of causing birth defects and twenty were identified as adversely affecting the human nervous system.

The GAO report also stressed that "many improvements in FDA's regulations could be made under its existing authority," including taking "regulatory action against violative manufacturers" and restricting the "use of hazardous cosmetic ingredients." And finally, the GAO urged the FDA to take action to require "appropriate precautionary labeling" and establish "tests to be used in evaluating cosmetic safety."

The FDA's response to this report was to issue no substantive response. Nor did Congress or the Carter Administration take up the challenge and push through legislative reforms to advance consumer protection. And nothing much has changed over the three decades since, except that the health threats have multiplied and the cosmetics and personal-care industry has grown much wealthier and considerably more powerful and skillful at sabotaging attempts to educate consumers about the safety of what they put on their bodies.

The FDA's regulatory failure is further detailed in several of my books, including the *The Safe Shopper's Bible*. The FDA's failure is also described in seventeen Cancer Prevention Coalition press releases from 1994 onward, and in two Citizen's Petitions filed with the FDA by the Cancer Prevention Coalition. The first petition, in 1994, asked the FDA to require products containing talcum powder to bear labels with a warning similar to "Talcum powder causes cancer in laboratory animals. Frequent talc application in the female genital area increases the risk of ovarian cancer." The second petition, in 1996, asked that a regulation be issued requiring a label on all cosmetics and personal-care products containing DEA, that warns consumers that DEA is a known cancer-causing agent; the petition also asked the FDA to conduct regular and routine analytical testing of products to determine if they were contaminated by NDELA, the result of the reaction between DEA and nitrites within products. Both petitions were rejected by the FDA.

A 2004 petition to the FDA filed by the Environmental Working Group, requesting warning labels on 356 personal-care products, received this 2005 response from the FDA: "The [Food, Drug, and Cosmetic Act] contains no provision that requires demonstration to

FDA of the safety of ingredients of cosmetic products . . . prior to marketing the product. . . . The Act does not authorize FDA to order a recall for a defective or possibly harmful cosmetic product."

With that official statement the FDA reiterated that it will not protect consumers from dangerous ingredients and products before the items enter the marketplace, and that it cannot require a recall of those cosmetic and personal-care products, even if they are harming consumers' health, unless the FDA proves in court that a product is misbranded or adulterated. But to do that, the agency must have clear evidence of harm, which is often difficult if not impossible to provide since the Agency is reliant on the manufacturer's interpretations of safety information. As a further barrier to public accountability, even if harm is clearly proven, without the court ruling, product recalls remain a voluntary action done at the discretion of the manufacturer.

In its petition to the FDA, the Environmental Working Group had requested that several categories of cosmetics products carry the warning label: "Warning. The safety of this product has not been determined," as allowed by FDA regulations. These categories were taken from an analysis of actions taken (or rather, not taken) by the Cosmetic Ingredients Review, an industry-funded science panel that has evaluated the safety of just 11 percent of the more than 10,000 ingredients used in cosmetics and personal-care products. By the EWG's estimate, 99 percent of all cosmetics and personal-care products contain one or more ingredients that have not ever been assessed for safety.

As the Environmental Working Group later reported:

> But in their response to our petition, FDA replied that it could not take action against these products, arguing that the Agency could not find them misbranded or adulterated, and could not require the warning label because it lacked the information to determine whether or not the ingredients were adequately substantiated for safety, or were causing acute injury. The FDA astoundingly claimed that the

industry panel recommendations were sufficient to
determine if ingredients are, indeed, safe.[4]

In other words, the FDA did not have the information necessary
to take steps protecting consumers, nor was the FDA interested in
obtaining it.

As a further insult to consumers, the FDA also declared in its
response to the petition that it refused to develop any guidelines for
manufacturers on what steps must be taken to substantiate product ingredient safety or what standards could be used to ensure that
products were safe before being marketed. In effect, the FDA was
proudly flaunting its impotence, proclaiming that manufacturers
know best about safety and implying that consumers deserve nothing more than their own uneducated guesswork.

Previous labeling petitions received similar treatment by the
FDA. A petition from the Environmental Health Network of California in 1999, for instance, supported by the Cancer Prevention Coalition, requested that the FDA require warning labels on all fragrances
marketed without prior safety testing. That petition and its concerns
were also dismissed.

Mounting Criticisms of the FDA

Criticism of the FDA's regulatory abdication has been increasing for
more than three decades, but with little or no impact on the Agency's policies. In 1997, the FDA proposed a reform bill to Congress
that ignored and further increased the risks of toxic ingredients in
cosmetics and personal-care products.

Included in the FDA's proposed bill was a sweeping rejection of
states' right to regulate any aspect of labeling. The FDA furthermore
proposed an exemption for the cosmetics and personal-care products
industry from requirements of the National Environmental Policy
Act, which requires that industries issue formal statements on possible toxic environmental impacts of their ingredients and products.
The FDA's proposal evoked strong criticism from Senator Edward
Kennedy and thankfully failed to pass.

Bisphenol-A Bias

An October 14, 2008, *New York Times* editorial criticized the FDA for conflicts of interest in a recent advisory committee on Bisphenol-A (BPA). The committee dismissed the dangers of BPA, a toxic plasticizer in baby bottles and liners for canned foods (as well as some cosmetics and personal-care products), saying that the small amounts that leach into food are not dangerous—after an outspoken critic of BPA regulation gave a donation of $5 million to a hospital whose director was the BPA advisory committee's head.

While the editorial did not claim to challenge either the advisory committee head's or the FDA's integrity, it did call for increased transparency regarding the FDA, urging that "consumers need to know that any decision on BPA is completely unbiased—and that the FDA is too."

What is astounding about this editorial is not its criticism of the FDA, though such criticism from a major media outlet such as *The New York Times* is rare. Rather, it is the editorial's lack of awareness of the FDA's decades-old indifference to toxic ingredients, including BPA, in cosmetics and personal-care products. As a result of such unawareness, the entire U.S. population remains exposed to these ingredients, from conception onward, without any warning whatsoever.

The FDA has mounted a series of damage-control initiatives, but these were more tokenistic than real. On December 9, 1999, the FDA's Office of Cosmetics Fact Sheet announced that it "takes the results of the 1997 National Toxicology Program study on the carcinogenicity of DEA very seriously, and has made the assessment of public health risks as one of its highest priorities for the cosmetic program." But the FDA failed to take any regulatory action.

Similarly, in its March 30, 2000, Office of Cosmetics Fact Sheet, the FDA warned that a high percentage of cosmetics and personal-care products contain carcinogenic nitrosamine contaminants, and that such contaminants "raise concerns." The Fact Sheet also extended this warning to the potent carcinogenic contaminant 1,4-dioxane. Nevertheless, the FDA has still taken no regulatory action against any of these avoidable carcinogens, nor made a real effort to warn unsuspecting consumers.

You cannot be faulted if, at this point, you are beginning to wonder whether the entire realm of cosmetics and personal-care products has somehow descended into a swamp of twisted logic, willful deceptions, and studied neglect. What use is the FDA regarding cosmetics and personal-care products if it has no legal power—or even the willpower—to monitor, much less to protect, consumer health and safety?

What Protection Does Labeling Afford Us?

You might think that since the FDA will not defend our health before harmful products are marketed, and cannot act after harmful products are in use, at least we have ingredient labels to fall back upon as a guide to making safe choices. But that's just wishful thinking. The reality is very different from what manufacturers want you to believe.

The only real legal requirement manufacturers adhere to, one that in theory could benefit consumers, is the listing of ingredients on product labels. Under the Fair Packaging and Labeling Act, manufacturers are required to list, in descending order of quantity, the ingredients of every cosmetic and personal-care product on its product label. But there are numerous significant loopholes in this law, and these loopholes negatively affect our choices as consumers and our ability to identify dangers to our health.

About half of all labels on 14,200 products examined by Environmental Working Group (EWG) researchers turned out to have mislabeled ingredients. Some ingredient names were misspelled; other names for the same ingredient varied according to the manufacturer. Even more damning, EWG identified forty-one online retailers of cosmetics that failed to post ingredient lists at all, rendering online purchasers unable to make informed buying choices. When the EWG urged the FDA to pressure these cosmetics companies to post ingredient information on their Web sites, the FDA replied that "there is no requirement that a manufacturer put an ingredient list on a Web site."[4] So much for the public's right to know!

Most cosmetics and personal-care corporations exhibit either outright disrespect for the public's right to know the dangers in everyday products, or else they abuse or attempt to redefine words such as "natural," so as to thwart the average person's best intentions at self-education and self-protection. While to any reasonable person "natural" implies something taken directly from nature, the law doesn't prohibit synthetic chemicals from being included in products labeled with the term. Some products labeled as natural even contain nothing *but* synthetic ingredients.

Some of the other major loopholes in labeling laws and practices:

- Generic terms on labels often hide the identity of some toxic ingredients. For example, the term "Fragrance Free" may sound as if it means no fragrance chemicals have been added to the product, but manufacturers can legally add unidentified fragrance ingredients to mask foul odors generated by other chemicals and still call the product "Fragrance Free." Since fragrances are treated as valuable trade secrets by fragrance and perfume manufacturers, hundreds of the chemicals that show up in fragrances in personal-care products are never listed on labels. And data compiled by the National Institute of Occupational Safety and Health indicated that of 3,000 ingredients commonly used by the fragrance industry, about 900 have been identified as toxic.
- Fragrances, generally, are exempt from labeling requirements, which means that ingredients such as phthalates, the proven hormone disrupters, are frequently not disclosed on labels on the specious grounds that, in the majority of products, they are components of fragrances.
- Still another labeling loophole is that products designated as "For Professional Use Only" and sold to salons do not need to

have their chemical ingredients labeled. That means consumers, as well as the owners and employees of salons, are completely at manufacturers' mercy when it comes to ingredient safety; they don't have the ability to exercise choice because they have no way of knowing what contaminants products contain.

- While the terms "hypoallergenic" (meaning that it contains no common allergens), "allergy tested," and "safe for sensitive skin" all have considerable promotional value for manufacturers and retailers, they have no real meaning under the law. Manufacturers are not required to do any skin testing to validate such claims, nor do these claims need to be proven to the FDA or any other regulatory body.

- Hidden carcinogens are also not identified on product labels. Because they are not in the product intentionally, there is no requirement to list them.

The trade secrecy laws that allow manufacturers to withhold product ingredients, such as those in fragrances, are nothing more than marketing strategies designed to manipulate consumers. The FDA supports trade secrecy and nondisclosure by manufacturers on the grounds that "consumers are not adversely affected—and should not be deprived of the enjoyment" of these products, as if disclosing toxic ingredients was somehow synonymous with deprivation. And the absurdity of the "protection" companies receive from trade secrecy laws comes into sharper focus when you realize that most product competitors have the technical expertise to back-engineer product ingredients created by their rivals—which means that it is really only consumers who are being kept in the dark about the identity of product ingredients.

A more subtle layer of public deception that shields dangerous chemicals from scrutiny is the result of the intimidation tactics sometimes used against experts who go public about health hazards. Some of the best examples illustrating this pattern of retaliation against dissent come from FDA and manufacturer responses to criticisms of pharmaceutical drugs. *New Scientist* magazine reported in 2007 how a well-respected physician who had raised concerns about serious side effects associated with the diabetes drug Avandia was attacked by the FDA, which sent news media organizations unsubstantiated allegations against the whistleblower. As a result of such tactics, scientists and physicians are often reluctant to publicize their concerns.

There are avoidable exposures to carcinogens that the public never learns about, and that the industry is able to suppress, because the FDA never points out dangers in cosmetics and personal-care products independent of the industry itself. The key player in this process is the industry's trade association. Founded in 1894, the Cosmetic, Toiletry and Fragrance Association (CTFA), comprising more than 600 manufacturers and distributors of cosmetic, fragrance, and personal-care products, as well as suppliers and packagers of raw materials for the industry, has been at the forefront of championing "voluntary self-regulation and reasonable government requirement." In 2007 the group changed its name to the Personal Care Products Council.

The Council maintains dozens of full-time lobbyists at the federal and state levels of government and with this highly paid team has pursued an aggressive political agenda against what it considers to be "unreasonable or unnecessary labeling or warning requirements." Among its many successes in stifling public disclosure was the blocking of a bill in the New York legislature that would have required a cancer warning label on cosmetic talc powder.

An essential part of the Council's work is to reassure consumers that everything they buy is safe, everything is under control, and no one needs to worry. As Stacy Malkan pointed out in her 2007 book *Not Just a Pretty Face*, the trade association had the following misleading claim posted on its consumer education Web site as of January 2007: "The FDA routinely conducts studies and tests to ensure the safety of all cosmetic products. . . . FDA's legal authority over cosmetics is comparable with its authority over FDA-regulated products, such as foods, nonprescription drugs, and nonprescription medical devices."

Why would the industry's mouthpiece be telling consumers something so blatantly false? The FDA has never "routinely" tested cosmetics and personal-care ingredients or products. The agency does not even require that manufacturers prove their ingredients and products are safe for human use and health. What this trade association and the industry it represents continue to count on is the passive acquiescence of consumers and their gullible acceptance of every reassurance, no matter how hollow, that the trade group propagates in furthering the industry's agenda.

The cosmetics and personal-care products industry successfully created the illusion of public safety, and so long as profits stay high, they will not be too concerned about liability issues associated with harmful ingredients in their products; they feel confident they can always create enough doubt about health claims to avoid account-ability in any court of law. Meanwhile, mainstream consumers are mostly content to believe that if the products they use contained threats to their health, the FDA would surely intervene and alert them. That same attitude prevails among the various state regula-tory agencies (with the exception of California's), resulting in those agencies' failure to exercise product oversight because they choose to believe that the FDA is already doing an adequate job. This attitude also pervades the U.S. Congress, where most members would rather not bother with a health issue unless the cause is easily traced and the deaths and injuries easily quantifiable.

While it may seem trite to say that consumers must assume responsibility for their own safety and health, the reality is that, in the absence of leadership from the various states, until Congress leg-islatively forces the Food and Drug Administration to do its job, we have only ourselves to rely upon.

PART TWO

Identifying Product Dangers

5 | Products Targeting Infants and Children

I f you have raised children, you know this loving ritual from firsthand experience: You pamper your infant with all the personal-care products at your disposal, bathing him or her with special infant formula soaps and shampoos, soothing his or her skin with lotions, and dusting his or her bottom with talcum powder. You go through this routine every day, thinking you're doing the right thing, never imagining you may be harming your child's health later in life.

The use of children's personal-care products has grown expansively over the past few decades. Not coincidentally, the incidence of many childhood cancers has increased up to 50 percent during the same period. Babies are about 100 times more sensitive to carcinogens than adults, a fact that is well documented scientifically. As we saw in chapter two, infants and young children have immature liver enzymes, meaning they have a limited physiological ability to detoxify carcinogens. Also, because their cells are dividing much more rapidly than those of adults, their bodies are more likely to develop genetic mutations that result in cancers later in adult life.

Given the exquisite sensitivity of infants and young children, the ingredients in each of their personal-care products must be safe—and safe without a doubt—or you could, quite unintentionally, be endangering their health and safety all the way into their adult life.

As this chapter will make clear, nearly all of the infant products on the market today are not safe. The first health threat is from chemicals that can disrupt children's (and their mothers') hormonal balance; the second is from all of the ingredients that still appear in personal-care products even though lab tests with animals have shown them to be causes of cancer.

From Mother to Fetus and Child

The external world actually begins to affect the health of your child well before his or her birth. A fetus is exposed to its mother's "body burden" of toxic ingredients from the cosmetics and personal-care products she has used, along with other toxins from the air she breathes, the water she drinks, the foods she eats, and the medicines she takes.

A few weeks before a baby is born, the umbilical cord pumps an estimated 300 quarts of blood daily between the placenta and fetus. As a result, much of a mother's own body burden of toxic contaminants cycles rapidly through her unborn child. Only breastfeeding rivals this period of development in its potential for a mother's own accumulated chemical contaminants to affect her child.

As a clear illustration of how easily the chemicals a mother uses on her skin end up in her fetus, consider these findings: An analysis of umbilical cord blood samples taken from twenty-seven European volunteers, in a 2005 study conducted by Greenpeace International and Britain's WWF (formerly known as the World Wildlife Fund), detected eight groups of contaminants.[1] These included fragrances used in perfumes and personal-care products, and synthetic musks, used to replace natural aromas in cosmetics, hand creams, perfumes, and soaps. The most common type of synthetic musk, known as HCB, turned up in almost all of the blood samples taken. Musk ambrette, another synthetic musk, was found in twelve of twenty-seven umbilical cords tested—despite the fact that this ingredient had been banned in European cosmetics (though not in U.S. cosmetics) as a toxin since 1995.

Another major group of contaminants called phthalates (pronounced "thalates"), which are used as solvents or fixing agents in perfumes, body lotions, and other cosmetics, were detected in most cord blood samples. The most commonly used phthalate, DEHP, was found in twenty-four of the twenty-seven samples. The report referred to numerous studies which, in the words of the researchers, "have shown a correlation between premature breast development in girls younger than eight years old and the concentrations of the phthalate DEHP in their blood. Other research suggests that exposure to some phthalates affects the sexual development of baby boys at exposure rates currently seen in the U.S."[2]

Still another contaminant found in half of the cord blood samples was triclosan, an antibacterial ingredient in toothpaste, deodorants, antibacterial soaps, and cosmetics. Lab studies on rats have shown that triclosan is toxic to normal liver enzymes. Of equal concern, triclosan persists in the environment and in our bodies, accumulating as it is passed up the food chain, and contributes to reduced resistance to antibiotics.

Commenting on these findings, a toxicopathologist and expert on the fetal effects of chemicals, Dr. Vyvyan Howard of Britain's University of Liverpool, pointed out how, at the fetal stage of life, "changes occur at exposure levels thousands of times lower than the safety limits that were set a few years ago. New studies show that many bulk chemicals that we thought were safe are actually biologically active and disrupt human systems. They don't work by having an acute toxicity effect. They work by hijacking development in the uterus. These chemicals can disrupt important cell signaling functions in the developing body."[3]

A second important study of umbilical cord blood, this one conducted in the U.S. by the Environmental Working Group in 2005, used the Red Cross to collect cord blood from ten babies born in U.S. hospitals. Altogether, 287 mostly industrial chemical contaminants were detected in them, ranging from pesticides to chemicals that had leached from nonstick cooking pans and plastic wrap. Nearly all of these chemicals had been linked in animal testing to cancer, birth defects, hormone disruption, and other health disorders.[4] Though these tests did not specifically target ingredients found in cosmetics and personal-care products, their results demonstrate the same principle: the toxins in the mother are passed also to the child. Once there, they inflict an unknown amount of harm. "For some of the chemicals, we know some safe levels for a single chemical in adults," commented Tim Kropp, a senior scientist with the Environmental Working Group. "In none of them, however, do we know what the safe level is in combination with each other and not what [the safe level] is in babies."

These tests were exceedingly expensive, about $10,000 for each umbilical cord tested, which helps explain why ignorance about the fetal absorption of contaminants has persisted for so long. Due to the costs involved, the testing has been limited in other ways, as well: this study only analyzed a few hundred industrial chemicals out of the tens of thousands humans can absorb during a normal lifetime.

Up until a few decades ago, most mainstream physicians and scientists believed that the placenta formed a barrier that prevented the mother's contaminants from entering the umbilical cord and circulating through the fetus. Subsequent research dramatically altered that viewpoint. Dr. Alan Greene, a Stanford University pediatrician, describes the placenta as a "free-flowing, living lake" inside mothers from which the umbilical cord draws nourishment for the fetus. Because of chemical absorption by mothers, this living lake has become contaminated, says Greene, and developing babies in today's world "mainline the contaminants through their umbilical cord, injecting them into their veins more potently than any IV drug administration."[5]

Why should we be so concerned by these findings about fetal exposure to chemicals? Four reasons stand out:

1. Fetuses are so much more sensitive to toxic chemicals than adults or even children, so the interaction of toxins is even more unpredictable, and could cause even greater damage.
2. The blood-brain barrier in fetuses is not fully developed, which means toxic chemicals may inflict neurological harm.
3. Female fetuses are born bearing eggs that will become their future children (should they choose to have them), which

means that future generations, too, can be affected by current toxic exposures.

4. Hormone-disruptive chemicals absorbed by the mother may feminize male fetuses and generally disrupt natural hormone development.

Once children are born, their sensitivity to toxic chemicals remains much higher than that of adults for two reasons we haven't yet discussed: children have faster metabolisms than adults, which speeds up the absorption of most contaminants; and children are not able to excrete contaminants, or store them away in fat tissues, as effectively as adults do. As a result, children's underdeveloped immune systems and blood-brain barriers are weakened further, increasing their susceptibility to toxic effects.

"Gender Bender" Chemical Effects

Hormone disrupters, technically known as endocrine disruptive chemicals (EDC) "gender benders," or more popularly, just "hormonals," are a group of natural and synthetic chemicals that interfere with the action of normal hormones. They can mimic, modify, or block the synthesis, release, binding, and/or metabolism of natural sex hormones. They can also disrupt other hormones, including thyroid hormones.

The presence of hormone disrupters in hundreds of industrial and consumer products is being blamed for twice as many girls as boys being born in some areas of the world. Hormone disrupters are also blamed for the birth defects and developmental disorders, especially in males, that have only been identified over recent decades.

Lab testing in animals has identified dozens of "gender bender" ingredients in common household products. One of these, Bisphenol-A (BPA), mimics the hormone estrogen, yet it is commonly used in polycarbonate baby bottles, cosmetics, and personal-care products, and even in some dental sealants for children.

A 2007 review of 700 studies involving BPA, published in the journal *Reproductive Toxicology*, found that infants and fetuses were the most vulnerable to adverse effects from this toxic substance. An accompanying study in the same issue of the journal by researchers at the National Institutes of Health found uterine damage in newborn animals exposed to levels of BPA consistent with normal human exposure. This finding may also implicate BPA as a cause of many reproductive tract disorders that occur in women later in life, decades after being exposed as fetuses and/or infants.[6]

Previous studies in the journal *Endocrinology* and elsewhere found evidence that BPA masculinizes the brains of female mice and feminizes the brains of male mice. One measure of the effects of these hormone disrupters on human males is the distance between the anus and genitals in infant boys, a standard measurement of normality for generations. Alarmingly, over the past decade there has been a significant reduction in that distance, which can be attributed to hormone-disruptive chemicals. The decrease in anogenital distance is clear-cut evidence of hormone disruption, and has been associated with a simultaneous decrease in sperm production, as measured in males worldwide.[7] In light of these dangers from BPA exposure, in early 2008 the Canadian government's Health Canada declared BPA to be a toxic chemical.

None of these developments should come as any surprise to us, since the hormonal effects of certain synthetic chemicals, particularly DDT, on wildlife have been well recognized since the 1950s, and were documented in Rachel Carson's classic 1962 book, *Silent Spring*. Carson's book described how predatory birds at the top of the food chain were producing thin-shelled and non-viable eggs due to the estrogen-like effects of DDT. On the basis of these concerns, particularly the cancer risks implied for human beings, the U.S. banned DDT in 1969. (I was the lead expert witness in this litigation, which was initiated by the Environmental Defense Fund against industry and the United States Department of Agriculture.)

The U.S. Congress passed the Food Quality Protection Act in 1996, which required the Environmental Protection Agency to start the Endocrine Disruptor Screening Program to test chemicals and environmental contaminants for their potential to disrupt the hormonal systems of wildlife and humans. Since that time, an increasing number of hormone disrupters have been shown to cause abnormal hormonal effects in many species of wildlife at very low levels and so has been recognized as environmental pollutants. Eggshell thinning, impaired fertility, and reproductive failure have been reported in adult birds exposed to hormone disrupters, coupled with reproductive, bone, and other abnormalities in their chicks. Other effects include small penis size and low testosterone levels in juvenile alligators from pesticide-contaminated lakes in Florida, and the feminization of trout in the Great Lakes.

Based on extensive evidence of hormonal effects in laboratory animals, males of all species have been found to be more sensitive than females. The abnormalities documented in male test animals include testicular atrophy; undescended, misplaced, or absent testes; benign tumors of the testes; infertility; and absent or malformed prostate and seminal vesicles. The results of these tests are consistent with a range of abnormal trends we have been seeing in humans over the past few decades, including declining sperm counts in industrialized nations; increased incidence of undescended testes in U.S. males, which is associated with increased risk of testicular cancer; and increasing incidence of prostate and breast cancers. There is clear evidence that fetuses, particularly male fetuses, are highly sensitive and vulnerable to multiple, cumulative exposures to hormone-disruptive chemicals.

The Six Families of Hormone Disrupters

The six major classes of hormone disrupters in many cosmetics and personal-care products include preservatives, detergents (or surfactants), solvents (or plasticizers), metalloestrogens, lavender and tea tree oil, and sunscreen ingredients.

PRESERVATIVES

Preservatives are the most widely used hormone-disruptive ingredients in cosmetics and personal-care products. They prevent bacterial contamination as well as maintain the stability of ingredients. Three types of preservatives pose major health concerns: parabens, triclo-san, and resorcinol.

Parabens—which include methylparaben, ethylparaben, propy-lparaben, butylparaben, and benzylparaben—are the most common of all ingredients in cosmetics and personal-care products. They are also widely used in foods and pharmaceuticals. It has been estimated that women are exposed to as much as 50 mg of parabens daily just from cosmetics and personal-care products.

Numerous studies over the last decade have shown that parabens pose weakly estrogen-like effects.[8] The level of their hormonal effects vary widely, from the most potent, butyl, which can affect the human body at levels 100,000 times lower than natural estrogen, to the less potent methyl.[9] In laboratory tests, parabens are readily absorbed through the skin of immature female rodents, and stimulate prema-ture uterine growth. Similarly, administering parabens to immature male rats decreases sperm counts and testosterone levels.[10]

One study showed the presence of parabens in the breast tissue of women with breast cancer, possibly originating from their use of underarm deodorants or antiperspirants (see chapter 10). The study also showed that methylparaben, the least potent hormone-disrup-tive chemical, was present at the highest concentration. Parabens' presence in breast tissue on its own incriminates them as a possible cause of breast cancer, but they have also been shown to stimulate the growth of estrogen-sensitive breast cancer cells in laboratory tests.[11]

In spite of extensive literature on the hormonal effects of para-bens, the 2006 industry Cosmetic Ingredient Review Compendium still trivialized such concerns by stating that these ingredients "must certainly be considered safe." The FDA agrees: "At the present time, there is no reason for consumers to be concerned about the use of cosmetics containing parabens."[12]

In another direct challenge to these reassurances, researchers at the Kyoto Prefecture University of Medicine in Japan have reported that methylparaben, at levels similar to those in cosmetics, increases skin damage, along with aging and cell death, following a person's exposure to ultraviolet radiation at levels comparable to normal daily exposure during summer months.[13] Other studies have shown that parabens readily permeate through the skin and accumulate in skin layers, from which they can pass into blood and enter body tissues. (See also chapter 10, for more information on paraben absorption and accumulation.)

The second type of preservative is triclosan, an active ingredient in many cosmetics and personal-care products, including nearly half of all commercial antibacterial soaps, deodorants, detergents, toothpastes, and mouthwashes. Triclosan and its chemically related cousin triclocarban have been shown to produce a variety of hormonal effects, including on the development of the thyroid gland in tadpoles,[13] and on sex ratios and fin length in fish. In humans, this preservative chemical has been linked to allergies, asthma, and eczema.[14] More importantly, in its role as an antibacterial, it has been directly linked to increasing resistance to a range of antibiotics commonly used for treating infectious disease, one potential contributor to the evolution of "superbugs" (particularly one known as Methicillin-resistant *Staphylococcus aureus* [MRSA]), now a major national concern.[15] Triclosan was mentioned previously this chapter as one of the contaminants found in umbilical cord samples collected by Greenpeace International and Britain's WWF. Surveys in Sweden have also found triclosan in the breast milk of 60 percent of women.

Triclosan interacts with free chlorine in tap water and degrades under sunlight to produce chloroform. It also produces a class of persistent, highly toxic, carcinogenic chemicals known as dioxins[16]— an ingredient in the Agent Orange defoliant used by the U.S. in the Vietnam War. In 2005, an advisory panel to the FDA concluded that triclosan and triclocarban posed "unacceptable health and environmental risks," but the FDA hierarchy still ignores this conclusion and its implications. (See chapter 10 for more on triclosan and triclocarban.)

The third preservative frequently used in cosmetics and personal-care products, resorcinol, is well-known to block the synthesis and transport of the thyroid hormone in humans, primates, and other species. In spite of claims of safety, industry consultants reluctantly admit their failure to identify safe exposure levels in rodent tests.[16]

DETERGENTS (SURFACTANTS)

Detergents, or surfactants, are used in such products as cleansers. They include phenol ethoxylate detergents, including some fifteen nonoxynols (nonylphenols) and twenty-five octoxynols (octylphenols), which have been shown to have hormonal effects in fish and other species[17] and also to persist in rivers, lakes, and seas.[18]

Strong evidence has emerged that at least one nonoxynol, 4-NP, poses risks of breast cancer[19] A variety of doses of 4-NP or of estrogen were administered to mice genetically engineered for increased susceptibility to breast cancer. A high percentage of mice given 4-NP developed breast cancer over a thirty-two-week period, while mice given equivalent doses of estrogen did not. This study concluded that "Long-term exposure to 4-NP could leave individuals at a significantly increased risk of developing breast cancer."[19]

In 2003, the Norwegian government banned "most" uses of ethoxylate detergents. This action is the first outright ban on "the production, use, and sale of the substances in pure form or in compounds," aside from some paint and industrial lubricant products, for which no alternatives had then been identified.

SOLVENTS (PLASTICIZERS)

Solvents, or plasticizers, are ingredients used to help dissolve other ingredients in water. There are two kinds of solvents commonly used in cosmetics and personal-care products: phthalates and Bisphenol-A.

Phthalates are used in deodorant, hair gel, mousse, hair spray, shampoo, lipstick, mascara, nail polish, and perfume, as well as in fragrances. These ingredients are often hidden, remaining undisclosed on product labels.

Phthalates have been well known as hormone disrupters since 1980, when dibutyl phthalate was shown to cause testicular atrophy in rats.[2] Since then, several studies have revealed that the administration of phthalates to infant male rats causes numerous toxic reproductive effects.[20] In fact, nine separate male abnormalities related to phthalate exposure have been documented in rodent studies:

- Hypospadias, an abnormality in which the opening in the penis occurs on the bottom of the organ rather than at the head.
- Absent prostate gland, a condition in which the prostate does not form.
- Absent testes, a condition in which testicles do not form at all.
- Undescended testicles, an abnormality in which the testes fail to descend into the scrotal sac.
- Ectopic testes, an abnormality in which the testes grow outside the scrotal sac.
- Testicular atrophy, a defect that reduces the capacity to produce male sex hormones and sperm.
- Malformed or absent epididymis, a defect of the structure where sperm mature and are stored.
- Absent or small seminal vesicles, a defect in structures that contribute to semen secretion.
- Reduced sperm count, a condition that leads to infertility or reduced fertility.

Of particular significance is that, while inactive in feeding tests, phthalates induce hormonal effects following application to the skin. This further incriminates them as dangerous in cosmetics and personal-care products.

A 2000 survey by the U.S. Federal Centers for Disease Control and Prevention identified high levels of phthalates, particularly diethylhexyl phthalate (DEHP), in the urine of approximately 300 women.[21] The highest levels were found in women of reproductive age. A subsequent study on urine phthalate levels in about 2,500 people over the age of six confirmed and extended these findings.[22] Even phthalates at low levels were toxic in screening tests for hormone disrupters.[23] The significance of these findings is bolstered by evidence that men with high levels of phthalates in their urine had reduced sperm counts, low sperm motility, and more deformed sperm.[24]

A subsequent pilot study reported genital abnormalities in male babies whose mothers were found to have high levels of four phthalate byproducts.[25] These abnormalities included a reduction in the anogenital distance mentioned earlier. Disputing the significance of these findings, Marian Stanley, manager of the industry's Phthalate Esters Panel, said, "The authors are not reporting any negative health effect on the male reproductive system"[26]—a statement that is clearly false.

Air tests done in 120 U.S. homes identified about seventy contaminants in air and dust, including six phthalates that were found in all of the homes.[27] High levels of phthalates have been identified in domestic wastewater as a result of bodily excretion and product-dumping down sinks and commodes.[28] Phthalates have also been identified in the urine of men shortly after the use of cologne, aftershave, hair products, and deodorants.[29] A study using men from an infertility clinic showed a strong relation between low sperm motility and levels of a phthalate metabolite in the urine.[30]

In spite of these findings, the industry still persists in refusing to list phthalates on product labels, using the highly misleading rationale that they are common ingredients in fragrances and thus exempt from labeling requirements because of trade secrecy laws. The 2007 Cosmetic Industry Review Compendium concludes that phthalates are "safe in the present practices of use and concentration in cosmetics."[31] However, the Compendium also admitted that oral administration of dibutyl phthalate "produced testicular atrophy in various test rodents." The American Chemistry Council is also dismissive of the toxicity of these ingredients, insisting that "phthalates are among the most widely studied materials in the world and have been researched and tested for more than fifty years."

Despite these protestations by manufacturers, and the FDA's advice to consumers that "there is no reason to be alarmed" by hidden risks posed by phthalates, the European Union examined similar study data and was alarmed enough to order the phase-out of common phthalates in 2005. An increasing number of companies, as well, including Dr. Hauschka, California Baby, Buddha Nose, and REN, are recognizing the danger and phasing out the use of phthalate ingredients.

Bisphenol-A (BPA), discussed earlier in the section on "gender bender" effects, is another plasticizer, one frequently used in the manufacture of polycarbonate water, baby, and cosmetic bottles, food can linings, microwave oven dishes, dental sealants, and medical devices. In addition to the effects outlined previously, exposure to very low levels in pregnant rodents—2,000 times lower than the Environmental Protection Agency's "safe dose"—resulted in sexual abnormalities in the rodents' offspring.[32,33] The offspring also had an increased number of "terminal end buds" in breast tissue, which are associated with a high risk of breast cancer.[34] An American Plastics Council spokesman publicly claimed that the human relevance of these findings is only "hypothetical."

BPA has also been found in human blood and placental and fetal tissues, and has been incriminated as a predisposing factor or cause of human prostate cancer.[35] The authors of the above study on BPA and breast cancer risk in rats also linked the reported incidence of endocrine-dependent human cancers, such as breast cancer, to even the minimal levels of estrogen-like chemicals, particularly BPA, to which pregnant women are exposed. An August 2, 2007, consensus statement by several dozen scientists warned that BPA, even at very low exposure levels, is probably responsible for many human reproductive disorders.[6]

Most recently, on October 3, 2008, *ScienceDaily* reported on a forthcoming article on phthalates and BPA set to appear in a special section of Environmental Research called "A Plastic World." Two articles reported on the very similar toxic reproductive effects in rats and in humans relating to fetal exposure to phthalates. Two other articles reported that fetal exposure to BPA disrupted the normal development of the brain and behavior in rats and mice. Two final articles reported that these chemicals are massively contaminating the oceans and harming aquatic wildlife.

LAVENDER AND TEA TREE OILS

Lavender and tea tree oils pose another kind of hormone disruption dilemma: breast enlargement, technically known as gynecomastia, has been reported in three boys, ranging from four to ten years old, following repeated use of scented soap, shampoo, and a "healing" balm containing tea tree or lavender oils.[36] Laboratory tests have also confirmed that both oils possess weak estrogenic and anti-testosterone effects. Lavender and tea tree oils are sold over the counter in pure form, and are also included in a wide range of soaps, shampoos, and lotions.

METALLOESTROGENS

Metalloestrogens are a new class of hormone disrupters, metals shown to have hormone disruption effects: aluminum, lead, cadmium, copper, and tin.[37,38] High concentrations of aluminum chloride, labeled or more commonly unlabeled, are the main ingredient in underarm and other antiperspirants, and also appear in sunscreens. And contrary to popular belief, they are readily absorbed through intact skin, particularly after shaving. A statistically significant association has been demonstrated between the long-term use of aluminum antiperspirants and Alzheimer's disease[39,40], and aluminum antiperspirants have also been shown to produce oxidative skin damage, notably wrinkles and aging (see chapter 10 for more details).

SUNSCREEN INGREDIENTS

See chapter 8 for details.

Special Phthalate Alert for Babies

Babies who had been recently shampooed, lotioned, or pow-dered with common brand-name baby products were found to have elevated levels of phthalates in their urine, according to a February 2008 study in the journal *Pediatrics*.

Researchers from two universities and the Centers for Disease Control and Prevention measured phthalate levels in the diaper urine of several hundred babies in three U.S. states within twenty-four hours of the use of lotions, powders, diaper creams, baby wipes, and shampoos. The highest phthalate lev-els came from the shampoos, lotions, and powders.

The higher the number of personal-care products used on a baby, the higher the baby's absorption of phthalates, espe-cially among the youngest infants. As the researchers conduct-ing this study noted, the youngest "may be more vulnerable to developmental and reproductive toxicity of phthalates given their immature metabolic system capability and increased dos-age per unit body surface area."

Detailed Guide to Safer Infant and Child Products

For a comprehensive guide to safer children's personal-care products—and hazardous brands to avoid—access the Envi-ronmental Working Group's cosmetic safety database: www. cosmeticsdatabase.com/special/parentsguide/.

Table 6: Toxic Ingredients in Products for Infants and Children

INGREDIENT	TOXIC EFFECT(S)
Benzyl alcohol	Allergen
Ceteareths	Contaminated with the carcinogens ethylene oxide and dioxane
Diazolidinyl Urea	Precursor of the carcinogen formaldehyde
DMDM Hydantoin	Precursor of the carcinogen formaldehyde
EDTA	Hormone disrupter and penetration enhancer
FD&C Red 40	Carcinogen
Lanolin	Allergen
Laureths	Contaminated with the carcinogens ethylene oxide and dioxane
Parabens	Hormone disrupters
Polyethylene glycol (PEG)	Contaminated with the carcinogens ethylene oxide and dioxane
Polysorbates	Contaminated with the carcinogens ethylene oxide and dioxane
Quaternium-15	Precursor of the carcinogen formaldehyde
Sodium lauryl sulfate	Penetration enhancer
Talc (talcum powder)	Carcinogen and lung irritant
Triethanolamine (TEA)	Precursor of the carcinogen nitrosamine

Safe Products for Infants and Children*

BABY WIPES
Avalon Organics Flushable Biodegradeable Baby Wipes
INGREDIENTS: demineralized water, organic aloe, organic chamomile, witch hazel, decyl glucoside, barbadensis juice, calendula extracts, citric acid, gluconolactone, sodium benzoate, vegetable glycerin
www.avalonorganics.com

Tushies Baby Wipes with Aloe Vera
INGREDIENTS: water, aloe vera, vegetable derived glycerin, vitamin E, allantoin, panthenol, tartaric acid, potassium sorbate
www.drugstore.com

DIAPER CREAMS
Aromababy Barrier Balm
INGREDIENTS: (all certified organic) evening primrose oil, vitamin E, cold pressed pure sweet almond oil, beeswax, cetostearyl alcohol, calendula oil, carrot oil, rose essential oil, neroli essential oil, chamomile essential oil
www.aromababy.com

LOTIONS/MOISTURIZERS
Aromababy Natural Baby Lotion
INGREDIENTS (certified organic): avocado oil, safflower oil, mango butter, evening primrose oil, jojoba oil, rosehip oil, vitamin E, hydroxymthlglycinate
www.aromababy.com

Cosmic Tree Essentials Simply Shea and Tamanu Body Butter
INGREDIENTS: shea butter, tamanu oil, rosemary extract
www.cosmictree.ca

---

*These listings, here and in the other chapters in Part Two, are based on information from company Web sites and also on listings of certified organic product companies from Table 15 in chapter 12.

Emily Skin Soothers Lotions
Emily Skin Soothers is a product line that uses no preservatives, fragrances, parabens, petroleum products, colorants, or "unpronounceable chemicals."
INGREDIENTS: olive oil, beeswax, Angelica Sinensis Root, Potentillae Chinensis herb, Haplocalyx herb
www.emilyskinsoothers.com

SHAMPOOS/CONDITIONERS
Aubrey Organics Natural Baby and Kids Shampoo
INGREDIENTS: deionized water, coconut oil, corn oil soap, hydrolyzed soy protein, extracts of fennel, hops, balm mint, mistletoe, chamomile and yarrow, citrus seed extract, xanthan gum, vanilla oil, almond oil
www.aubrey-organics.com

Dr. Bronner's Castile Liquid Soap
INGREDIENTS (certified organic): water, saponified organic coconut, organic palm, organic olive oil, organic hemp oil, organic jojoba oil, essential oils, citric acid, vitamin E
www.drbronner.com

Jason 2-in-1 Shampoo & Body Wash
Contains no parabens, lanolin, sodium lauryl, or laureth sulfates.
INGREDIENTS: organic chamomile and marigold extracts, lavender, beta glucan
www.jason-natural.com

SOAPS
Dr. Bronner's Baby Mild Organic Bar Soap
INGREDIENTS: saponified organic coconut, palm, and olive oils, water, organic hemp oil, organic jojoba oil, citric acid, vitamin E
www.drbronner.com

Emily Skin Soothers Soap
INGREDIENTS: shea butter, avocado oil, coconut oil, olive oil, palm oil, Angelica Sinensis Root, Potentillae Chinensis herb, Haplocalyx herb
www.emilyskinsoothers.com

Vermont Soap Organics
INGREDIENTS: hypoallergenic vegetable base of organic coconut, palm, olive, and palm kernel oils, aromatherapy essential oils, rosemary extract
www.vermontsoap.com

BABY POWDER

Any brand of talcum powder or baby powder with talc must be avoided. The use of talcum dusting powder in infants is dangerous. It can result in inhalation of significant amounts of powder, causing acute or chronic lung irritation, known as talcosis, and also possible risk of lung cancer. (Unlike with genital application in premenopausal women, it does not pose a risk of ovarian cancer. See chapter 6 for more details.)

Organic cornstarch powder is a reliable, safe, and readily available alternative to talc for the dusting of a baby's genital areas.

Special Warning: Titanium dioxide is sometimes used to whiten dusting powders. This additive further heightens the cancer risk to infants because, in powdered form, it is a frank carcinogen, as documented by inhalation exposure in rodent testing. The International Agency for Research on Cancer cites several studies from 1985 that found lung cancer in rats following their exposure to titanium dioxide powder. Infants should never be exposed to this substance. (See the box on page 97 and chapter 8 for more information on titanium dioxide.)

CHILDREN'S TOOTHPASTE

Peelu Company Spearmint Toothpowder
INGREDIENTS: peelu powder, natural oil of spearmint
www.peelu.com

Healing-Scents Spearmint Toothgel
INGREDIENTS: spearmint, myrrh, thyme essential oils, neem seed oil, baking soda, zinc oxide, titanium dioxide, kaolin clay, water, glycerine, cellulose, xanthan gum
www.healing-scents.com

the U.S. contain ingredients that "the U.S. cosmetic industry's own safety panel has determined to be unsafe when used as directed." The analysis also revealed that 751 personal-care products marketed in the U.S. either "violate industry safety standards or cosmetic safety standards in other industrialized countries."[4]

Perfumes and fragrances, including essential oils, are the largest single category of personal-care product. Fragrances are especially common as a component of hair, facial, eye, and nail products. And the most prominent dangers in perfume and fragrances are allergens.

Allergens are a large group of natural and synthetic chemicals that cause immunological sensitization of the skin, known as allergic contact dermatitis. This is entirely different from non-specific dermatitis, also known as irritant contact dermatitis, which originates with skin irritation from dryness and other damage.[5]

Allergic contact dermatitis involves two distinct stages. First, the skin comes into contact with an allergen, which sensitizes specific "memory cells" to that allergen. Subsequent exposure to the allergen, some five to ten days later, causes the sensitized cells to release specific molecules (known as cytokines), which trigger an allergic reaction. This reaction can range from mere itching and transient redness, to swelling, blistering, and ulceration. While this reaction is initially localized to the immediate area of the allergen-exposed skin, it may spread and require treatment with antihistamines and cortisone, or even hospitalization. Fatal anaphylactic shock has even been reported as a rare complication.

There have been many and varying estimates on the frequency of allergic contact dermatitis in the general adult population, though the consensus is that the incidence of allergic contact dermatitis in most nations has expanded significantly over recent decades. Probably one of the best estimates is provided by a Danish study done on people between fifteen and sixty-nine years of age.[6] It showed that the overall incidence of sensitization in the Danish population, which in 1990 was 15 percent, had increased to 19 percent by 1998.

Numerous allergenic ingredients are present both in perfumes, which are used mostly by women, and in fragrances, which are added to most cosmetics and personal-care products used by everyone, and there is a clear link between exposure to these allergens and the dramatic increase we have seen in allergies over the past few decades. A large-scale survey by the North American Contact Dermatitis Group found that the incidence of cosmetic allergy, which from 1992 to 1994 was 11 percent of the population, increased to 14 percent from 1994 to 1996[7]—an increase of millions of people, mainly women. Perfumes and fragrances are, by far, the most common causes of allergic contact dermatitis. In fact, the incidence of cosmetic allergy in the U.S. population (about 14 percent) is twice that of food allergy (about 7 percent), which is noteworthy in view of recent legislation requiring consumer-friendly label warnings for food allergens.[8]

This is particularly critical to know because the synthetic fragrance market is currently growing by leaps and bounds—and it is likely synthetics that are causing most of the trouble. The chemicals that give perfumes and fragrances their aromas are manufactured in one of three ways: chemical synthesis from petrochemicals; chemical modification of isolates from natural sources; or direct extraction from natural sources. In various combinations, perfumes and fragrances use at least 5,000 different ingredients, and about 95 percent of these are synthetic, A single American or French designer perfume can contain up to sixty ingredients, nearly all synthetic. These synthetic ingredients can appear at concentrations up to 35 percent in perfumes, though they are used at much lower concentrations in fragrances. The discovery of highly potent "aroma boosters," which can be added to synthetic fragrances and perfumes to give them more power, means products will need less of the organic ingredients to achieve the same intensity of aroma. (Some of these boosters are also toxic in their own right. The latest of these boosters is cyclooctane carbaldehyde, which has been shown to be highly toxic to the kidneys.[3])

Another link between fragrances and allergens: fragrances may also be involved in causing asthma. Asthma is a chronic allergic condition that affects more than 20 million people in the U.S., according to the Centers for Disease Control and Prevention, and about

300 million people worldwide, based on World Health Organization statistics. More than half of all asthmatics have reported experiencing asthma attacks triggered by fragrances or odors, and numerous allergenic ingredients have been identified in perfumes. Warning labels for twenty-six of them are already required by the European Union. This may also provide a clue as to why one in ten people in the U.S. suffers from bouts of asthma, compared to only one in twenty of the world's population. The U.S. has long been the world's leading innovator in adding fragrances to products, especially cosmetics and personal-care products. Also, "The prevalence of asthma (in the U.S.) has been increasing since the early 1980s for all age, sex, and racial groups," reports the National Institutes of Health's Heart, Lung, and Blood Institute, and that jump in the incidence of asthma coincides with the immense surge of fragrances being added to consumer products in the 1970s and '80s.[6]

Allergens are not, however, the only, or even the most serious, danger of perfumes and fragrances. In 2007, *Consumer Reports* financed lab testing of eight perfumes selected at random found hormone-disruptive phthalates DBP and DEHP in every one of them.

And in a 1986 report to a committee of the U.S. Congress, the National Academy of Sciences labeled certain fragrance ingredients as neurotoxins. And yet, despite this finding about the impact of fragrance chemicals on the human brain, the FDA rejected citizen petitions urging that product labels clearly list fragrance ingredients so consumers could, at the very least, make informed choices.

A revealing summary on the absence of regulatory oversight of the fragrance industry and the potential health problems associated with the regular use or exposure to fragrances appeared in a 2002 issue of *Flavor and Fragrance Journal*. It is worth quoting a few passages from that paper to illustrate the challenges that consumers faced then, and still face today:

> There is little information available on the materials used in fragrance. Fragrance formulas are considered trade secrets and components that make up

the fragrance portion of the product are not revealed on labels. Fragrance is increasingly cited as a trigger in health conditions such as asthma, allergies and migraine headaches. In addition, some fragrance materials have been found to accumulate in adipose tissue and are present in breast milk. Other materials are suspected of being hormone disrupters. The implications are not fully known, as there has been little evaluation of systemic effects. There are environmental concerns as well, as fragrances are volatile compounds, which add to both indoor and outdoor air pollution. At present there is little governmental regulation of fragrance. The fragrance industry has in place a system of self-regulation. However, the present system has failed to address many of the emerging concerns.[9]

Talcum Powder and Your Risk of Cancer

The mortality of ovarian cancer, a relatively rare cancer at any age, has escalated dramatically in women sixty-five years of age and older since 1975: 16 percent in white women, and 52 percent in black women. There are about 15,300 deaths from ovarian cancer each year, making it the fourth most common fatal cancer in women, after breast, colon, and lung cancer. Even though talcum powder is strongly linked to ovarian cancer, an estimated one out of every five women regularly applies it to her genital area, whether directly or via application to sanitary pads, tampons, and diaphragms.

As early as 1992, a publication in *Obstetrics & Gynecology* reported information that frequent talc use on the genital area increases a woman's risk of ovarian cancer threefold—using information that was already a decade old. "The most frequent method of talc exposure," the study reported, "was use as a dusting powder directly to the perineum [genitals]. . . . Brand or generic 'baby powder' was

Table 7: Allergens in Perfumes and Fragrances

Alpha isomethyl ionone
Amyl cinnamal*
Amyl cinnamyl alcohol*
Anise alcohol*
Balsam of Peru*
Benzyl alcohol*
Benzyl benzoate*
Benzyl cinnamate*
Benzyl salicylate*
Butylphenyl/methylpropional*
Cetyl alcohol
Cinnamal*
Cinnamic aldehyde*
Cinnamyl alcohol*
Citral*
Citronellol*
Clove oil
Coumarin*
Eugenol*
Evernia furfuracea (treemoss
    extract)*
Evernia prunastri (oakmoss
    extract)*

Farnesol*
Fennel oil
Geraniol*
Hexyl cinnamal*
Hydroxycitronellol*
Isoeugenol*
Isomethyl ionone*
Jasmine absolute
Lanolin and lanolin alcohols
Lavender oil
Lemongrass oil
Limonene*
Linalool
Methyl coumarin
Methyl-2 octynoate*
Narcissus absolute
Nitro musks
Oakmoss*
Phthalates
Resorcinol
Vanillin
Ylang-ylang*

---

*Warning labels required by the European Union

used most frequently and was the category associated with a statistically significant risk for ovarian cancer."[10]

In 1994 and again in 1996 (as related in chapter 4), the Cancer Prevention Coalition and the New York Center for Constitutional Rights, endorsed by the Ovarian Cancer Early Detection and Prevention Program and leading scientists, submitted a Citizen's Petition to the FDA demanding that talc genital dusting powder be labeled with an explicit cancer warning. The FDA inexplicably denied the petition.

How to Diagnose Allergic Dermatitis

Diagnosing the cause of allergic dermatitis is done based on the location of the rash, coupled with information on recent product of use. For instance, a rash on the neck or wrists is commonly associated with the recent use of perfumes at these sites, while a rash on the head is generally associated with the recent use of hair dyes. A rash on the fingertips suggests a reaction to nail polish.

Diagnosis may be more difficult if a patient is not seen by a dermatologist until weeks after allergic dermatitis's onset. By this time, the dermatitis may have spread well beyond the originally exposed area, and the patient may be hazy about their past product use. In these circumstances, diagnosis generally requires a diagnostic test known as the patch test.

In a patch test, a drop of liquid containing a mix of commonly known allergens is applied to the skin. The skin is then covered by an occlusive tape, and after two days the tape is removed and the skin inspected. Local redness and swelling indicate that the reaction is due to one of the allergens in the test mix. In the absence of any local reaction, the test is repeated with a different mix of allergens, particularly those recently used in products.

Commercial patch test kits are available as a "fragrance mix" (FM) of seven common allergens. Included in both the North American and the European Standard Patch Test trays: balsam of Peru; hydroxycitronellol; cinnamyl alcohol; cinnamic aldehyde; oakmoss; eugenol; and geraniol. The highest concentration of FM allergens is found in prestige perfumes. However, the FM test fails to identify up to 30 percent of fragrance allergens. Among the most important are essential oils, particularly lemongrass, jasmine absolute, and ylang-ylang.

"Fragrance-Free" and "Hypoallergenic"

Some cosmetics, and other fragranced products, are labeled "fragrance-free" even if they contain fragrance ingredients. Also, some companies misleadingly label their cosmetics, if they do not contain any of the few allergenic ingredients tested for in Standard Patch Test trays, as "hypoallergenic." While the "hypoallergenic" label, not to mention other labels such as "allergy tested" and "safe for sensitive skin," have considerable promotional value, they can mean just about whatever any particular company wants them to mean. Manufacturers of these products are not required to do any testing to validate these claims.

In the continuing absence of any action or response from the FDA, on May 13, 2008, the Cancer Prevention Coalition, with endorsements from leading scientific experts and consumer organizations, including the International Association for Humanitarian Medicine, the Organic Consumers Association, and Dr. Faye Williams of the National Congress of Black Women, submitted a second petition to the FDA, further updating the scientific evidence on the lethal effects of talc. It requested that the FDA require that all cosmetic talc products bear labels with a warning such as: "Frequent application of talcum powder in the female genital area substantially increases the risk of ovarian cancer."

Evidence supporting the petition was based on twelve science articles published in such medical journals as *Cancer, The Lancet Oncology,* and the *International Journal of Cancer* since the previous petition was denied. These convincingly confirmed the causal link between genital application of talc and ovarian cancer. One of these major studies, in 2003 for the journal *Anticancer Research*, did what is known as a "meta-analysis" of sixteen other published studies involving a total of 11,933 subjects. This confirmed a statistically significant 33 percent increased risk of ovarian cancer associated with the genital use of talc.

As stated in the 2008 petition, J. Mande, Acting Associate Commissioner for Legislative Affairs of the Department of Health and Human Services, admitted in August 1993 that

> We are aware that there have been reports in the medical literature between frequent female perineal talc dusting over a protracted period of years, and an incremental increase in the statistical odds of subsequent development of certain ovarian cancers. . . . (However) at the present time, the FDA is not considering to ban, restrict or require a warning statement on the label of talc containing products.

Also noted in the petition: In an August 12, 1992, *New York Times* article, manufacturer and retailer of talc dusting powder Johnson & Johnson also admitted that frequent genital dusting with talc increases risks of ovarian cancer threefold—a risk belatedly admitted in 2008 by the industry's Cosmetic Toiletry and Fragrance Association as well. And in 2002, Edward Kavanaugh, president of the industry's Cosmetic Toiletry and Fragrance Association, acknowledged that talc is "toxic" and "can reach the human ovaries."

The 2008 petition goes on to point out how in 1997, Senator Edward Kennedy, in a statement to the U.S. Senate, had urged the FDA to place a cancer warning on the label of talc products, along with other products containing known carcinogens. More than a decade later, the Agency still remained unresponsive.

As noted in chapter 4, the FDA's response to this petition is still pending as of this writing.

What Is Really in Your Lipstick?

The practice of coloring one's lips to appear more attractive to potential romantic partners has been around since the time of Cleopatra, who painted her lips with carmine and henna to give them a fashionable appeal for her Roman suitors. It turns out, however, that many of those colored kisses are poisoned: most brand-name lipsticks sold in the U.S. contain detectable levels of lead that can be toxic

Beware of Powdered Titanium Dioxide

Titanium dioxide loose powder is used by cosmetics companies as a whitening agent in facial powders, which are marketed mainly to women.

Powdered and ultrafine titanium dioxide dust is a carcinogen that has been implicated in respiratory tract cancer in rats exposed during laboratory testing. Canada's Centre for Occupational Health & Safety issued an alert in 2006 warning employers to "review their occupational hygiene programs to ensure that exposure to titanium dioxide dust is eliminated or reduced to the minimum possible." Manufacturers were advised to alter product labels to reflect this danger.

The Canadian alert was based on the International Agency for Research on Cancer's classification of titanium dioxide as a carcinogen in 2006. By 1995 the National Institute of Occupational Safety and Health had also confirmed that titanium dioxide induces lung cancer in rodents following inhalation and that there is no safe exposure level.

The U.S. Department of Labor's Material Safety Data Sheet on this substance further warns: "Precautions: Do not breathe dust. Causes respiratory tract irritation." It also notes: "Protective Equipment: Be sure to use an approved respirator" if handling the powder.

Titanium dioxide powder particle size is very fine, less than one micron, which is why it is readily inhaled deeply into human lungs. Though titanium dioxide appears in sunblocks, toothpastes, and other non-powdered products, it poses no similar threat to health in those non-powder forms. But dozens of women's facial powders containing titanium dioxide are widely available on store shelves, often without indicating titanium dioxide's inclusion on product labels because it is not considered an active ingredient. Barbers and hairdressers sometimes fluff the powder on their customer's faces. Actors

continued on the next page

Beware of Powdered Titanium Dioxide, *continued*

and actresses, along with others who appear frequently on television, also have high exposure levels.

Manufacturers of some "natural" lines of cosmetics remain wholly uninformed or misinformed about titanium dioxide's carcinogenic risk. Earth Beauty Cosmetics, for instance, advertises its Real Purity product as containing titanium dioxide. Our survey of other brands of "natural solutions" cosmetic powders, such as Logona Cosmetics and Sante Kosmetics, also found titanium dioxide to be a common additive.

Skin Whiteners

Skin whiteners or lighteners are now being intensively marketed to women of African and Asian descent. These lighteners are now the world's fastest growing product category, and comprise 10 percent of the Asian cosmetic market.

Whiteners contain two active ingredients, the potent natural hormone cortisone and the frank carcinogen hydroquinone (an ingredient banned in Europe that poses risks of leukemia and genetic damage[11]). This combination inhibits the natural production of melanin, the compound responsible for dark pigmentation of the skin.

to the wearer, according to a 2007 study by the Campaign for Safe Cosmetics. Of thirty-three brands of lipstick sent to an independent laboratory for analysis, 61 percent contained lead. Many lead levels were much higher than what the FDA allows for candy (0.1 parts per million)—the only standard we can use to measure against, because the FDA has set no limits for lead in lipstick.[12]

What the report fails to take into account is that the lead in lipsticks is a contaminant, *not* an ingredient, and as such is not subject to any regulation.

The four worst offending brands were:

- L' Oreal Colour Riche "True Red"
- L'Oreal Colour Riche "Classic Wine"
- Cover Girl Incredifull Lipcolor "Maximum Red"
- Christian Dior Addict "Positive Red"

A year earlier, a television station in Pittsburgh, Pennsylvania, had five brands of lipstick tested by a laboratory, and lead was detected in every sample. Other similar tests initiated by media outlets in other parts of the country found lead in lipstick to be about four times the FDA safety limit for lead in candy sold in stores.[13] Lead as a contaminant has also been found in lip glosses and lip conditioners.

This is bad news for most women and for the two-thirds of girls ten years old and younger who experiment with lip products. Each time a woman or girl wearing lipstick wets or licks her lips, especially when eating, she ingests some of the lipstick's chemicals. Those same chemicals are also absorbed directly through her lips and into her bloodstream. The subsequent lead exposure can result in slow poisoning, as lead accumulates in the body over time. Lead is readily absorbed by the body, accumulates in bone, remains highly persistent, and is highly toxic to the nervous system, particularly in embryos, and babies born with lead exposure that occurred in the womb, as well as children exposed to lead, can develop serious complications, including decreased attention span, impulsiveness, lowered IQ, seizures, aggressiveness, and even brain damage.

"The problem with lead in the body is that it mimics other biologically important metals such as iron, calcium, and zinc," says Dr. Edward C. Geehr, former Clinical Associate Professor of Medicine and Surgery at the University of California, San Francisco. "By taking the place of these metals in certain proteins and molecules, lead interferes with normal biological processes. For example, it hampers certain neurotransmitters responsible for learning and brain development. Lead also interferes with enzymes critical to the production of red blood cells, leading to a form of anemia similar to that caused by iron deficiency. Gastrointestinal symptoms of lead poisoning include constipation, diarrhea, vomiting, metallic taste, and weight loss."[14]

Unsafe Lipsticks Versus Safer Lipsticks

Out of 393 brands of lipsticks rated on the "Skin Deep" Web site (www.cosmeticsdatabase.com) maintained by the Environmental Working Group, only six were given a top rating of safest (and one of these contained an ingredient potentially contaminated by toxins), while seventy-eight were categorized as hazardous based on the toxicity of their ingredients. The rest of the brands fell somewhere in between on a scale of 0 (most safe) to 10 (most hazardous).

The highest hazard lipsticks in the database:

- Avon Color Trend Essential Lipstick
- Avon Ultra Color Rich
- Color Me Beautiful Class Cream
- Dior Addict Lipstick
- Estée Lauder Pure Color Cystal
- Palladio Lipstick
- Philosophy the supernatural Cream Lipstick
- Philosophy word of mouth lipstick
- Revlon Moisture Cream Lipstick
- Revlon Moisture Frost (all colors)
- Revlon Moon Drops (33 different variations)
- Revlon Super Lustrous (21 different variations)
- Studio Gear Luxury Lipstick
- Sue Devitt Studio Matte Lipstick (4 different variations)
- Sue Devitt Studio Sheer Lipstick (4 different variations)
- Vincent Longo Cream Frost Lipstick, Natural
- Zhen Cream Lipstick

Five of the safer lipsticks from the study are listed under "Safe Products for Women" in this chapter. (The sixth, Afterglow Cosmetics lipstick, contains the potentially contaminated ingredient lanolin.)

Unfortunately, even after you find a brand of lipstick that has been tested for lead content and found safe, there is yet another safety hurdle to overcome. Laboratory tests done in 2004 by the National Environmental Trust discovered unlabeled hormone-disruptive phthalates in Revlon Moondrops Lipstick, as well as in other well-known brands.[15]

Table 8: Toxic Ingredients in Products for Women

INGREDIENT	TOXIC EFFECT(S)
Benzyl alcohol	Allergen
Ceteareths	Contaminated with the carcinogens ethylene oxide and dioxane
Disodium EDTA	Penetration enhancer and hormone disrupter
Limonene	Carcinogen
Parabens	Hormone disrupters
Phthalates (DEHP and DEP)	Hormone disrupters
Polyethylene glycol (PEG)	Contaminated with ethylene oxide and dioxane
Laureths	Contaminated with ethylene oxide and dioxane
Talc (talcum powder)	Carcinogen
Triethanolamine (TEA)	Precursor of the carcinogen nitrosamine

Safe Products for Women

PERFUMES
Bella Mira Organic Angelica Root Essential Oil
One of several dozen fragrances in this product line with no chemical solvents.
INGREDIENTS (organic): steam-distilled angelica root essential oil
www.aundantlifeessentials.com

Coastal Classic Creations "Quiet Waters" Tuberose Perfume
INGREDIENTS: organic sweet almond oil, organic tuberose oil
www.coastalclassiccreations.com

Cosmic Tree Essentials Chocolate Cosmos Botanical Scent
INGREDIENTS: caprylic/capric trigyceride, theobroma cacao (cocoa) absolute, vanilla planifolia (vanilla) absolute
www.cosmictree.ca

GENITAL POWDER
Any common brand of talcum powder poses a threat to health.
At least forty published scientific studies have found evidence that women who dust themselves with powder containing talc particles for hygiene purposes substantially raise their risks of ovarian cancer.

Organic cornstarch powder is a reliable, safe, and readily available alternative to talc for the dusting of genital areas and also for feminine hygiene.

LIPSTICKS
Barefaced Mineral Cosmetics Natural Lipstick
INGREDIENTS: Castor oil, Sesame oil, Coconut oil, Cocoa oil, Candelilla wax, Meadowfoam Seed oil, Cocoa butter, Mango butter, Shea butter, Tocopherol, Iron Oxides
www.barefacedminerals.com

CARGO Reverse Lipliner for Gloss or Lipstick
INGREDIENTS: titanium dioxide, iron oxides, hydrogenated palm kernel glycerides, hydrogenated palm glycerides, hydrogenated vegetable oil, talc, tocopherol, caprylic/caprictriglycerida, Japan wax, ascorbyl palmitate
www.drugstore.com

Musq Lipstick
INGREDIENTS: castor seed oil, jojoba seed oil, mica, carnauba wax, candelilla wax, shea butter, orange peel oil, tocopherol, titanium dioxide, iron oxides, ultramarines, pigment violet
www.musq.com.au

RJ Mineral Cosmetics Lipstick
100 percent vegan in twenty-six shades.
INGREDIENTS: castor seed oil, jojoba seed oil, mica, carnauba wax, candelilla wax, shea butter, orange peel oil, tocopherol, titanium dioxide, iron oxides, ultramarines, pigment violet
www.rjmineralcosmetics.com.au

Valana Minerals Sparkle Lips Vegan Lipstick
INGREDIENTS: cocoa butter, candelilla wax, castor oil, meadowfoam seed oil, avocado butter, macadamia nut oil, mica, titanium dioxide, iron oxide
www.valanaminerals.com

MASCARAS
Dr. Hauschka Skin Care Mascara
INGREDIENTS: water, pyrus cydonia seed extract, alcohol, saccharum officinarum (sugar cane) extract, sorbitol, mica, ricinus communis (castor) seed oil, acacia senegal gum, cetearyl alcohol, beeswax/cera flava, camellia sinensis leaf extract, melia azadirachta leaf extract, euphorbia cerifera (candelilla) wax, lysolecithin, euphrasia officinalis extract, silk/serica powder, hydrogenated jojoba oil, rosa damascena flower wax, rosa damascena flower oil, fragrance/parfum, citronellol, geraniol, linalool, hectorite, maltodextrin, ferric ferrocyanide/CI

77510, carmine/CI 75470, iron oxide/CI 77491, iron oxide/CI 77499, titanium dioxide/CI 77891, ultramarines/CI 77007
www.drhauschka.com

Jane Iredale Purebrow Fix & Mascara
INGREDIENTS: water, PVP, glycerin, glyceryl polymethacrylate, carbomer, panthenol, aloe barbadensis leaf extract, hydrolyzed wheat protein, algae extract, vanilla tahitensis fruit extract, prunus amygdalus dulcis (sweet almond) seed extract
www.janeiredale.com

SKIN CLEANSERS/FACIALS
Mountain Girl Botanics Aspen Spa Soap
INGREDIENTS: saponified oils of olea europaea (olive, organic), cocos nucifera (coconut, organic), elaeis guinnesis (palm, organic), mel (honey), Persea gratissima (avocado, organic) oil, avena sativa (oatmeal, organic), lavandula officinalis (lavender, organic) flower, calendula officinalis (calendula, organic) flower, matricaria chamomilla (chamomile, organic) flower, rosemarinus officinalis (rosemary) extract, essential oils of pelargonium graveolens (geranium), eugenia caryophillata (clove bud, organic), juniperus communis (juniper berry), and pogostemon patchouli (patchouli)
www.mountaingirlbotanics.com

Pangea Organics Facial Cleanser, Egyptian Calendula & Blood Orange
INGREDIENTS: purified water, organic lavender alcohol, organic coconut oil, organic extra virgin olive oil, organic hemp seed oil, organic jojoba oil, caprylic/capric triglyceride derived from coconut oil, soy lecithin, natural vegetable glycerin, almond oil, organic rice bran extract, organic shea butter, organic argan oil and evening primrose, safflower seed oil, pumpkin seed oil, vitamins E and C
www.pangeaorganics.com

7 | Products Targeting Beauty and Nail Salons

S tep into any beauty or nail salon and the first thing you are likely to be aware of is the unmistakable odor of synthetic chemicals. As these fumes assault your nose and then your lungs, you are being exposed to numerous toxic chemicals. The impact on salon workers, who are exposed for long hours every day, is so severe that their job description should come with a warning label.

To complicate matters for salon employees, cosmetology schools are unaware of, or fail to inform their students about, the hazards of carcinogenic and other toxic ingredients in beauty products. Most states use standards for their cosmetology schools that are generally similar in how their curricula are structured to meet licensing requirements. For instance, the Georgia State Board of Cosmetology requires students to complete a minimum of nine months and 1,500 credit hours of training divided into six courses: skin and nail care; permanent waving; hair coloring; hair and scalp treatments; hair cutting; and hairdressing.[1] Following an initial 250 credit hours of instruction, the students advance to practical application by performing supervised services for clients. This curriculum touches on sanitation and sterilization, and the chemistry of how products affect skin and hair, but no instruction is given on how ingredients pose serious threats to the health of the stylists and, to a lesser extent, their clients.

Judy Le, a student in one of California's cosmetology schools, recalled in a 2006 interview with the National Asian Pacific American Women's Forum how she first learned about cancer-causing ingredients in beauty products only while doing independent research outside of her cosmetology school. She then confronted her instructors, who admitted that they knew little or nothing about chemical hazards. "The program didn't talk much about harmful ingredients," she related. "We weren't given this information. The program didn't focus on health hazards. It focused on the money-making aspect."[2]

Products used in hairdressing and beauty salons contain many unlabeled toxic ingredients. These include carcinogens, hormone disrupters such as phthalates and parabens, allergens, and penetration enhancers. BBC News reported on November 21, 2008, that Professor Paul Elliot of the Imperial College London had found that male infants of hairdressers and beauty salon therapists exposed to hairsprays during pregnancy developed anogenital abnormalities, which were attributed to the endocrine disruptive effect of phthalates (see chapter 5).[3]

Salon products are often dispensed from bulk containers without readily available ingredient labels. Of even greater concern is the cumulative contamination of the air in salons with volatile ingredients, as well as fine particles from hair sprays, known as aerosols, which penetrate deep into the lungs.

Workers in the hair and nail care businesses tend to drift in and out of these jobs, so epidemiological studies to ascertain impacts on health with certainty are hardly feasible. But we do know that toxic effects experienced by salon workers include respiratory illness and asthma, nausea, sleep disorders, fatigue, and numbness and pain in the fingers. We've had substantial evidence as to these effects on the health of hairdressers, barbers, and to a lesser extent, beauty stylists since the 1970s.[4] Even then, health effects included skin irritation, allergic contact dermatitis, and acute lung irritation, as well as increased incidence of asthma and chronic bronchitis. And in spite of the explicit and long-standing evidence, salon employees, let alone their clients, still remain mostly unaware of these risks.

The Problem with Hair Dyes

An estimated 35 percent of women and 10 percent of men in the U.S., Japan, and Europe use hair dyes either regularly or infrequently. For most, almost every time they do, they put their health at risk. As of December 2005, the Danish Consumer Council had received complaints from more than 300 women of acute toxic effects following the use of hair dyes, including inflammation and serious hair loss.[5] The cosmetic giant L'Oreal subsequently made out-of-court settlement payments to consumers who suffered toxic effects from the use of their dyes, but refused to admit liability.

Black and dark brown permanent and semi-permanent dyes contain numerous frank and hidden carcinogens including paraphenylenediamine (ppd) (which is also an acute irritant, and an allergen), preservatives, nitrosamine precursors, detergents, and much less commonly, lead acetate in products for men.

Ppd is known to cause cancers, particularly non-Hodgkin's lymphoma, Hodgkin's disease, multiple myeloma, bladder cancer, and breast cancer. There is suggestive evidence that it was Jackie Kennedy's frequent use of these hair dyes that resulted in her premature death from non-Hodgkin's lymphoma. In fact, frequent and prolonged use of these dyes has been associated with significant risks for a range of cancers, including acute and chronic leukemia, multiple myeloma, Hodgkin's lymphoma, non-Hodgkin's lymphoma, and bladder and breast cancers. It is estimated that use of these dyes accounts for more than 20 percent of all non-Hodgkin's lymphoma in women, the incidence of which escalated by 70 percent from 1975 to 2004.[6]

Evidence on the carcinogenicity of hair dye ingredients has been well recognized since 1979[7], but remains trivialized or ignored by the manufacturers of these products. The European Union banned twenty-two hair dye ingredients in 2006 because of the evidence of bladder cancer risk, and also because the industry had failed to submit safety files on 115 other ingredients in currently used products.[8]

While we're on the subject of hair, there is one more danger to be aware of: thioglycolic acid hair straighteners. A 2007 *New York Times* article referred to thioglycolic acid straighteners as "new reducing agents," which combined with a "heat protein" and a nichrome wire heat panel was at that time boosting sales at a group of Momotaro Hair Salons in New York.[9] However, it has been well known for more than three decades that thioglycolic acid straighteners are highly toxic, causing hair to become brittle and break in addition to irritating the scalp and causing pustular and other allergic reactions.[10]

Safe and Natural Hair Colorings

A unique line of certified organic herbal hair color natural powders and creams has been developed by a German company called Logona. Logona's hair dyes contain only 100 percent natural botanical coloring and conditioning ingredients. These include henna, indigo, cassia, walnut, buckthorn, rhubarb, rhatany, coffee, curcuma, and beetroot, with essential oils to improve fragrance. These products achieve many stable and long-lasting colors, ranging from copper blond to henna black.

A Closer Look at Nail Salons

According to *Nails* magazine, a nail trade publication, nail salons are a nearly $7 billion industry nationwide, with at least 57,000 nail salons operating in the U.S. and employing 380,000 nail technicians, most of them young Asian and African women, usually immigrants, of an average age of thirty-eight years. Approximately 1,000 new salons open each year and most are small operators employing just two or three technicians.[11]

Nail salon workers often spend ten to fourteen hours a day at work—which means they spend ten to fourteen hours a day handling

The Problem with Eyelash Salons

Eyelash extension procedures and false eyelashes are in wide use both in high-end hairdressing and beauty salons and in small neighborhood nail salons. These silk and polyester threads, numbering up to 100 or so and designed to mimic natural lashes, are dipped into glues and applied using sharp tweezers, one at a time, to the root of individual lashes on the upper eyelids. This procedure has to be repeated every one to two months to achieve the intended cosmetic purpose.

Application of the lashes is a potentially dangerous procedure, because of the toxicity of the glue used, as well as its repeated use of sharp, fine-pointed tweezers close to the eyeball. The Riverside, California–based Lavish Lashes, one of the few large eyelash extension companies, is very explicit about the potential dangers of eyelash extensions, and requires salon technicians to be carefully trained before selling its products, which are made available only to high-end salons.

Eyelash tinting is illegal in New York and Colorado because of the risks of blindness or eye injuries, but there are still no such regulations in either state for lash extensions. California and Washington now also require eyelash extension professionals to be licensed.

and breathing in chemical ingredients toxic to their health. Not surprisingly, data compiled from salon worker organizations reveal many health problems, including skin allergies and respiratory abnormalities. A 1994 study in the medical journal *Epidemiology,* examining cosmetologists in North Carolina, even found a heightened risk for spontaneous abortions among salon workers involved in manicuring or nail sculpturing.[12]

"Most kinds of house paint are less toxic than what you find in nail polish," said Cora Roelofs, assistant professor at the University of Massachusetts School of Health & Environment and a researcher who specializes in health problems associated with nail salon employees. In a 2007 interview with *The Nation* magazine, Professor Roelofs makes an important point that the health hazards in nail salons and their products are not just the effects of individual chemicals: "we do not understand how these chemicals interact with each other in the salon environment."[13]

In the nail care industry alone at least 10,000 chemicals are used, 89 percent of which have never been safety tested individually by an independent agency. Few if any have been tested for their synergistic effects. And there are plenty of opportunities for different chemicals to interact: nail polish alone contains one of the more potent brews of toxins in all cosmetics and personal-care products.

Nail polish formulas are proprietary, but usually include the following basic ingredients:

- Pigments, for color and covering power.
- Film former, to make the polish hard and shiny following drying. The most common is nitrocellulose.
- Resins, notably tosylamide or formaldehyde, to make the polish tough and resilient.
- Solvents, to facilitate application of the polish. These include toluene and ethyl acetate.
- Clay, to suspend the ingredients and facilitate application.
- Plasticizer, particularly dibutyl phthalate (DBP), to prevent chips and cracks.
- UV stabilizer, to prevent fading from light, particularly sunlight.

Artificial fingernails, also known as sculpted or acrylic nails, have also become increasingly popular. Before an artificial nail is applied, any old color on the natural nail is removed, and the natural nail is filed or sanded to create a rough surface. The stylist then dips a small brush applicator into liquid ethyl methacrylate (EMA) and then into a powdered primer, which catalyses the liquid into a solid polymer. The mixture is brushed onto to each nail before the artificial nail is applied. The artificial nail is then shaped and filed, generating fine dust.

In most salons, the stylist sits opposite the client on one side of a small table, and sculpts and files nails about one to two feet below her face. During this time, both clients and stylists are exposed to this EMA vapor and dust. Salon employees sometimes wear simple cotton or other masks in attempts to filter the dust released in filing acrylic nails, but these masks do not protect them, or their clients, from chemical fumes. Many nail salon owners have resisted installing more efficient (and thus more costly) ventilation systems in their salons to make the air safer, and they worry about the psychological effect on customers if their workers were to wear carbon filter masks and gloves while doing nails, so even these minimal health precautions are often not taken.

EMA is actually a relatively new addition to the chemical mix, a replacement for methyl methacrylate (MMA). As early as the 1970s, it had been recognized that MMA was a common cause of both irritant and allergic contact dermatitis.[4] Following increasing complaints of its toxic effects, the FDA banned the use of liquid MMA in 1974. (Despite this ban, some nail products still contain MMA because manufacturers have recklessly found ways to disguise its presence.)

However, EMA is not any safer than MMA—in fact, it may be less safe. Toxic effects reported in the brains and spinal cords of rats exposed to EMA are consistent with neurological toxicity seen in exposed workers. Nevertheless, the Cosmetic Industry Review Compendium dismisses such concerns, and insists that "this ingredient is safe as used, when application is accompanied by directions to avoid skin contact."[14] Complicating matters, EMA is a virtually permanent adhesive, which can only be removed from nails with extreme difficulty.

EMA is far from the only chemical health threat in nail salons. Nail varnishes and polishes include such toxic ingredients as formaldehyde, a carcinogen; parabens and phthalates, both hormone disrupters; and toluene and other petrochemical solvents, some of which are not only toxic but also highly volatile. Many nail polishes contain the phthalate dibutyl pthalate (DBP), so it should not have been a surprise when the U.S. Centers for Disease Control and Prevention tested the blood of 289 people in 2000 and detected DBP in every person's body. The highest levels were recorded in women twenty to forty years of age, the prime childbearing years—a major cause for concern since DBP has been linked to birth defects and reproductive problems.[15]

A subsequent survey of nail polish brands conducted by the Environmental Working Group found DBP in thirty-seven of the most popular nail polishes, topcoats, and hardeners. In 2007, a coalition of organizations led by the consumer health group Women's Voices For the Earth took urine samples from thirty-three people selected from seven states. The lab tests performed detected another phthalate, DEHP, in every single sample.[11]

In response to rising public alarm about DBP and DEHP, two major nail polish manufacturers—Procter & Gamble and Estée Lauder—announced in 2004 that they would phase out those two chemicals from their nail products by reworking their formulas. These companies have also removed the other ingredients from their nail polishes necessary to meet European Union regulatory guidelines. In 2006 two more major nail polish companies, Orly International and OPI of Los Angeles (the nation's largest manufacturer of nail polishes and nail treatment products), phased out DBP.[16] Additionally, Sally Hansen, a branch of the giant Del Laboratories and the leading drugstore brand, agreed to phase out the use of formaldehyde, toluene, and dibutyl phthalate.[17] Responding to public pressure, OPI announced in 2007 that it was also removing toluene from its nail products. Toluene, along with DBP, is on California's list of chemicals known to cause reproductive abnormalities and cancer. However, OPI and many other major companies do continue to use formaldehyde in nail hardener products.[18]

As the scope of nail salon services gradually expanded over the past decade from just manicuring to pedicuring, massaging, cleansing, and beautifying hands and feet, and soaking them in spa water tubs, reports began surfacing of outbreaks of bacterial infections of hands and feet in unsanitized salons. These developments create a whole new set of challenges for salons and for regulatory agencies.

A final word to the nail product buyer: As with other products, even when nail products promote themselves to consumers as "natural," which presumably means containing few if any toxic chemicals, buyers should beware. A case in point comes from OPI, which marketed a "Natural Nail Strengthener" that contained eleven toxic ingredients, according to the Environmental Working Group's "Skin Deep" report.[19]

Some Needed Reforms

Chapter 11 addresses many necessary reforms in cosmetics and personal-care products, but there are some reforms specifically needed in beauty and nail salons.

Currently, federal regulatory jurisdiction requires the Environmental Protection Agency (EPA) and the Occupational Safety and Health Administration (OSHA) to monitor indoor air quality and levels of toxic ingredients in both hair and nail salons. But the OSHA Permissible Exposure Limit guidelines were created in the 1960s for industrial workplaces, not the salon environment. Moreover, these outdated regulations fail to take into account the long-term effects of chronic exposure in salons, nor do they address the effects of exposure to multiple toxic chemicals. As a further barrier to proper oversight, OSHA's exposure limits are based on inhalation and do not consider absorption through the skin.

And the EPA's efforts? In 2004 the Region 6 office of the EPA, based in Texas, published "A Guide to Protect the Health of Nail Salon Workers and Their Working Environment," a laudatory effort at educating salon workers about health hazards. It even made this declaration: "Nail salon products may contain many potentially harmful chemicals that can be a major cause of occupational asthma as well as other health and environmental concerns." But following complaints from the nail products industry about this and other wording in the guidebook, the national Washington, D.C., EPA office, in collaboration with industry, ordered the text to be drastically revised and the warning watered down.[20]

In the absence of federal regulation, regulatory action by individual states, as well as manufacturer responsibility, can readily reduce, if not eliminate, health risks to both salon workers and clients.

These actions include:

- Routinely testing the air in nail salons for DBP and other contaminants.
- Routinely testing the blood of nail salon employees to determine exposure levels to toxic ingredients.
- Establishing efficient ventilation in all hairdressing and beauty salons. Local exhaust ventilation should be made available at every location, and designed to evacuate air through filters to the external air. The efficiency of each ventilation system should conform to standards established by nationally certified ventilation engineers, and compliance should be checked regularly.
- Supplying at least 25 cubic feet per minute of outside air per stylist, continuously, as recommended by industrial hygienists, notably the American Society of Heating, Refrigeration, and Air-Conditioning Engineers.
- Fitting each manicure table with a commercially available downdraft vapor extraction exhaust system, with a capacity of at least 235 cubic feet per minute, in order to reduce the levels of volatile nail products in the air.
- Requiring stylists to wear latex or vinyl gloves, and also dust masks when working with nail powders or buffing artificial nails.
- Detailing all ingredients in all products used in salons, including their risks and necessary precautions, and making this information readily available to all stylists in Material Safety Data Sheets (already required by OSHA regulations for all workplaces with more than ten employees, just not reliably enforced). This information should also be made available to clients.
- Banning pressure-spray products. They release very fine aerosol particles, which are readily inhaled deep into the lungs where they can irritate and cause toxic effects. Pump spray products are much safer, as their particles are tenfold or more larger, large enough for the nose to mostly filter them out.

- Banning polyvinyl pyrrolidine (PVP), a common ingredient in hair sprays that is designed to increase smoothness and flexibility of hair, but it can cause chronic lung damage, known as thesaurismosis. PVP should be phased out and replaced by safe organic resins, such as pine and jojoba.
- Banning liquid EMA. EMA polymers, commonly known as nail powder, are safer, though care should be exercised that they are not contaminated by residues of unreacted EMA.

Is There Mercury in Your Mascara?

You may not realize it, but many brands of mascara, as well as eyeliners and skin-lightening creams, used in salons and available for purchase in beauty supply stores contain mercury, which is legally added as a preservative and germ killer. Under federal law, up to 65 parts per million of mercury can be added to beauty products.

Mercury is known to retard brain development in children and can cause neurological damage in adults who experience high or long-term exposure. As a result, many toxicologists recommend avoiding contact with mercury, at *any* level, whenever possible.

Even from small doses, mercury accumulates in the human body over time. Even mercury fumes that collect in jars of skin cream or in tubes of mascara, and are inhaled when the containers are opened, add to the cumulative body burden. Placing mercury directly on exposed skin, as with eyeliners and skin creams, heightens the absorption.

In late 2007 Minnesota became the first state to ban mercury in cosmetics, with fines for retailers who knowingly sell mercury-laden cosmetics and penalties of up to $10,000 levied on manufacturers that fail to disclose mercury additives on product labels.

However, even EMA polymers can be replaced by safer alternatives.

- Discontinuing use of polishes containing formaldehyde, dibutyl phthalate, and toluene, in favor of water-based products.
- Reducing, if not eliminating, the use of polishes and conditioners, in favor of film-adhesive systems, which can be applied by women themselves.
- Regularly inspecting all salons. These inspections should be performed by local health authorities, and safety certification should be prominently posted on salon windows.

Table 9: Toxic Ingredients in Hair Dyes

INGREDIENT	TOXIC EFFECT(S)
Coal Tar Dyes	
CI Disperse Blue 1	Carcinogen
D&C Red 33	Carcinogen
HC Blue No. 1	Carcinogen
p-Phenylenediamine	Carcinogenic following oxidation
Detergents/Solvents	
Ceteareths and laureths	Contaminated with the carcinogens ethylene oxide and dioxane
Diethanolamine and triethanolamine	Precursor of the carcinogens nitrosamines
Humectants	
Polyethylene glycol	Contaminated with the carcinogens ethylene oxide and dioxane
Preservatives	
DMDM-hydantoin	Precursor of the carcinogen formaldehyde
Imidazolidinyl urea	Precursor of the carcinogen formaldehyde
Quaternium-15	Precursor of the carcinogen formaldehyde
Other	
Lead acetate	Carcinogen

Table 10: Toxic Ingredients in Beauty and Nail Salons

INGREDIENT	TOXIC EFFECT(S)
Ethyl methacrylate	Neurotoxin and allergen
Glyceryl	Allergen
Lead acetate	Carcinogen
Methyl methacrylate	Neurotoxin and allergen
Parabens	Hormone disrupter
p-Phenylenediamine	Carcinogen
Phenol formaldehyde resin	Allergen
Phthalates	Hormone disrupter

Table 11: Natural Safe Hair Colorants

COMMON NAME	CHEMICAL NAME
Alkanet	Natural Red 20
Amaranth	–
Ammonia sulphate caramel	–
Annatto, bixin, norbixin	Natural Orange 4
Anthocyanins	–
Azorubine, carmoisine	–
Beetroot, betanin	–
beta-apo-8'-carotenal	Food Orange 6
beta-carotene	Food Orange 5
Camwood, deoxyisosantalin	Natural Red 22
Canthaxanthin	Food Orange 8
Caramel	Natural Brown 10
Caustic sulphate caramel	–

Chamomile, apigenin	Natural Yellow 12
Charcoal (black)	Pigment Black 8
Chlorophyll, chlorophyllins (green)	Natural Green 3
Clover, pratol	Natural Yellow 10
Cochineal, carminic acid	Natural Red 4
Copper complex of chlorophyll, chlorophyllins	–
Cucumin, turmeric	Natural Yellow 3
Ethyl ester of beta-apo-8'-carotenal	Food Orange 7
Flavine	Natural Yellow 10
Henna, lawsone (red)	–
Indigo	Natural Blue 1
Indigo (blue/mauve)	Vat Blue 1
Isosantalin	Natural Red 22
Lutein	–
Luteolin	Natural Yellow 2
Lycopene (orange)	–
Marigold	–
Mixed carotenes	Natural Yellow 26
Monascus	Natural Red 2
Osage orange, morin	Natural Yellow 8, 11
Paprika, capsanthin, capsorubin	–
Persian berry	–
Plain caramel	–
Riboflavin	–
Riboflavin-5'-phosphate	–
Saffron, crocetin	–
Saffron (crocin)—Golden	Natural Yellow 6
Sandalwood, santalin	Natural Red 22
Sulphite ammonia caramel	–
Vegetable carbon (black)	Pigment Black 7

Safe Products and Ingredients for Beauty and Nail Salons

HAIR DYE

Logona Herbal Hair Colors
INGREDIENTS: henna, indigo, cassia, walnut, buckthorn, rhubarb, rhatany, coffee, curcuma, beet root, essential oils
www.logona.com

NAIL POLISH

Acquarella Nail Polish
Water-based and vegan. Contains no formaldehyde, phthalates, EMA, or any chemical solvents such as toluene.
www.acquarellapolish.com

Honeybee Gardens WaterColors Peel Off Polish
Water-based. Contains no formaldehyde, phthalates, EMA, or any chemical solvents such as toluene.
www.honeybeegardens.com

8 | Products Targeting Sun Worshippers

Picture a white sand beach in Southern California on a typical summer weekend. Thousands of sun worshippers of all ages lounge on the beach or wade and swim in the ocean water, their bodies glistening and lathered with sunscreens or sunblocks. While this may seem like a benign scene, something subtle but dangerous is happening just below the surface of both their awareness and their skin.

During the last few decades, we've been told over and over again about the dangers of sun exposure. The consequences of ignoring the risks include not just the telltale pink flush, tender skin, and eventual peeling of sunburn, but longer-term effects: accelerated aging, premature wrinkles, and skin cancer. To protect ourselves, we've been encouraged to apply sunscreen daily, or even more frequently if going out in the sun for extended periods of time. What we haven't been told is that sunscreens can be dangerous, to our health and to the environment.

How could this be? How could sunscreen, a product that so many people rely upon, a product that has been championed by health agencies the world over as essential to protecting the skin, harbor silent threats to our health and well-being?

Let's first look at the history of the product. Being tan was not always in vogue. Prior to the twentieth century, if you were of

European origin, having tanned skin associated you with manual laborers, who spent time in the sun because they had to, while a pale complexion was admired as a sign of wealth, health, and beauty. Our ancestors usually tried to avoid direct sunlight either by covering themselves with hats and other garments or by staying in the shade whenever possible. In cultures where exposure to intense sunlight was unavoidable, formulations of oils and sand were used to protect the skin.

The intentional tanning of skin, as with the use of cosmetics, first arose from the desire to be fashionable. By some accounts, the trend began with French designer Coco Chanel, who accidentally sunburned herself on a boat in the 1920s. Her afterglow started a fashion trend among Hollywood starlets that hasn't abated to this day.

In 1944, Miami pharmacist Benjamin Green developed a suntan cream called Red Vet Pet, which he made from a mixture of cocoa butter and jasmine, cooked on his wife's stove, and tested on his own bald head. Sun worshippers on Florida beaches were his target consumers. His creation later became Coppertone Suntan Cream, the first mass-produced sunscreen. Mainstream consumers soon took note, and a multibillion dollar industry was spawned.

When twentieth century scientific research identified the ultraviolet wavelengths of sunshine—generally categorized as short (UVB) or long (UVA) wavelengths—and their relationship to sunburn, it prompted cosmetics manufacturers to create two types of products to protect against sun exposure: absorbers (sunscreens) and reflectants (sunblocks).

What Sunscreens Do

Sunscreens act by absorbing short-wave ultraviolet light, or UVB, the wavelength responsible for sunburn. To gauge how much protection each sunscreen product affords you against burns, a Sun Protection Factor (SPF) was created in 1962 as an international standard, and embraced by sunscreen makers and the regulatory and health agencies of most governments. The higher the SPF number on the label, the higher the level of protection the product theoretically affords. A SPF of 30, for instance, supposedly guarantees you that the product will enable you to remain in the sun thirty times longer, safely, than if you had not used sunscreen at all.

Though the SPF standard feels comforting, it is based on a faulty premise, and so provides only the illusion of safety. There are several problems with relying on a product's SPF. First, when we swim in water, or even just sweat, we lose the product's protective value (unless it is continually reapplied). Second and even more importantly, because few people apply sunscreens "at the same rate of application at which the product was tested in the laboratory," in the words of New Zealand physician and sunscreen expert Dr. Steve Taylor, "no one should think that their sunscreen gives them anything more than two hours protection at best," no matter how high the SPF.[1]

As Dr. Taylor further explains in his 2002 online book, *Two Fingers To Sunscreen? An Essential Guide for the Effective Use of Sunscreens*, "For testing purposes all sunscreens, whether they be creams, lotions, or gels, are applied at an internationally agreed application rate of $2mg/cm^2$, and it is from this rate of application that the product's SPF is determined. . . . Studies have shown, however, that in reality most people apply only a fraction of that amount. This varies between 10 percent and 75 percent of the test quantity. On average, people apply about one-third of that amount. So the SPF they actually achieve on their skin is nowhere near what they expected."

When consumers slather themselves with sunscreens boasting high SPFs, they do so with false expectations about their safety, especially given that nowhere on product labels is a warning posted about the necessary application rate. Taylor estimated that two-thirds of the population of his home country New Zealand will contract skin cancer during their lifetimes, in part because they have been lulled into a false sense of security about the effectiveness of the sunscreens they apply and so remain in the sun far longer than they should or otherwise might have.

A certain amount of sunshine is healthy, as it stimulates the body to produce vitamin D, and can counteract depressive disorders, but that amount is generally no more than fifteen minutes of sun exposure a day. And supplements also provide an effective antidote for vitamin D deficiency, so there's no good health reason to purposefully expose yourself to the sun. "Deliberately setting out to get a suntan should not be seen as being 'cool,' nor 'attractive,' nor 'desirable,'" observes sunscreen expert Dr. Taylor. "It should be seen for what it really is: rather absurd and irresponsible."

What Sunscreens Don't Do

The extra sun exposure this false sense of security results in may contribute to why the greatest increases in the incidence of the dangerous skin cancer malignant melanoma have occurred in those areas of the world where sunscreen use is the most prevalent. But it's only part of the reason. The rest is because of something sunscreens don't do, no matter how effectively they're applied: block long-wave ultraviolet radiation (UVA).

It has been well documented that dark-skinned people and people who tan well are less likely to develop skin cancer than persons who are light- or red-skinned, though they do still face the same risk of damaging their skin and causing premature aging. The reduced skin cancer risk is due to the fact that dark skin contains much higher levels of the natural black pigment melanin, which is very effective in blocking long-wave UV radiation.

A study published in a 1992 issue of the *American Journal of Public Health,* provocatively titled "Could Sunscreens Increase Melanoma Risk?", first introduced this idea into public debate.[2] Sunscreens clearly encourage people to remain in the sun for extended periods of time, and even if their sunscreen is effectively absorbing the short-wave radiation that causes sunburn, they are still exposing themselves to increased long-wave radiation. This radiation penetrates into the deep layers of the skin, breaking down the protein and collagen that keep the skin firm and plump, and is responsible for the classic signs of skin aging, including wrinkling and discoloration. More seriously, UVA radiation is well recognized as the major cause of malignant melanoma, which is now the fastest rising cancer in the world. Since 1975, its incidence in white men and women has increased by 243 percent and 172 percent, respectively, while its mortality rate has increased by 55 percent and 24 percent, respectively.[3] (In sharp contrast, there has been no increase in the incidence and mortality of malignant melanoma in black men and women, who are protected by the pigment in their skin.)

This exposure seems to be particularly dangerous during childhood and adolescence; years of research data has clearly shown a relationship between the number of sunburn episodes before the age of fifteen and the subsequent development of skin cancer later in life.

More Problems with Sunscreens

The Environmental Working Group did an analysis of 868 sunscreen products sold in the U.S. and discovered that 83 percent contained ingredients that either raised health safety concerns or were inadequate in protecting the wearer from the sun despite assurances made by the product manufacturers. In a 2007 document presented to the FDA, this group made a series of claims against many of the sunscreens marketed in this country:

- They provide inadequate protection from the sun.
- They are labeled with misleading promises about the product's effectiveness.
- They may be less safe than similar products sold in other countries.
- They contain ingredients with significant concerns about their impact on human health.

Furthermore, the group charged that because the FDA fails to review the accuracy of claims made about new sunscreen products, "manufacturers are using unapproved sunscreens in products, [and] listing them as inactive ingredients" despite basing their marketing claims on these ingredients' inclusion. The group concluded, "Our analysis of marketing claims on hundreds of sunscreen bottles shows that false and misleading marketing claims are common. Claims like 'all day protection,' 'mild as water,' and 'blocks all harmful rays' are not true, yet are found on bottles."[4]

Not only do these sunscreen ingredients not do what they claim, they also have direct negative effects on the body. When sunscreen ingredients are absorbed through the skin, they generate something called "free radicals." Free radicals interact with and damage molecules in the skin, which can result in skin damage and skin aging, along with sharply increased risks of skin cancer. A 2006 study in the science journal *Free Radical Biology and Medicine* reported finding that three commonly used chemicals in sunscreens to filter ultraviolet rays—octyl-methoxycinnamate and benzophenone 3—are penetration enhancers that cause the sunscreen to soak into deeper skin layers after application, leaving top skin layers vulnerable to UVB radiation and reacting to UVA light in those deeper layers to generate free radicals.[5] Another common sunscreen or sunblock, butyl-methoxydibenzoylmethane, also known as avobenzone, not only rapidly converts light into chemical energy, which is released in the body as free radicals, but rapidly degrades in sunlight, becoming ineffective within one hour. This was the only sunscreen allowed in Europe as of 2007, but even its safety is clearly questionable.

One of the other chief dangers of sunscreens is that they are often also hormone disrupters. The evidence that most sunscreen ingredients have hormonal effects comes largely from experiments demonstrating their ability to stimulate proliferation of human breast cancer cells, and to induce the production of breast cancer protein in laboratory tests.[6] The sunscreen chemicals Bp-3, 4-MBC, and OMC increased uterine growth when fed to immature rats,[7] and the painting of the skin of immature female rats with 4-MBC, using concentrations of the chemical similar to those found in common sunscreens, significantly increased uterine growth. Bp-3 has been detected in urine up to four hours after skin application of sunscreens, and both Bp-3 and OMC accumulate in the body, as evidenced by their detection in human breast milk. Yet, if you read through the industry's Cosmetic Industry Review Compendium, it makes no reference to the hormonal effects of Bp-3 or any other sunscreen ingredient.[8]

Oxybenzone, a chemical similar to estrogen in its effects, is another hormone disrupter commonly found in sunscreens. Its effects have been highlighted by a University of California-Riverside research teams' discovery of evidence in 2006 that oxybenzone had transformed the males of two coastal fish species into feminized fish carrying ovary tissue. Two-thirds of the male fish examined had been feminized in this way.[9]

Oxybenzone is not the only chemical ingredient inflicting harm on aquatic life. These chemicals wash off sunbathers when they enter the ocean water, or when they later bathe or shower. If the latter, the chemicals then pass largely unaffected through wastewater treatment plants and back into the sea, where they settle in ocean sediment to be absorbed by fish as they feed. Accumulations of hormone disrupters in sunscreens have been reported in fish caught in Switzerland and in rivers throughout Europe.

Oxybenzone was detected in the bodies of 97 percent of 2,500 U.S. residents who were tested by the U.S. Centers for Disease Control and Prevention in 2005, and women and girls were found to have higher levels than men and boys, a disparity that may be due to heavier female usage of sunscreens and other body care products. At least two common hormone disrupters in sunscreens—oxybenzone and octyl-methoxycinnamate—have been detected in human breast milk, further demonstrating how readily the human body absorbs them, and how easily these chemicals can be passed on to infants.[9] The subsequent release of such feminizing ingredients through the placenta into unborn children increases the prospect that male babies will be feminized, or will develop hormonal imbalances later in their lives. As well, a March 2008 study in the science journal *Environmental Health Perspectives* presented evidence that mothers with a higher body burden of oxybenzone were more prone to giving birth to underweight baby girls. Low birth weight could make children more susceptible to coronary heart disease, type 2 diabetes, and other maladies once they are adults.[10]

Hidden Sunscreens

Some sunscreen ingredients are now being incorporated in beauty and anti-wrinkle creams, lipsticks, skin lotions, hair products, and bubble baths, in order to maintain the products' light stability and durability. These ingredients are usually not identified on the product labels.

Why Are Nanoparticles in Sun Protection Products?

There are significant safety differences between sunscreens and sunblocks. All sunscreens are unsafe for two reasons: they encourage people to stay longer in the sun, and they have hormonal effects. Sunscreens do not protect against the dangerous long-wave ultraviolet radiation, while sunblocks, especially those including zinc oxide and titanium dioxide, are highly protective; they block long-wave ultraviolet light by reflecting radiation off the skin's surface. If you must be out in the sun, don't use sunscreen, use sunblock.

Even sunblocks, however, are not a sure, safe bet for sun protection. Borrowing a technique used by the pharmaceutical industry in skin patch tests, cosmetic manufacturers often add "penetration enhancer" ingredients to their products, including sunscreens and sunblocks, to decrease skin resistance and drive chemicals deeper into body tissues. Their reasoning is that by increasing the absorption of these chemicals, the products become more effective and longer lasting.

The rise of nanotechnology has been a huge step forward in penetration enhancement, a development comparable to the technological leap that occurred when plane propellers were eclipsed by the development of jet engines. By shrinking chemical particles to 100 nanometers wide, or about 1/100,000 of the thickness of this sheet of paper and far smaller than the smallest blood vessels, these "nanoparticles" are able to penetrate human skin more rapidly and much more deeply that was ever before possible.

Nanotechnology has been put to good use in a variety of products: stain-resistant clothing and textiles, computer microchips, plastics, and even razors and food-storage containers, to which nanoparticles of silver have been added as an antibacterial agent. And by the end of 2007, at least 300 sunscreen and sunblock products contained nanoparticles of titanium dioxide or zinc oxide, making this the most common use for nanotechnology among all consumer products. An Australian government health agency estimated that about 70 percent of sunblocks that include titanium dioxide and 30 percent of sunscreens that include zinc oxide contain these materials in nanoparticle form.

Once titanium dioxide or zinc oxide is reduced in size, the chemical becomes transparent, losing its usual white coloration when applied to the skin. Both nanoparticle versions still block harmful ultraviolet radiation, but allow visible light to pass through, making them a more appealing product to consumers previously repulsed by the white sheen sunblocks left on their skin.

Because both titanium dioxide and zinc oxide have been traditionally regarded as safe materials without any impact on human health, manufacturers are blithely assuming that nanoparticle

---

Lip Gloss Can Magnify the Sun's UV Rays

A consumer alert from dermatologists, widely publicized in April 2008, warned that lip glosses can act like magnifying glasses, concentrating the UV rays of the sun in a way that allows more light rays to penetrate directly into the lips. As a result, the wearer's risk of contracting squamous cell carcinoma, a cancer of the lips, could be increased—though it must also be noted that, as of this writing, no medical studies had been conducted to confirm a cancer link.

Just to be safe, however, one option to reduce risk is to mix lip gloss with zinc oxide, which has a protective effect, rather than use lip gloss alone.

versions will not pose a health risk either. A common assurance given by sunscreen and sunblock manufacturers is that nanoparticles of titanium dioxide and zinc oxide remain on the surface of the skin, never penetrating into your skin cells or into your bloodstream (and through it, the rest of your body). But at least four major independent science studies between 2003 and 2008 have emerged to convincingly refute that claim.[12] By 2004, two dozen toxicology publications had reported that nanoparticles pose unique and unpredictable risks.[13]

While titanium oxide and zinc oxide are harmless and beneficial as topical sunblock agents, having those chemicals distributed more deeply throughout our bodies may create unknown health risks. A perceptive article about nanotechnology in *The Economist* magazine (November 22, 2007) summarized the health concerns associated with their use this way: "Research on animals suggests that nanoparticles can even evade some of the body's natural defence systems and accumulate in the brain, cells, blood and nerves. Studies show there is the potential for such materials to reach the lung and cause inflammation; to move from the lungs to other organs; to have surprising biological toxicity; to move from within the skin to the lymphatic system; and possibly to move across cell membranes. Moreover, these effects vary when particles are engineered into different shapes."

Studies by the DuPont Company have shown that injection of nanoparticles into the lungs of rats resulted in very high mortality. Other studies have found that small nanoparticles penetrate deeply into the lungs of rats where they produce severe inflammation.[14] They also rapidly diffuse into the blood, resulting in coagulation disorders. And at least one variety of nanoparticles used as penetration enhancers in sunscreens has the potential to cause neurological damage to humans, according to the results of a study in 2006 by a research laboratory at the U.S. Environmental Protection Agency. While examining the effects of nanoparticles of titanium oxide on cultures of mice cells called microglia, which protect brain neurons, researchers found that the particles provoked these cells to go into dangerous overdrive, producing free radicals in an attempt to destroy the invading nanoparticles. This is a serious risk to health because free radicals don't just attack the nanoparticles; they can also damage neighboring cells. The result is oxidative stress in the brain, which is theorized to be a cause of Alzheimer's and Parkinson's diseases.[15]

"The chemicals industry has blithely assumed that if large grains are safe, smaller ones will be too," commented an article about the study in the science journal *Nature*. "But that assumption is coming under increasing scrutiny and is not necessarily always valid." Previous studies had indicated that nanoparticles of titanium oxide might also be toxic to skin, bone, and liver cells.[16]

A July 2007 issue of *Consumer Reports* reported on the magazine's test of nineteen sunscreen products. Of those nineteen products, eight contained nanoparticles, but only one disclosed their presence on the label. Not only that, but the magazine found no correlation between the presence of nanoparticle ingredients and increased product effectiveness.

Even with products marketed as containing only "natural" ingredients, you will need to read the labels carefully to detect nanoparticles, if they are identified on the label at all. Caribbean Blue Natural Basics, for example, is advertised as a "100% all-natural sunscreen formula" that contains "natural zinc oxide in a new patented transparent form" to prevent skin whitening. When I phoned the manufacturers to inquire about the new transparent form of zinc oxide

A Warning on Sunblocks

When buying sunblocks, be very careful to check the ingredient list, as often, products are labeled sunblocks despite not actually including ingredients that block the sun's rays. Neutrogena Age Shield Sunblock, Aveeno Continuous Protection Sunblock Spray, and Hawaiian Tropic Ozone Spray Sport Sunblock all claim to be sunblocks, but contain neither zinc oxide nor titanium dioxide. Only if one or both of these ingredients appear as the active ingredient on the label is a product a true sunblock!

in the formula (called "microfine" in the ingredient list), I was told this language referred to a nanoparticle ingredient. (Other than this major flaw, the product seemed safe, made from a natural base of oils extracted from coconut, seaweed, safflower, almond, sesame, and macadamia nut, plus other vitamins and essential oils.)

An Emerging Regulatory Nightmare

Nanotechnology research and development, and the addition of nanoingredients to products, have advanced far faster than the ability of scientists and health agencies to evaluate their impact on human health. Currently, toxicologists do not even have the technology to measure all of the ways in which nanoparticles escape into the environment, much less measure all of their effects once inside the human body.

The first public revelation of the cosmetics industry's use of ultra-fine particles came in a January 8, 2005, article in *The New York Times* with a headline proclaiming, "Cosmetics Break the Skin Barrier: Sophisticated Science Being Used to Deliver Creams Behind the Lines." The products the article discussed were designed to force powerful anti-wrinkle, anti-aging, moisturizing, and other ingredients deep into the skin. Examples cited included Procter & Gamble's use of invisible small ball-bearing-like particles in its Olay brand body lotions; Freeze 24/7's new line of anti-wrinkle creams, which combines the muscle relaxant gamma-amino-butyric acid, which does not penetrate skin, with gynostemma, a plant extract that does penetrate; and Esteé Lauder's use of cell vectors, small spheres of protein that encapsulate anti-wrinkle ingredients, to penetrate the skin, where the vectors are slowly dissolved by enzymes, releasing their contents.

Despite the cosmetic industry's hype, nanotechnology is already hitting some unexpected snags. European consumers have reacted with alarm, much as they did in response to genetically engineered foods, dubbed "Frankenfoods." The cosmetics industry should not be surprised if European campaigns and boycotts of "Frankencreams" follow.

Some developments that may herald this trend:

• A nanoproduct aerosol bathroom spray was recalled by German health authorities in 2006 after eighty people reported severe respiratory problems. Six people were hospitalized with fluid in their lungs.

• The International Center for Technology Assessment, together with a range of other organizations, petitioned the FDA in 2006 to monitor products containing nanoparticles—including more than 100 cosmetics and sunblocks—for their toxic effects. This petition was filed in conjunction with the release of a comprehensive report on the dangers of nano-cosmetics by Friends of the Earth.[17]

• A British health agency issued a report in 2004 urging that nanoparticles be considered "new chemicals under European and U.K. legislation"[18] As such, they would be subject to safety testing by an independent safety committee before they could be used in cosmetics and other consumer products.

• A 2006 report, "Project on Emerging Nanotechnologies," commissioned by the Woodrow Wilson International Center for Scholars, featured former Deputy FDA Commissioner Michael Taylor criticizing the ability of his former agency to regulate nanotechnology. "Unless the FDA addresses potential nanotechnology risks now, public confidence in a host of valuable nanotechnology-based products could be undermined . . . There are important gaps in FDA's legal authority that hamper its ability to understand and manage nanotechnology's potential risks, (particularly) in the area of cosmetics . . . and in the oversight of products once they reach the market." Taylor's criticisms were strongly supported by activist groups, notably the Consumers Union and the Organic Consumers Association.

The FDA issued a statement in 2007 that it would not require any special labeling or regulations for nanoparticles added to cosmetics because, the Agency claimed, there was no scientific evidence of any major safety risks. But to the contrary, there is now more than enough evidence to demonstrate that nanoparticles pose serious and irreversible health hazards. Under no circumstances should nanoparticle cosmetics be evaluated in humans, let alone be further commercialized, until thorough toxicological investigations have been undertaken by industry, and rigorously evaluated by independent experts.

Led by the International Center for Technology Assessment, a group of consumer and environmental groups filed a petition in early 2008 with the U.S. Environmental Protection Agency requesting the regulation of more than 200 consumer products that contain nanoparticles of antimicrobial silver to kill germs. These nano-sized particles of silver are considered more lethal to beneficial and harmful microbes both. The petition asked that the nanoparticles of silver be treated as a type of new pesticide, a regulatory category that would require safety analysis and oversight before products containing them could be released to the public. The FDA had not responded as of this writing.

Nature Provides Sunscreen Options

Research into sun care products that utilize natural active ingredients has advanced rapidly over the past decade. This new generation of ingredients mined from nature may actually protect body cells from UV radiation damage rather than just blocking or absorbing the rays as conventional sunblocks and sunscreens do.

Some examples of this welcome trend:

- Broccoli extract contains a chemical called sulforaphane that may reduce UV damage by up to 37.7 percent, based on findings from a study in 2007 conducted at the Johns Hopkins University School of Medicine. This chemical stimulates the cell's own protective mechanisms to inhibit the activation of carcinogens. It also continues to support the cell's innate protective system for several days after the extract dissipates from the body.
- Black tea, with its antioxidant components, seems to have the ability to help repair skin damage from UV

---

exposure. Research published in an October 2007 issue of the *International Journal of Cosmetic Science* reported that when an extract from black tea leaves was topically applied to skin that was then exposed to UV radiation, burning was prevented, apparently because the extract absorbed the UVB rays within cells, protecting DNA against damage from sun exposure.

- Scientists at Israeli Biotechnology Research, a private company that investigates natural non-toxic ingredients for cosmetics, released experimental results in 2007 showing how the carotenoids phytoene and phytofluene provide double protection against UV radiation by limiting free radical damage and absorbing the more damaging rays. Carotenoids are a class of 600 or so natural fat-soluble pigments found primarily in plants. The most publicized is carotene, from carrots.

- Risks of melanoma can be reduced, to a limited degree, by the addition of vitamin E to sunscreens. Of interest in this connection is evidence that a skin lotion spiked with caffeine or green tea extract, containing the antioxidant EGCG (epigallo-catechin-3-gallate), reduced the risk of skin cancer in hairless mice following repeated exposure to high levels of UVB radiation.[19] The protective effects of caffeine, however, were shown to be a result of its ability to induce cell suicide among sunburn-damaged cells, technically known as "apoptosis," rather than its effectiveness as a sunscreen.

- Soyscreen, a combination of two natural plant ingredients, ferulic acid and soybean oil, has been reported to be a highly effective "green" sunscreen and was licensed by the USDA in 2005. It also has the advantage of being water resistant. Another natural plant ingredient, gamma oryzanol, from rice bran, is an effective, safe sunscreen as well as a sunblock.[20,21]

Sunscreen Regulations

On August 23, 2007, the FDA proposed new regulations for the informative labeling of sunscreens. Almost a year later, however, they had still remained pending.

In response to the FDA's inaction, and mounting concerns about SPF, Connecticut attorney general Richard Blumenthal wrote to the FDA on July 24, 2008, criticizing its failure to regulate the sunscreen industry and prevent it from making "dangerously misleading claims" about the safety and effectiveness of its products. A week later, Senators Jack Reed and Christopher Dodd introduced the "Sunscreen Labeling Act of 2008." As of this writing, the Act will be introduced into the Senate for ratification in February 2009.

Table 12: Toxic Ingredients in Sunscreens and Sunblocks

INGREDIENT	TOXIC EFFECT(S)
Benzophenone-3	Penetration enhancer, hormone disrupter, and allergen
Octyl-methoxycinnamate (OMC)	Penetration enhancer and hormone disrupter
Oxybenzone	Hormone disrupter
Nanoparticles ("micro-fine," "ultra-fine")	Penetration enhancers
Parabens	Hormone disrupters

Safe Products and Ingredients for Sun Worshippers

SUNSCREEN
There are no safe sunscreen products on the market.

Mexoryl SX is a combination sunblock and sunscreen said to achieve protection against UVB rays with an SPF of about 90, which if true would make it more effective than any other sunscreen currently being sold.

SUNBLOCK
Zinc oxide and *titanium oxide* are safe and effective sunblock ingredients, and most common sunblock products contain these substances. Be aware, however, that nanoparticle versions of these ingredients have not been fully tested, and evidence points to potential negative health effects. The presence of nanoparticles is sometimes indicated by the words "ultra-fine" or "micro-fine," but often is not indicated on labels at all.

Burt's Bees Chemical-Free Sunscreen*
Active ingredient: titanium dioxide (8.58 percent) Inactive ingredients: water, cannabis sativa (hemp) seed oil, glycerin, stearic acid, fragrance, helianthus annuus (sunflower) seed oil, hydrated silica, sucrose distearate, calendula officinalis (calendula) flower extract, crataegus oxyacanthus (hawthorn) stem extract, hamamelis virginiana (witch hazel) extract, hydrastis canadensis (golden seal) extract, symphtum officinale (comfrey) extract, rosmarinus officinalis (rosemary) leaf extract, alginic acid, acacia senegal gum, xanthan gum, beta carotene, sucrose stearate, lecithin, aluminium hydroxide, sodium borate, glucose, sodium chloride, canola oil, glucose oxidase, lactoperoxidase
www.burtsbees.com

---

*Burt's Bees Chemical-Free Sunscreen calls itself a sunscreen, but the presence of titanium dioxide makes it a sunblock.

CLOTHING

Solumbra

A sun-protective line of clothing created by Shaun Hughes after he was diagnosed with malignant melanoma. Solumbra offers swimsuits and everyday-wear clothing for people of all ages, with 97 percent protection from both UVA and UVB rays.

www.solumbra.com

9 | Products Targeting Youth Seekers

The quest to regain one's lost youth is an ancient human obsession, most famously embodied in the sixteenth-century Spanish adventurers who searched the Americas for a rumored fountain of youth. But perhaps no period in history even remotely compares to the last fifty years in terms of the preoccupation. Anti-aging products are currently the fastest growing sector of the cosmetics industry.

Products and advice claiming to retard or reverse age began to appear in the late eighteenth century. German physician Christopher Hufeland's 1797 collection of diet and lifestyle recommendations was probably the first formula for anti-aging, but not long afterward, the search for rejuvenation took a dramatic turn into wishful thinking and charlatanism. A potion that consisted of crushed and liquefied dog testicles, and reputedly would cause senior citizens to experience their youth again, sold widely in Western countries in 1889, and was typical of the era's offerings.

In 1984, at a Society of Cosmetic Chemists meeting, Dr. Albert Kligman, a dermatologist seeking a way to describe products that did more than color the skin but less than what pharmaceutical drugs are designed to do, coined the term "cosmeceutical." Cosmetic companies were developing products that altered the function and structure of the skin, and the industry was afraid the FDA would be tempted to regulate cosmetics if any of these products were labeled as having drug-like effects. "Since everything applied to the skin produces change," Kligman told an interviewer in 2005, for an article in the journal *Dermatologic Surgery*, "we needed a third category of products known as cosmeceuticals."[1]

Cosmeceuticals claim to protect and lighten the skin, reduce wrinkling, eliminate cellulite, and even reverse the aging process; essentially, a cosmeceutical is any product that biologically alters the skin. "Ninety percent of all cosmetics sold in the world today are probably cosmeceuticals," Kligman said in that same 2005 interview. "The terminology regarding the distinction between cosmetics and drugs is a marketing game in the U.S. If you reverse aging, you are a drug. If you smooth skin, you are a cosmetic. Categorization depends more on the language on the bottle than the product in the bottle."

Some cosmeceuticals have also been embraced by dermatologists as treatments for diseases of the skin. The clever promotion of these products by a growing number of dermatologists, many of whom earn hefty fees consulting for cosmeceutical companies or produce and market their own products, raises disturbing questions about professional conflicts of interest which may tempt dermatologists to inflate cosmeceutical product claims.

With so many claims for the effectiveness of cosmeceuticals relying on anecdotes, these products have understandably been characterized as a "voodoo science"[2,3]. Evidence used to claim effectiveness for most of the products sold as cosmeceuticals has not been supported by rigorous clinical trials or other science-based data. Only a double-blind clinical trial* that lasts from four to six months, the gold standard of laboratory testing, can prove the worth of these products, and few such trials have been performed.

---

*In double-blind clinical trials, study patients are randomly assigned to receive either the study treatment/substance or an alternative treatment/substance. Neither the patient nor the researcher conducting the study knows which treatment is being given to which patient until after the results have been tabulated.

The Mayo Clinic issued a warning in June 2007 that cosmeceutical products contain "powerful active ingredients that can affect biological processes," and emphasized how these ingredients have not been subjected to rigorous safety testing. Anti-wrinkle creams, lotions, and related skin treatments use complex and potent chemicals with drug-like properties that stimulate skin cell production but in doing so also alter the biological processes that regulate the structure of the skin. These biological changes pose unknown and untested potential dangers to human health. In addition, the

Blow Your Whistle on Overpriced Products

We are bombarded with claims for the greater effectiveness of high-priced cosmeceutical products with fancy packages and exotic-sounding ingredients. These claims, unsurprisingly, are misleading. The first loud whistle blown on this trend came in late 2006, when a *Consumer Reports* magazine story concluded that there is no correlation at all between the price and the effectiveness of anti-wrinkle creams. ("The best advice is prevent those wrinkles in the first place," the magazine stated. "Stay out of the sun and don't smoke."[18])

In a January 4, 2007, *New York Times* report, "The Cosmetics Restriction Diet" by Natasha Singer, highly qualified academic dermatologists were quoted making statements such as "the cheapest products work just as well as the more expensive ones," and this one about the origins of product ingredients, which should really get your attention: "all these skin-care products come out of the same vat in New Jersey." The article goes on to point out how moisturizers "don't do much except for creating a smooth surface so that make-up can go on without drag." If you want to be a smart buyer, then you should "cut down on the $100 skin care product and cut your skin care budget." Still another expert is quoted as saying that "it is difficult to determine how well creams work, whether they cost $10, $100, or $1,000."

overwhelming majority of cosmeceuticals draw no distinction between the supposedly active ingredients in their products and other ingredients, further confusing consumers interested in the identity of ingredients in the products they purchase.

Why are manufacturers so reluctant to conduct adequate safety testing on their products? As Dr. Mary P. Lupo of the Tulane University School of Medicine, in an article for a 2005 issue of *Dermatologic Surgery*, observed, "manufacturers make a calculated decision not to make claims that will result in scrutiny by the U.S. Food and Drug Administration of the product as a drug. Clinical testing could also draw the attention of the FDA, so some manufacturers opt instead to allow the consumer arena to become the test market."[4]

Without either manufacturers or the FDA evaluating the safety and toxicity of the ingredients in these products, consumers who buy cosmeceuticals quite literally become guinea pigs in a vast uncontrolled experiment where the only benchmark to measure safety will be how many people suffer health consequences from using the products—a standard for measuring cause and effect that is so flawed as to be useless, since cosmeceutical users simultaneously absorb chemicals from many other personal-care products and cosmetics. This means there is no definitive way to differentiate which products may be responsible for any observed health problems.

And there are likely to be health problems. What has been reliably demonstrated in tests on cosmeceutical ingredients is that many of these products contain dangerous, often undisclosed ingredients that remain hidden behind slick marketing campaigns.

Skin Peelers

One of the dangerous ingredients is hydroxy acids: alpha-hydroxy acids (AHAs), and the less common beta-hydroxy acids (BHAs). AHAs are used in many products—up to 10 percent of moisturizers, 6 percent of sunscreens, and more extensively in anti-wrinkle and anti-aging skin creams—to increase the permeability of the skin. Products that contain hydroxy acids are being used increasingly not just by individuals at home, but in cosmetic salons and even by dermatologists.

In a March 2007 article in *O, The Oprah Magazine*, writer Jenny Bailly warned of "pain, scabs and bruises" that could result from non-surgical anti-aging procedures and cosmeceutical products, but misrepresented hydroxy acids as just "lift[ing] away dead cells on the surface of skin, revealing fresher smoother skin underneath."[5] It's a common misperception. But even the industry's Cosmetics Ingredient Review Compendium admits that AHAs are not only skin irritants, but also "can act to remove a portion of the skin surface" known as the stratum corneum, which absorbs long-wave ultraviolet radiation from sunlight and tanning beds.[6] The Compendium also admits that a statistically significant increase in the number of sunburn cells was seen in guinea pig skin treated with AHAs, and that "pre-treatment with AHAs could increase skin damage produced by ultraviolet radiation." Apart from increasing the risk of sunburn, products containing AHAs are thus likely to increase the risk of skin cancer, particularly malignant melanoma.

Despite these concerns, the Compendium claims that AHA ingredients can be safely used at concentrations up to 10 percent in personal-care products and at concentrations as high as 30 percent in salon products. One problem that complicates this advice is that the industry still fails to disclose the concentration of these ingredients in most products. Worse still, AHAs are used in an estimated 5 percent of all products without appearing on the label at all.

The FDA issued a consumer warning in 1992 that the use of "skin peel" products like those containing hydroxy acids, advertised to remove wrinkles, blemishes, blotches, and acne scars, "could destroy the upper layer of the skin, causing severe burns, swelling and pain"[7]—an unprecedented action by the FDA. But in spite of these warnings, or more likely because these warnings have been poorly publicized, the public's use of these products has increased dramatically, thanks to reckless but seductive industry claims about how they supposedly enhance the youthful appearance of skin.

Products containing hydroxy acids should never be used, regardless of those products' claims. But there is one category of product in which the use of hydroxy acids is downright ludicrous: sunscreens. Following over a decade's review of AHAs, studies sponsored by the FDA finally warned that AHA ingredients in sunscreens increase susceptibility of the skin to damage following exposure to sunlight— the very thing sunscreens are supposed to protect against—and thus increase the risk of skin cancer.[8] These studies also identified a doubling of UV skin damage among people using products containing AHAs. While typically failing to take any regulatory action, in this case the FDA proposed the following contradictory recommendation: that sunscreen users should be warned to "limit sun exposure while using these products and for a week afterward."[9]

Twelve Categories of Cosmeceutical Ingredients

Including hydroxy acids, the second most common kind of cosmeceutical, there are twelve major cosmeceutical ingredients and product categories currently on the market. Some are outright dangerous; others simply have shown no measurable positive or protective effect. While a few have actually shown some benefit, these are very much in the minority.

The other eleven:

1. **Retinoids.** Vitamin A or carotenoids, and their synthetic retinoid derivatives (including retinol and tretinoin), are the most common cosmeceuticals on the market. As antioxidants, they protect cells from free radical damage. Local application of the synthetic tretinoin (vitamin A acid) is used to bleach pigmented spots and smooth wrinkling caused by excessive or prolonged sunlight exposure. Despite their popularity, retinoids have shown only limited effectiveness. They are not, however, dangerous.

2. **Antioxidants**. Antioxidants are natural substances that protect our bodies against damage from free radicals. Skin is continually exposed to damage not only within, from free radicals, but without, from heat, cold, air pollutants, and, most importantly, UVA long-wave radiation. Antioxidant

cosmeceuticals claim to reduce or reverse this damage. Anti-oxidant cosmeceutical ingredients include vitamins such as B-5 (and its synthetic derivative panthenol), C, E, and nicotinamide; lycopene; polyphenols such as coffeeberry in coffee plant fruit and resveratrol in grapes; genistein, the isoflavone in soy milk and fermented soy; EGCG (epigallo-catechin-3-gallate); pycnogenol, an extract of French marine pine bark; grape seed extract; and DMAE, found in cold-water fish, particularly salmon. While they may be useful, there has been no clinical evidence as to their effectiveness in cosmeceuticals. There are no dangers associated with their use.

3. **Botanicals**. Botanicals are extracts taken from natural plants. Well over sixty natural botanicals are currently marketed in chemically pure or concentrated forms, in an increasingly wide range of products. They include grape seed, horse chestnut, German chamomile, curcumin, comfrey, allant-oin, aloe vera, and virgin olive oil. They also include green and black tea, soy, pomegranate, and date, some of which have been found to be effective in clinical trials.[2] As with antioxidants, there has been no clinical evidence as to their effectiveness in cosmeceuticals. Also as with antioxidants, there are no dangers associated with their use.

4. **Mica**. Mica is the name for a group of fine crystallized min-erals that create a light glow in facial cosmetics by increas-ing the reflection of light. They can be colored or colorless. Mica is harmless, except when inhaled as a fine dust, when it can cause acute or chronic lung irritation.

5. **Tyrosinase Inhibitors**. Tyrosinase inhibitors are a diverse group of natural whitening agents that inactivate tyrosinase, the enzyme responsible for skin darkening due to its role in the formation of the natural pigment melanin.[10,11] They include vitamin C, kojic acid, arbutin, azaleic acid, licorice, mulberry, and burner root extract. The most recent of these is melanostat, a patented synthetic peptide. (See also num-ber 8 below, for other uses of peptides in cosmeceuticals.)

There is no scientific evidence that these are effective. While they may or may not be useful, their use at least appears to pose no serious health threat.

6. **Anti-Cellulite Creams**. Anti-cellulite creams supposedly treat cellulite, the normal skin puckering or dimpling adult women develop, to varying degrees, as part of the normal hormonal process of aging. However, there is no evidence whatsoever that any creams can reduce or have any beneficial effect on cellulite—though they do at least appear to have no negative effect.[12] Advertisements claiming these effects, such as Unilever's New Dove Firming Lotion, or Esteé Lauder's much more expensive Body Performance Anti-Cellulite Visible Contouring Serum, are problematic at best.[13]

7. **Bisabolol.** Bisabolol, like hydroxy acids (though less commonly used), is a dangerous skin peeler and penetration enhancer that facilitates the absorption of other ingredients into the skin.

8. **Peptides**. Peptides are chains of amino acids often used in anti-wrinkle products. Peptides cannot penetrate the skin barrier alone; they are often paired with a penetration enhancer to drive the peptide deep into the skin. The evidence for their effectiveness is very limited, and due to their pairing with penetration enhancers, their presence can pose a serious threat.

One expensive anti-wrinkle cosmeceutical, StriVectin-SD, aggressively marketed as an "Anti-Aging Breakthrough" and "Better than Botox," is based on a chain of amino acids known as Pal-KTTKS (sold under the trade name Matrixyl). In the product, Pal-KTTKS is chemically linked to the penetration enhancer palmitic acid. StriVectin-SD is claimed to increase skin's strength by stimulating enzymes to produce more collagen, thus reducing wrinkling. However, the effectiveness of the product is based on short-term clinical trials with a relatively small number of women,[10] without any subsequent follow-up. More seriously, StriVectin contains toxic ingredients, particularly five hormone-disruptive parabens, and also PEG, which is usually contaminated by potent carcinogens.

Argireline, or acetyl hexapeptide, is a cheaper anti-aging cosmeceutical marketed by the New Jersey–based Janson Beckett company.[14] This product is a peptide chemically

---

Nanoparticles Creep Into Cosmeceuticals as Penetration Enhancers

Many cosmeceuticals work—or are claimed to work—because they also include nanoparticles that let their ingredients penetrate into the skin.

Take the Men's Skin Care line developed by dermatologist Dr. Nicholas Perricone, who is perhaps best known as the author of three *New York Times* bestselling books, including *The Perricone Prescription*. Here is how Perricone's Web site describes his products: "Dr. Perricone has developed a patented technology exclusive to this line, called Fullerene. Fullerenes are highly stable, microscopic hollow spheres that carry the active ingredients into the skin. They bring the intriguing and transformative world of nanotechnology to the fine art and science of high performance skin care." Fullerenes, with an average size of 1/10,000 of a millimeter, have been introduced into a growing number of anti-aging products, particularly skin creams touted as reducing wrinkles and firming up the skin surface.

An equally alarming and similarly unproven yet overhyped anti-aging trend is the use of nanoparticles ingredients in foods that, when eaten, allegedly prevent wrinkles by promoting skin cell regrowth.

As with sunscreens and sunblocks, the addition of these ultraminute nanoparticles to anti-aging skin products—and foods!—races ahead of safety concerns to create a potential public health hazard.

linked to a different penetration enhancer, acetic acid residue, and is claimed to fight signs of aging in skin by reducing muscle movements that cause wrinkling.

9. **Restylane**. Restylane, or Perlane, is an anti-wrinkling agent manufactured by Q-Med, a Swedish biotechnology company.[15] It is based on the natural biodegradable ingredient hyaluronic acid, the effectiveness of which is well documented.[16] In fact, restylane has been shown to be more effective than collagen in double-blind clinical trials six months after injection by dermatologists in the naso-labial folds, wrinkles that run from the bridge of the nose to the corners of the mouth. It's also cheaper than collagen. Injections that combined restylane and the prescription drug Botox (botulinum toxin) were also reported to be more effective than injections of either product alone.

10. **Mexoryl SX.** Mexoryl SX, which we discussed last chapter as a highly effective new sunscreen and sunblock, is also claimed to have "proven anti-aging benefits." But this claim is based on a clinical test of only "32 women . . . in just two weeks." Mexoryl SX is a proprietary ingredient in L'Oreal's Revitalift UV cream (a product that, notably, also contains hormone-disruptive parabens and the dangerous sunscreen ingredient avobenzone).

11. **Pro-Xylane**. A more recent L'Oreal product, Skin Genesis, containing the innovative natural ingredient Pro-Xylane, has been claimed to be an effective long-term anti-aging product.[17] However, there is no available scientific evidence on either its effectiveness or its safety.

Green Tea and Other Natural Skin Enhancers

Numerous clinical studies have demonstrated the multiple therapeutic benefits of natural green tea due to its anti-carcinogenic, antioxidant, and anti-inflammatory properties. In a 2005 trial of green tea extracts published in the journal *Dermatologic Surgery*, it was revealed that topical and oral formulations of green tea polyphenols can prevent or modify skin damage caused by UV radiation exposure. Forty women with moderate photoaging of the skin were randomly assigned to either a placebo group, where they drank a harmless but inactive potion, or a group that followed a regimen of 10 percent green tea cream and 300 mg twice-daily green tea oral supplements. The clinical trial lasted for eight weeks.

"Participants in this trial confirmed the well-established ability of green tea derivatives to prevent skin damage following UV radiation exposure."[19]

In an unrelated clinical trial done in 2002, study participants topically applied date palm oil to their eyelids twice daily for five weeks. Researchers found that "a statistically significant reduction in wrinkle surface (27.6%) and wrinkle depth was achieved."[20]

A physician associated with Oregon Health Sciences University surveyed the medical literature in 2005 for the safe and active use of botanicals in cosmeceuticals and came to this conclusion: "The most significant human cosmeceutical data have been generated with formulations containing green and black tea, soy, pomegranate, date, and a grape seed–based mixture."[2]

Distorting the Meaning of "Natural"

One of the Estée Lauder companies, Origins, launched a new line of anti-aging cosmetics products in late 2006 that it called "a totally integrative approach to skin care . . . to help your skin be as healthy as possible, [and] optimize its defenses against age accelerators." The line of products is marketed under the brand name of Dr. Andrew Weil for Origins, and the use of that name alone seemed designed to emphasize the natural-ness of these products; Dr. Weil is a bestselling author who extols the virtues of natural health and healing. Origins fur-ther bills itself as using "natural resources from many different cultures and alternative healing traditions," in product formu-lations that "ensure our products are authentic and as natural as can be."

What I found among the ingredients when I studied the product labels surprised and disturbed me. These products being touted as "natural" contained a long list of toxic synthetic ingredients. For instance, Origins' Plantidote Mega-Mushroom line, which consisted of a face serum and face cream, included the harmful ingredients limonene, parabens, butylene glycol, and bisabolol.

Here is a listing of the most harmful ingredients (and why they're harmful) from a survey I did of the complete Origins product line:

- Limonene, a skin irritant also rated as a carcinogen in 1990 by the National Toxicology Program.
- Ethoxylated detergents, which unless purified (and labeled to that effect) are contaminated with high con-centrations of the potent carcinogens ethylene oxide and dioxane.
- Parabens, which even at very low concentrations can produce toxic hormonal effects, particularly in male embryos and infants.

- Butylene glycol, a skin irritant related to the antifreeze ethylene glycol.
- Bisabolol, a penetration enhancer that drives other harmful chemicals deeper into the skin.

Not only are the claimed anti-aging effects of these Origins products not based on any clinical trials, but when I communicated the list of dangerous ingredients to the CEO of Origins, she responded that she was uninformed about the "scientific technicalities" of what the company's products contained. A senior scientist for Estée Lauder even attempted to challenge evidence on the carcinogenicity of limonene on the irrelevant grounds that a European Council Directive relating to limonene's allergenic effects had made no reference to its carcinogenicity.

The company maintained that its ingredients "are all acceptable in cosmetic formulations throughout the industry"— which is, of course, part of the problem!

A Truly Natural Way to Reduce Wrinkles

Much as with any other muscles in the body, our facial muscles need to be exercised in order to stay toned. Facial yoga has been heralded as a face-muscle training technique that can provide people with a natural facelift, one without the side effects and hazards of chemicals and surgery.

New York yoga teacher Annelise Hagen's book, *The Yoga Face: Eliminate Wrinkles with the Ultimate Natural Facelift*, utilized these facial exercises include smiling slightly while pursing your lips (the Smiling Fish), transferring air from cheek to cheek while puffing out your face (the Satchmo), and blowing kisses while trying to keep your forehead smooth (the Marilyn).
continued on the next page

A Truly Natural Way to Reduce Wrinkles, *continued*

A *Time* magazine article in late 2007 brought the techniques to a national audience and quoted practitioners as claiming that it had taken years off their faces. They said the most obvious differences after a month of doing the exercises could be seen around the eyes and on the forehead. "It's like natural Botox," declared Leta Koontz, who holds Fresh Face Yoga workshops at a studio in Pittsburgh, Pennsylvania.[21]

While no clinical studies have been done to support facial yoga's effectiveness, at least you know there's no danger from toxic or unknown ingredients!

Table 13: Toxic Ingredients in Products for Youth Seekers

INGREDIENT	TOXIC EFFECT(S)
Bisabolol	Penetration enhancer
Hydroxy Acids	Penetration enhancers and skin irritants
Limonene	Carcinogen
Nanoparticles ("micro-fine," "ultra-fine")	Penetration enhancers
Parabens	Hormone disrupters

Safe Products and Ingredients For Youth Seekers

ANTI-WRINKLE PRODUCTS

Numerous medical studies have found several *natural botanicals* to be safe and effective, particularly date palm oil for eyelid wrinkles and topical green tea cream for sun damage to skin.

The anti-wrinkling agent *restylane*, or *Perlane*, used in products made by Sweden's Q-Med, incorporates a natural biodegradable ingredient called hyaluronic acid that has been shown to be both safe and effective.

Botox injections have been in use long enough to be considered relatively safe, but must be injected by a qualified dermatologist.

10 | Products Targeting Everyone

I magine for a moment that you are in your bathroom in the morning, beginning your daily routine. First, you use the toilet, and then spray an air freshener. You take a shower, using soap, shampoo, and hair conditioner. Afterward, you stand at the mirror and apply underarm deodorant or an antiperspirant and brush your teeth.

It's a routine that seems—even feels—harmless. Examine each of these modern conveniences and how they interact with each other through the lens of scientific research, however, and the picture is very different.

What Is Really in Your Air Freshener?

About three out of every four U.S. households keep air freshener products in their bathrooms. Most of these products contain variable amounts of phthalates, hormone disrupters suspected of causing a range of reproductive abnormalities, sometimes without labeling. Phthalates are used to dissolve and absorb fragrances, enabling aroma from the products they're used in to linger for longer periods of time. A 2007 survey by the Natural Resources Defense Council evaluated fourteen air fresheners purchased from U.S. store shelves and twelve were found to contain phthalates, either diethylphthalate

(DEP) or dibutyl phthalate (DBP), ranging in concentrations from a few parts per million up to as high as 7,000 parts per million. Only two products were virtually free of phthalates: Febreze Air Effects and Renuzit Subtle Effects.[1]

Your exposure level to air freshener ingredients is determined by the size of the room the fresheners are sprayed in and the length of time you stay in that room. Since most bathrooms are small enclosed, and improperly ventilated—and because freshener mist is designed to linger in the air for many minutes—the longer you stand in front of the sink performing your morning ritual, the more phthalates you inhale and absorb through your skin. When researchers at the U.S. Centers for Disease Control and Prevention tested 289 persons for phthalate contamination in 2000, seven types of phthalates were found in subjects' blood. DBP, the phthalate most often found in air fresheners, was detected in every person.[2]

But air fresheners alone should not be the focus of our concern: when a coalition of environmental and public health groups contracted with a major laboratory in 2002 to test seventy-two cosmetic products for phthalates, three-quarters of the products contained them, including nine of fourteen deodorants, fourteen of eighteen hair sprays, and all seventeen fragrances. As reported in the "Not Too Pretty" report by the Environmental Working Group (EWG), DEP and DBP were found in 71 percent and 8 percent of the products, respectively. None of the personal-care items containing phthalates listed them on the ingredient label.[3]

A subsequent study by two consumer groups in Britain and Sweden found that 79 percent of personal-care products on their store shelves carried phthalates, and more than half of them contained multiple phthalates.[4] Nor was the situation any different in Asia. A women's group in South Korea had twenty-four products tested in 2003 and found that 100 percent contained phthalates; half contained more than three different types.[5]

Because phthalates have become so prevalent, we have countless opportunities to absorb them every day. These exposures are cumulative, so have a much greater potential for affecting our health than any one phthalate from any one product has on its own. One study found high concentrations of DEP in the urine of men after they used cologne or aftershave, and also found that phthalate levels in men's bodies increased by 33 percent with the application of each additional personal-care product.

In the aftermath of news coverage about the discovery of so many phthalates in common toiletries, medical researchers began looking anew into the possible relationship between this class of chemicals and reproductive abnormalities in humans. One of the first significant findings came from a human study at the University of Rochester that measured phthalate levels in pregnant women and then, after the birth of their children, compared the results to the physical condition of their male infants. The study discovered "a significant relationship" between abnormal changes in male infant genitals and the phthalate levels in their mother's bodies while pregnant, suggesting that the phthalate contaminants had been passed on to the fetuses affected their development.[6]

More evidence for a link between phthalates and reproductive abnormalities emerged from a 2006 study, published in *Epidemiology*, that tested men in an infertility clinic. Harvard School of Public Health researchers determined that the men with low sperm quality also had the highest levels of the phthalate DBP in their blood.[7] Other work by the same researchers, measuring the phthalate DEP in men with fertility problems, connected high phthalate blood levels with genetic abnormalities in the men's sperm.[8]

In EWG's "Not Too Pretty" report, a survey was done of all the medical science literature pertaining to phthalates and possible human reproductive disorders. "Scientists have shown that phthalates can damage the female reproductive system," the report observed, "but it is the male reproductive system that appears to be more sensitive." (See chapter 5 for more on phthalates' effects on the male reproductive system.)

What Is Really in Your Shampoo and Conditioner?

Did you ever stop to think about what produces all of that foam and lather when you use shampoo? It is usually one of a group of harsh detergents: sodium lauryl sulfate, sodium laureth sulfate, or one of its related ingredients.

In addition to acting as penetration enhancers for other potentially toxic ingredients, these and other ethoxylate detergents—any ingredient with myreth, oleth, laureth, ceteareth, or any "eth," in their names, in addition to PEG, polyethylene, polyethylene glycol, polyoxyethlene, or oxynol—are invariably contaminated with high concentrations of the volatile and carcinogenic ethylene oxide and 1,4-dioxane. Both of these are readily absorbed through the skin, and can also be inhaled.

Ethylene oxide is a potent carcinogen which induces brain, breast, and lung cancer in rodents. It has also been incriminated as a cause of lymphomas in exposed workers.[9] In the medical journal *Cancer*'s 2007 review of mammary carcinogens, dioxane was one of the 216 chemicals they identified as producing breast cancer in rodent tests. Its carcinogenicity in rodents was first reported in 1965 and subsequently confirmed in 1978. The predominant cancer caused in rats was nasal cancer; cancer was also found in the livers of mice.

As far back as 1985, the FDA recognized these dangers, and requested that manufacturers voluntarily limit dioxane levels in cosmetics and personal-care products to 10 parts per million. Unfortunately for consumers, the industry has remained unresponsive. *Los Angeles Times* staff writer Marla Cone in February 2007 reported that all eighteen child and adult personal-care products she had tested by an independent laboratory were contaminated by high levels of dioxane, three of these exceeding the FDA's recommended upper limit. The industry trade group, the Personal Care Products Council, responded that "Consumers should not be concerned about the levels in this data."[10]

Other carcinogenic contaminants include acrylates, which appear in a range of complex ingredients known as acrylate polymers or copolymers.

Contaminants are one source of toxic concern in shampoos and conditioners; chemical reactivity is another. Diethanolamine (DEA) is a common ingredient in shampoo, and readily reacts with nitrite preservatives or contaminants to create nitrosodiethanolamine (NDELA), a known and potent carcinogen.

These contaminants are also particularly easy, and dangerous, to absorb through the skin. A 1989 study showed that 13 percent of the carcinogenic preservative butylated hydroxytoluene (BHT) and 50 percent of the carcinogenic pesticide DDT (a common contaminant of commercial-grade lanolin derived from sheep's wool), are absorbed through skin very rapidly.[11] And evidence cited in an October 22, 1996, Citizen Petition to the FDA "Seeking Cancer Warning on Cosmetics Containing DEA" concluded that NDELA is readily absorbed through human skin.

Meet Your Local "Penetration Enhancers"

For decades, the drug industry has used a group of ingredients known as "Penetration Enhancers" to decrease the resistance of the skin and increase drug absorption up to a hundred-fold.[12] In spite of possible hazards, the personal-care industry still makes extensive use of penetration enhancers, as we've discussed in chapters 8 and 9. Penetration enhancers fall into four major categories: Gentle Detergents; Harsh Detergents; Hydroxy Acids; and the unrelated but much more hazardous Nanoparticle Ingredients.

1. **Gentle Detergents.** The most common penetration enhancers in use are the gentle detergents monoethanolamine, diethanolamine, and triethanolamine, which are also used as emulsifiers and thickeners. They facilitate the absorption of other ingredients through the skin by damaging the skin to increase its permeability.

   Another gentle detergent, ammonium lauryl sulfate, is widely used as a cleansing agent. However, in its action as a penetration enhancer, it also has a degenerative effect on cell membranes, particularly at concentrations over 1 percent.

continued on the next page

Meet Your Local "Penetration Enhancers," *continued*

2. **Harsh Detergents.** Harsh detergents act as penetration enhancers by damaging the skin and increase its permeability to varying degrees. Two of the most widely used harsh detergents are sodium lauryl sulfate and glyceryl laurate.

As admitted by the industry's Cosmetic Ingredient Review Compendium, sodium lauryl sulfate is a strong irritant that "causes severe epidermal changes of the skin of mice," including damage to skin protein and degeneration of skin membranes.[13] The Compendium further admits that products containing this ingredient are only "designed for brief discontinued use, following which they are thoroughly rinsed from the surface of the skin." As reported by Danish Institute of Public Health studies, a single twenty-four-hour exposure to sodium lauryl sulfate damages skin proteins and causes prolonged disruption of "the skin barrier integrity," allowing the ready penetration of carcinogens.[14, 15]

A related detergent, sodium lauryl sarcosinate, can also react with nitrates to yield a carcinogenic nitrosamine.

3. **Hydroxy Acids.** See chapter 9 for details.
4. **Nanoparticle Ingredients**. See chapters 8 and 9 for details.

Other penetration enhancers include bisabolol, a naturally occurring terpene alcohol derivative widely used as a skin conditioner and also an anti-aging ingredient (see chapter 9), and ethylenediamine tetra-acetic acid (EDTA), a sodium salt that binds to calcium normally present in skin and disrupts the normal bridges connecting cells. EDTA is also a hormone disrupter.

What Is Really in Your Deodorant or Antiperspirant?

The biggest concern about antiperspirants in recent years has been whether their contents contribute to the risk of breast cancer in women. Though the jury is still out, one study in particular, done in 2006, did ring a lot of people's alarm bells. An article in the *Journal of Applied Toxicology* reported evidence that aluminum chloride, which appear in concentrations of up to 25 percent in some antiperspirants, exhibits the same effects as estrogen in a way that could stimulate the onset of breast cancer, making aluminum chloride a hormone disrupter.[16]

There are several reasons for concern about the possible relationship of aluminum chloride to breast cancer, as cited by study author Philippa Darbre, Ph.D., of the University of Reading in Britain. Aluminum chloride–laden antiperspirants are applied to the underarm, near the breasts. The aluminum chloride remains on the skin, allowing continuous exposure. Shaving the armpits may damage the skin enough to allow aluminum chloride direct chemical access to underlying tissue—though studies have shown that aluminum chloride also has no trouble passing through intact human armpit skin.

What particularly concerned Darbre was the impact of the multiple chemicals in deodorants and antiperspirants acting together. Most studies examine one chemical at a time, and these alone may not have measurable effects on people, meaning that study results can project an illusion of safety. "Each of these agents on their own may not have a powerful effect, but we need to see what happens when a number of them act together," she commented. "It could be that this would have a significant effect on diseases like breast cancer."[17]

Even products where responsible manufacturers have made honest attempts to limit the toxicity of their products—by eliminating aluminum, for instance—can still fall short of safety. Nature's Gate Spring Fresh deodorant, which is aluminum-free, still contains diethanolamine.

Another kind of ingredient in deodorants and antiperspirants that may contribute to breast cancer are hormone-disruptive parabens, discussed in more detail in chapter 5. At least a dozen rodent tests since 1998 have documented parabens' hormonal effects. Notably, parabens' estrogen-like effects did not occur when the animals were fed the parabens, but did show up when parabens were applied to their skin.[18] "To date there is no concrete scientific evidence to support a link between parabens and breast cancer," observed the two physician authors of a 2007 study of parabens in the journal *Skin & Aging*. "Nevertheless, these studies brought to light the possibility that parabens might affect endocrine function and breast cancer development. Given that underarm deodorants or antiperspirants that contain these parabens are used daily for millions of people and the close proximity of the axilla and breast tissue, this possibility should be considered and further work done in this area."[19]

It was long thought that parabens did not accumulate in the body because they were quickly metabolized by the liver and kidneys. This turned out to be untrue, at least when parabens are absorbed by the skin. A 2007 study in the *International Journal of Cosmetic Science*, which assessed three different parabens in three commercial cosmetic creams, found strong retention rates. The three types studied—methylparabens, ethylparabens, and propylparabens—displayed some variation in this retention; methyl was the highest, with a 60 percent retention rate, followed by ethyl at 40 percent and propyl at 20 percent.[20] A 1999 report for the Ministry of Health and Welfare of Japan found the main metabolite of parabens present in blood and breast milk. And in a subsequent study of 100 demographically diverse adults, methyl- and propylparabens were discovered in nearly every sample of urine, while other parabens were detected in more than half of the samples.[21]

What Is Really in Your Toothpaste?

Maybe you have noticed that most brands of toothpaste carry this poison warning, or a variation of it, on their labels: "Keep out of reach of children under six years of age. If you accidentally swallow more than used for brushing, seek professional help or contact a poison control center immediately." The main reason is the presence of fluoride in most toothpaste products; fluoride can be highly toxic,

Deodorants That Do and Do Not Contain Phthalates

Here are the deodorants in EWG's "Not Too Pretty" report in which lab testing uncovered the presence of phthalates (measured in parts per million, or ppm):

- Arrid Extra Dry Ultra Clear Ultra Fresh Spray: 200 ppm of DBP
- Arrid Extra Dry Ultra Clear Ultra Clean Spray: 150 ppm of DBP
- Arrid Extra Dry Maximum Strength Solid: 2900-3300 ppm of DEP
- Arrid Extra Dry Ultra Clear Ultra Clean Spray: 1100-1200 ppm of DEP
- Ban Delicate Powder Roll On: 400 ppm of DEP
- Degree Original Solid Antiperspirant & Deodorant: 140 ppm of DEP
- Dove Solid Antiperspirant Deodorant: 110 ppm of DEP
- Secret Powder Fresh Aerosol: 63 ppm of DEP
- Secret Sheer Dry Regular: 49 ppm of DEP
- Sure Clear Dry Antiperspirant & Deodorant: 20 ppm of DEP
- Secret Sheer Dry Regular: 33 ppm of DMP

Five lab-tested deodorants had no detectable levels of phthalates, which demonstrates that manufacturers are capable of making effective products free of phthalates if they so choose. Those deodorants:

- Certain Dri Antiperspirant Roll-On
- Dove Powder Antiperspirant Deodorant
- Lady Speed Stick Soft Antiperspirant
- Secret Antiperspirant & Deodorant Platinum Protection
- Soft & Dri Antiperspirant Deodorant Clear Gel

Note: These phthalate levels and product formulations may have changed since the "Not Too Pretty" test results were released in 2002. Additionally, the products tested represented only a small selection of deodorants on the market.

even if it does help to prevent cavities when applied topically to your teeth.

But the warning could also apply to some other common ingredients contaminating toothpastes. In a court settlement little noticed outside of California, the state where the lawsuit was filed, the Procter & Gamble Manufacturing Company conceded in the summer of 2005 that its Crest brand of toothpaste products contained high levels of lead.[22]

The lead in this product was not discovered by any government agency, or even by the manufacturer. Instead, the analytical testing of numerous toothpaste products that uncovered this information was initiated by the Palo Alto–based American Environmental Safety Institute under California's Proposition 65, a landmark consumer health initiative statute passed by voters that requires warnings be given to consumers about the presence of hazardous chemicals in the products they purchase in California.

"The research demonstrated that almost all toothpaste products contain significant levels of lead, a heavy metal known to the State of California's health experts to be hazardous to human health by causing cancer and birth defects," declared Institute researchers. Crest was singled out as one of the worst offending brands due to its additional inclusion of hydrated silica, an abrasive cleanser found to be laced with even more lead. Eighteen other toothpaste manufacturers also used lead-laced hydrated silica.

Procter & Gamble agreed to settle the lawsuit brought by the American Environmental Safety Institute by paying the group almost $400,000 to cover its research costs and attorney fees.[22] In addition, Procter & Gamble agreed to reduce by 25 percent the lead levels of toothpaste sold in California through testing and product reformulations.[22] The FDA was not involved.

Contrast this to what happened during the 2007 consumer scare over the discovery of diethylene glycol in toothpaste imported from China. The FDA quickly got involved, issuing an alert to retailers and consumers and stepping up its scrutiny of personal-care products made in China. Under the brand names of Excel and Cool, the oversea manufacturer had substituted diethylene glycol, known as

DEG, for a more expensive chemical normally used as a sweetener and thickening agent. The syrupy DEG constituted up to 4 percent of each toothpaste tube's overall weight. But according to an FDA statement, "it does not belong in toothpaste even in small concentrations" because it can lead to organ failure and death. Toxic DEG exposure is of particular concern for children and people with kidney or liver problems. When DEG had been added to cough syrup in Panama, up to 100 people died.[23]

The question naturally arises: Why would the FDA pay so much attention to foreign products and foreign manufacturers when it fails to give equal scrutiny to the safety of domestic products?

What Is Really in Your Soap and Cleanser?

In addition to whatever phthalates and parabens soaps and other cleansers may contain, there are two preservative ingredients common to antibacterial soaps and cleansers which pose particular dangers: triclosan and triclocarban, first discussed in chapter 5.

Just since 2000, more than 1,500 new antibacterial products have entered the marketplace. In a 2006 study, John Hopkins University researchers found that 75 percent of the bacteria-killing ingredients found in these products survive wastewater treatment processes and end up contaminating waterways or the sewage sludge that is commonly spread on farm fields. These ingredients accumulate in soil and water (and perhaps in human bodies), and help create super germs resistant to antibiotics.[24] Indeed, water testing studies by the U.S. Geological Survey have found that triclosan and triclocarban are among the top ten persistent contaminants in U.S. rivers, streams, lakes, and underground aquifers.[25]

Triclosan, which is also a hormone disrupter, is present is many liquid soaps. Ironically, unexpected volatility has been documented when the triclosan in these liquid soaps and other common household products comes into contact with water—something one assumes would happen during every use. At Virginia Tech University a team of researchers in April 2005 reported that some toothpastes and soaps create a chloroform gas when the triclosan in these products reacts with chlorinated water. Chloroform is known to cause liver problems, depression, and cancer if inhaled or absorbed through the skin.[26]

Even more troubling evidence has emerged about the health impacts of triclocarban, which is used in bar soaps, deodorants, toothpaste, and even baby toys. A study published in the science journal *Endocrinology* in late 2007 revealed that this chemical, too, is also a hormone disrupter; feeding triclocarban to test rats resulted in abnormally enlarged prostate glands.[27]

In contrast to most other hormone disrupters, which either block or decrease natural hormonal effects, triclocarban, as this study showed, abnormally increases hormonal effects. "This finding may eventually lead to an explanation for some rises in some previously described reproductive problems that have been difficult to understand," commented study co-author Professor Bill Lasley, a University of California at Davis expert on reproductive toxicology.

Are There Fragrances That Are Safe to Use?

Today, fragrances appear in almost all our cosmetics and personal-care products. Since even skin patch tests fail to identify up to one-third of known fragrance allergens, you should avoid all fragranced products unless they are labeled "contains no known allergens."

This recommendation is strongly endorsed by the Perfume Foundation, a Belgium-based non-profit organization established in 1995 "to be the leading authority on health and environmental issues related to fragrances and scents, while contributing to the cultural heritage of perfumes." The Foundation also works in collaboration with leading independent scientists and non-government organizations "in order to reduce the toxicity of perfumes," and is also developing a "seal of approval" for non-toxic perfumes and related products.

Table 14: Toxic Ingredients in Products for Everyone

INGREDIENT	TOXIC EFFECT(S)
4-methyl-benzylidene camphor (4-MBC)	Hormone disrupter
Ceteareths	Contaminated with the carcinogens ethylene oxide and dioxane
Diethanolamine (DEA)	Carcinogen
Ethylenediamine tetra-acetic acid (EDTA)	Hormone disrupter and penetration enhancer
Laureths	Contaminated with the carcinogens ethylene oxide and dioxane
Parabens	Hormone disrupters
Polyethylene glycol (PEG)	Contaminated with the carcinogens ethylene oxide and dioxane
Phthalates	Hormone disrupters
Polysorbates	Contaminated with the carcinogens ethylene oxide and dioxane
Triclocarban	Hormone disrupter
Triclosan	Hormone disrupter

Safe Products and Ingredients For Everyone

AIR FRESHENERS
Nearly all air fresheners on the market contain dangerous levels of either DEP or DBP phthalates. The exceptions, according to a 2007 Natural Resources Defense Council study, are *Febreze Air Effects* (www.febreze.com) and *Renuzit Subtle Effects* (www.renuzit.com).

SHAMPOO/CONDITIONER
Erbaorganics Shampoo
INGREDIENTS: organic aloe barbadensis (aloe vera) leaf juice, sodium coco-sulfate, sodium lauroyl oat amino acids, sodium olivamphoacetate, sodium levulinate, glyceryl oleate (and) coco-glucoside, sodium chloride (sea salt), citric acid, organic lavandula hybrida (lavandin) oil, organic lavandula angustifolia (lavender) oil, organic citrus nobilis (mandarin orange) peel oil, organic anthemis nobilis (roman chamomile) flower oil, sodium phytate, potassium sorbate, citric acid
www.erbaorganics.com

Nurture My Body Shampoo—Fragrance Free
INGREDIENTS: water, decyl glucose, lauryl glucose, coco protein, seaweed extract, organic herbal infusions of coltsfoot, chickweed, nettles, horsetail, slippery elm, marshmallow root, comfrey root, calendula blossoms, chamomile flowers and oatstraw, sea buckthorn CO_2, grapefruit seed extract
www.nurturemybody.com

DEODORANTS
Erbaviva Jasmine Grapefruit Organic Deodorant
INGREDIENTS: organic grain alcohol, organic essential oils extracts of jasmine, grapefruit, ginger, safe, cedarwood, orange, and lemon
www.erbaviva.com

TOOTHPASTES AND MOUTHWASHES

Dentarome's Thieves Toothpaste

Dentarome's line of toothpastes use a formula of mostly plant-derived ingredients, including baking soda and peppermint and wintergreen essential oils. Their Web site challenges: "Go ahead and eat it! Our selection of powerful, non-fluoride toothpastes without the sodium lauryl sulfate are completely edible."
www.secretofthieves.com

Jason Natural Sea Fresh Toothpaste

INGREDIENTS: calcium carbonate, glycerin, purified sea water, blue green algae, sodium cocoyl glutamate, carrageenan, aloe bara-badensis gel, sodium bicarbonate, bambuse arundinaces, stevioside, perilla seed extract, parsley extract, silica, grapefruit seed extract, spearmint
www.jason-natural.com

PerioPaste

INGREDIENTS: phytoplenolin (*Centipeda Cunninghamii Extract*), bio-chelated extracts of echinacea purpurea tops (*Echinacea Purpurea*), calendula flower (*Calendula Officiinalis*), olive leaf (*Olea Europea*), black walnut green hulls (*Juglans Nigra*), gotu kola herb (*Centella Asiatica*), chamomile flower (*Chamomilla Recutita* [*Matricarla*]), green tea leaf (*Camellia Sinensis*), prickly ash bark (*Zanthoxylum Ameriicanum*), grapefruit seed (*Citrus Grandis*), bio saponins, folic acid, CoEnzyme Q10, aloe vera phytogel ,sodium bicarbonate, colloidal silica, lysine, xylitol, xanthan gum, chlorophyll, essential oils of peppermint, oregano, clove, thyme, lavender, cinnamon, and eucalyptus
www.bioprodental.com

Tom's of Maine Mouthwash Oral Moistening Peppermint

INGREDIENTS: water (from branch brook), glycerin (from kosher vegetable oil), witch hazel (non-alcoholic, from hamelis virginiana plant), aloe vera juice, sodium bicarbonate (from purified sodium bicarbonate from the earth), poloxamer 335 (processed from natural

gas and oil), xylitol (from birch trees), peppermint oil, menthol from Brazilian cornmint oil
www.tomsofmaine.com

SOAP/CLEANSER

Aubrey Organics Meal & Herbs Exfoliation Skin Care Bar
INGREDIENTS: palm oil, coconut fatty acids, peanut oil, shea butter, almond meal, oatmeal, walnut meal, coconut oil, water, almond essential oil
www.aubrey-organics.com

Chandrika Ayurvedic Soap (produced in India)
INGREDIENTS: coconut oil, wild ginger, lime, soda, soap stone powder, chandrika thilam, chandrika kashayam
www.chandrikasoaps.com

Erbaviva Awaken Body Wash
INGREDIENTS: de-ionized water, olivoil glutinate, decyl glucoside, cocamidopropyl hydroxysultaine, soyamide DEA, quilaja saponaria extract, sodium hydroxymethylglycinate (preservative at 0.3 percent), essential oils of melissa, organic lemongrass, rose, organic ginger, organic roman chamomile, and organic lavender
www.erbaviva.com

PART THREE

Getting Us Out of Danger

11 | Reforming the Cosmetics and Personal-Care Products Industry

As you've seen, cosmetics and personal-care products present a minefield of potential dangers that the FDA has done criminally little to protect us against. These products are the single largest avoidable cause of disease in the U.S., and yet the information you've read here remains undisclosed by the industry and the FDA.

The products we use every day are plagued by a wide range of toxic ingredients; some are unintentional contaminants and others purposeful additions. Our cumulative body burdens of chemicals keep growing. Clearly, we need to do something to put a stop to this. The question is, what?

There Are Safer Options

Aubrey Organics was one of the first manufacturers to abandon the use of the carcinogen DEA in its products. As Aubrey Hampton, director of that company, assured me back in 1996: "None of our products perform less effectively because they do not contain DEA. There are many alternative bases available without DEA that can be used by cosmetic manufacturers. The removal of DEA does not pose a manufacturing problem to the cosmetics industry." By 1998, Neways International had also phased out the use of DEA, as well as subsequently pioneering a series of initiatives to phase out carcinogens and other toxic ingredients in its products. (Under recent new management, the company's pledge of increased safety has become more aggressive. Neways has, with my collaboration, now eliminated all toxic ingredients in its new products.)

DEA isn't an isolated example. For every single one of the toxic ingredients we've discussed in this book, there are safe alternatives available. Responsible companies have demonstrated how toxic ingredients can be economically removed from cosmetics and personal-care products, and their example provides a roadmap for what other manufacturers and distributors can accomplish if they place the interests of public health and safety ahead of a reliance on risky shortcuts to higher profitability.

Though most manufacturers have historically relied upon hormone-disruptive parabens as preservatives to keep their products from going bad, safe alternatives include chlorophenesin, phenoxyethanol, and caprylyl glycol. Grapefruit seed extract has also been claimed to be a safe alternative to parabens, but its preservative action is actually due to contamination by the highly toxic hormone disrupter triclosan, or sometimes by the less toxic benzethonium chloride. Pure grapefruit seed extract has no preservative action whatsoever.[1]

Phthalates are the most commonly used solvents, but cosmetic-grade petroleum distillate (or petroleum jelly) is just as effective. At high concentrations petroleum distillate can be an irritant, especially in mascara and other eye make-up products, but is generally highly purified and non-toxic, and a great substitute for other solvents in conditioning, protective, and hairdressing creams.

Safe whitening ingredients—based on the synthetic peptide Melanostat, which suppresses tyrosinase, the enzyme responsible for the production of black pigment in skin cells—are becoming increasingly available. And there has been much promising research into safe, natural sunblocks (see chapter 8). Current safe sunblocks using zinc and titanium dioxide can even be made transparent using "encapsulated" ingredient formulas rather than untested nanoparticles.

For ingredients that frequently carry unsafe contaminants, there are often ways to remove those contaminants. Ethoxylate detergents, commonly used in shampoos and other cleansing products, can be largely purified of their hidden carcinogens, ethylene oxide and 1,4-dioxane, through a simple, inexpensive vacuum-stripping process. Steam-stripping is even more effective, particularly for ethylene oxide. (You can usually tell when ethoxylates in a particular product have been decontaminated, because they are labeled "ultra-purified.")

Even purified, however, ethoxylates still contain low levels of these two carcinogens. Better to avoid ethoxylates entirely, and instead use organic ingredients such as coconut and babassu palm oils and their sulfates, which are very safe, effective detergent alternatives.

There are also ways to minimize the toxic effects of many ingredients. There are many safe herbal hair dyes readily available, but if you do use a toxic dye, preventing contact between the dye and your scalp by using a plastic cap, with holes through which hair strands can be pulled before they are painted or streaked with dye, will at least minimize contact.

If there are such reasonable safe alternatives available, why don't more companies use them? The answer is twofold. The first part is economic; companies save a little, though not a lot, of money. Most unsafe ingredients are cheaper than their alternative—at least for now. The second part is plain irresponsibility. With no government agency standing watch over them, most manufacturers simply don't take consumer health as seriously as they do corporate profitability.

Needed Reforms

Convincing companies to discontinue their use of toxic ingredients means making it more cost-effective to change than to continue as they are. One way to do this is through the power of the marketplace. If enough citizens boycott hazardous products in favor of safer ones, companies will be forced to alter their products to compete. And the first step toward making that a reality is re-establishing the consumer's right to know.

RE-ESTABLISHING YOUR RIGHT TO KNOW

Being able to find out the identity of product ingredients and whether they are harmful to their user's health should be a fundamental, inalienable right. But it is a right we are unlikely to get without some kind of government regulation.

Dr. Donald Kennedy, FDA Commissioner from 1977 to 1979, and one of the few if only activist and scholarly experts to ever hold that position, once stressed how "information strategy," particularly the need for labeling of consumer products with explicit warnings of health risks, should be an integral function of regulation:

> Regulation arises as a consequence of the generation of public costs by private activity. **The best regulation is a clear signal that identifies these costs and allows members of the public to avoid them voluntarily.** Sometimes the regulator has to do more, as when the costs are impossibly cryptic or public understanding is inadequate. **In most cases, the regulator's task is to provide information. This role puts the Food and Drug Administration in the middle of the health-education business** [*emphasis added*].

Kennedy never had the reforming effect on his Agency that he sought, but his position remains a vigorous statement on the government's responsibility to intervene, even if only by supplying information, to protect the public.[2] His vision of the government's role remains just as pertinent and essential in this century as when he made those remarks decades ago.

While the full and accurate labeling of product ingredients is a necessary first step, product labeling per se is still inadequate to protect consumer health. Products that contain hazardous or problematic ingredients need to be accompanied by "Red Flag" warnings that spotlight the health risks uncovered during laboratory testing, similar to the cancer warnings mandated to appear on packs and cartons of cigarettes. But product label warnings should not be used as a justification for the authorization of new carcinogens or for the continued use of carcinogenic products already on the market. It must be stressed that product label warning is no substitute for ingredient phase-out or a ban on products containing clearly harmful chemicals. Absolute prohibition should be placed on the introduction of new carcinogenic products and untested new technologies. Human health and safety should rank above economic and political concerns.

All of this is impossible while industry claims of confidentiality and trade secrecy still present a serious obstacle to our obtaining the information we need to know to issue such warnings. There is an urgent need for international rules that restrict claims of confidentiality by corporations trying to withhold information on ingredients and their toxic effects. Information on the carcinogenic and otherwise toxic risks of products must be automatically and fully released

---

According to Horst Rechelbacher, CEO of Intelligent Nutrients

"Lowering safety and production standards and product quality to increase bottom-line profits, while knowingly and deceptively selling consumers inferior, defective, or unhealthy products, has long been a standard business strategy. Every day, substandard, defective, toxic, even dangerous products are knowingly released onto the market and sold to the public. At the same time and in the same way, we are also being denied a fundamental consumer right—the right to know exactly what we are being sold and are consuming, and what the effects of the things we are sold and consume can have on our bodies, our health, and on the environment. Today's business and government have become so completely and often covertly enmeshed that the denial of these citizen and consumer rights now defines and affects every aspect of our lives."

From Rechelbacher, Horst M. *Minding Your Business: Profits That Restore the Planet*. Earth Aware Editions: San Rafael, California, 2008.

to the public. As well, right-to-know regulations should be extended to the overseas operations, particularly in lesser developed countries, of U.S. corporations and those of other major industrialized nations, encompassing not just testing practices, but environmental and human rights practices as well.

MAKING COMPANIES PAY

Except for their operations in European Union countries, most of the global cosmetics and personal-care product industry has been essentially self-regulating (though that situation may be changing). Many nations still emulate the U.S. and rely on industry to ensure product safety, to determine the way cosmetics are labeled, and to decide the number of ingredients that are prohibited or restricted. There are no regulatory requirements for pre-market testing of ingredients and products. Nor, with few exceptions, are there any requirements for labeling products with cancer warnings or other dangers. Clearly, removing government from the equation does not work. Government regulation can be very useful not only in protecting our right to know, but in encouraging companies to adopt safer product standards—both by offering incentives for positive steps and threatening sanctions for violations of law.

Granting tax incentives for the development of safe alternatives to toxic-based, conventional technologies and ingredients, as well as tax penalties for failure to adopt available safe alternative technologies and ingredients, could encourage the active interest of mainstream industry in such initiatives—the surest way to stimulate belated reform of the mainstream cosmetic and personal-care product industry.

Consideration should also be given by state and federal government to using laws on white-collar crime—which are now applied largely just to crimes of economic motivation with adverse economic consequences—against crimes of economic motivation with adverse public health consequences, consistent with a major legislative initiative that I proposed nearly three decades ago.[2] Penalties could be levied against industry managers, executives, and consultants who knowingly manipulate, distort, or suppress information on the environmental, occupational, and consumer hazards of their products and manufacturing processes. There is currently a double standard of justice in the U.S.; as Ralph Nader has repeatedly commented, "Jail for the crime in the streets, but bail for crime in the suites."

More general reform of toxics use would have a positive impact as well. Following a well-organized political campaign by environmental groups and far-sighted industry representatives, the Commonwealth of Massachusetts unanimously passed the "Toxics Use Reduction Act" in 1989, which created the Massachusetts Toxics Use Reduction Program. The act is a specific form of pollution prevention that focuses on reducing the use of toxic chemicals by improving and redesigning industrial products and processes, and provides a useful model for state, national, and international legislation.

Thanks to this act, Massachusetts has reduced its generation of toxic wastes from 1989 to 1997 by 50 percent, by reducing toxics use by 20 percent; promoted reduction in the production and use of toxic chemicals; and enhanced and strengthened the enforcement of existing environmental laws, among other achievements.

Most recently, on August 14, 2008, Congress passed the Consumer Product Safety Modernization Act, the most comprehensive modernization of consumer product safety legislation in the last three decades. The act bans the sale of children's products, such as games and toys, containing more than 0.1 percent of any phthalate. The act also requires the appointment of a Chronic Hazardous Advisory Panel within eighteen months of the act's passing to consider and examine the following concerns:

- All potential health dangers, in isolation and in combination, for all consumer products intended for children under the age of twelve years.
- The health effects of exposure to phthalates from ingestion and skin contact.
- The likely levels of phthalate exposure in children, pregnant women, and others, based on products' estimated normal use and also abuse.

- The cumulative effect of exposures to phthalates in children's products, including personal-care products.

In addition, the legislation increases civil penalties, and possible criminal penalties, for companies that endanger consumers' health. Large fines and even imprisonment may be imposed upon a company's directors and officers, regardless of whether they are aware of the violation involved.

Most importantly, the Consumer Product Safety Modernization Act reflects explicit recognition of the FDA's reckless abdication of responsibility for the regulation of toxic hormonal ingredients in cosmetics and personal-care products. The scope of this act is likely to be expanded to include a wide range of other toxic ingredients, and offers an example of regulation on which we might base more comprehensive future regulation that protects consumers.

There are other successful models, both at home and abroad, we can look to in reforming our chemical safety policies as well, especially in terms of cosmetics and personal-care products—specifically, in California and in Europe.

California Pioneers U.S. Legislative Change

California often acts as a bellwether for the rest of the country, and in 2005 its state legislature enacted a Safe Cosmetics Act that requires cosmetic companies to disclose to a state agency any ingredients in their products that cause cancer or hormone disruption. Repeated failures in the U.S. Congress to enforce the FDA's compliance with the Food, Drug, and Cosmetic Act helped inspire California Assemblywoman Judy Chu to introduce landmark legislation, in 2004, that would have banned the use of phthalates and required disclosure of all carcinogenic, hormone-disruptive, and otherwise toxic ingredients in cosmetics and personal-care products, including their hidden use in perfumes and fragrances. Backed by a coalition of consumer, women's, occupational, and church groups, but opposed by mainstream industry interests, the legislation failed to pass. But this shot across the bows of industry marked the beginning of nationwide initiatives to protect consumers from undisclosed dangerous ingredients in cosmetics and personal-care products.

A second attempt in the California Legislature in 2005, also vigorously opposed by the cosmetics industry, proved successful. The result was the California Safe Cosmetics Act, which Governor Arnold Schwarzenegger signed into law in 2007. It requires cosmetic companies to disclose to the State Department of Health Services any ingredients in their products that have been identified as causing cancer or hormone disruption. The department can then require the manufacturer to disclose these ingredients and their toxic effects on a Web site for public viewing. California state officials can also demand that products handled by salon employees meet minimum safety standards. Though the law does not require products to include warning labels for dangerous ingredients, the hope behind this legislation was that once companies were forced to publicly disclose product ingredients to the state, they would begin reformulating their product lines to remove questionable chemicals. Whether or not the law will achieve this goal remains to be seen.

The Safe Cosmetics Act was vigorously supported by activist groups including Health Care Without Harm, a coalition of environment and health groups; the National Environmental Trust; and the San Francisco-based Breast Cancer Fund, founder of the Campaign for Safe Cosmetics (which demands that all U.S. and international companies marketing their products in the U.S. pledge to conform to the guidelines developed by the European Union). By January 2007, over 500 cosmetic and personal-care product manufacturers, but none of the major corporate players, had endorsed the Campaign for Safe Cosmetics' "Compact for the Global Production of Safe Health and Beauty Products," pledging to eliminate hazardous ingredients and replace them with safer alternatives. Additional support for the act came from public health and labor organizations, particularly those representing nail, hairdressing, and beauty salon workers, and the Screen Actors Guild.

California's highly progressive initiative has motivated changes in other parts of the country as well. The act helped inspire the Oregon state legislature to pass a joint resolution in 2007 telling the U.S.

Congress that it wants the federal government to mandate accurate labeling of all ingredients in cosmetics and personal-care products. The resolution also urged Congress to require the FDA to test the safety of all products used on the skin. In addition, thanks to efforts by the Campaign for Safe Cosmetics, a series of grassroots initiatives has taken hold in cities and small towns across the U.S. One of these initiatives occurred in the town of Belmont, Massachusetts, population 25,000, where in early 2008 the Sustainable Belmont committee embraced the precautionary principle as part of a program to educate local consumers on which harmful personal-care product ingredients to avoid and which companies are taking positive steps to make their products safer.

Europe's Seventh Amendment

In beginning to reform our own policies, we would also do well to look to the legislative initiatives adopted in Europe, which have rewritten the rulebook for how cosmetic and personal-care product companies must operate in the twenty-first century in order to satisfy public concerns about health and safety.

The most important European initiative is the European Union's Seventh Amendment, which went into effect in 2005, and attempts to ensure the safety of cosmetics and personal-care products sold in European Union countries.[3] Three major classes of toxic ingredients are regulated by the amendment: carcinogens; mutagens (toxins that can cause genetic damage); and reproductive toxicants (or hormone disrupters). Ingredients are further broken down into three categories; those in Categories 1 and 2 (almost 1,000 total) are banned entirely, and those in Category 3 are permitted pending further investigation. The Seventh Amendment also requires the labeling of twenty-six additional fragrance ingredients that may cause allergic reactions, contact dermatitis, and asthma in sensitive users.

Driving these public policy reforms throughout Europe has been a groundswell of consumer demand for natural ingredients in personal-care products, coupled with a rejection of (most) synthetics as being unnecessary safety risks. Where most other countries (particularly increased risks of breast, colon, and prostate cancers) from consumption of genetically engineered (rBGH) milk.[4]

Problems with the Seventh Amendment

While important and well intentioned, the Seventh Amendment isn't perfect. It's marred by several problems and errors, such as:

- The well-known carcinogen formaldehyde is omitted from Categories 1 and 2 (which do include lead and mineral spirits), and instead is incorrectly listed in Category 3.
- Parabens are omitted from Categories 1 and 2.
- Dibutyl phthalate is listed in Category 1, but no other phthalates appear in any category.
- There are no hidden carcinogens, notably nitrosamine precursors, formaldehyde releasers, or ingredients that often carry contaminants, listed in any category.

In spite of these limitations, the Seventh Amendment has already had a profound impact on global cosmetic companies. Industry giants Revlon and L'Oreal reformulated their products in compliance with the amendment (and also in anticipation of California's January 2007 law, which we'll look at later in this chapter). Unfortunately, less responsible companies have opted to market new "green" products in Europe while continuing to supply U.S. and other markets with unsafe old products. This strategy is limited, however, by the fact that the EU has become the largest trading partner with every continent worldwide, except Australia.

The Seventh Amendment has also led to the ban of ingredients already on the market. In 2006, the EU announced a ban on twenty-two hair dye ingredients for which industry had not submitted any safety files.[5] The Scientific Committee on Cosmetic Products, an advisory committee involved in the Seventh Amendment's development, previously warned of epidemiological evidence that incriminated the long-term use of hair dyes in bladder (including our own) make consumer and environmental policy deci sions based solely on a cost/benefit analysis of risk, European Union countries approach chemical safety with a directive to "do no harm," even if an ingredient is only suspected of causing harm to human health. The European Union follows the "precautionary principle," a moral and political principle based on the idea that harm need not be completely established for corrective action to be taken. The principle mandates that industry must provide unequivocal evidence that any new candidate products do not pose potential or recognized human or environmental risks. The principle further absolves citizens and regulatory agencies from the heavy burden of proving such a risk, and allows the banning of suspect products in circumstances of scientific uncertainty. In addition, the raw data on which industry claims of safety are based must be fully disclosed and evaluated by an independent agency at industry's expense.

This approach is essential to excluding bias and manipulation, of which there is a well-documented track record in the petrochemical and other industries. An illustrative example comes from a review of 161 studies in the National Library of Medicine files on four heavily regulated industrial chemicals—formaldehyde, perchloroethylene, atrazine, and alachlor. While only 14 percent of industry studies reported toxic or carcinogenic effects, such effects were disclosed in 71 percent of studies done by independent researchers.

Policies based on the precautionary principle are clearly preferable to our method, the deliberate acceptance of risks followed by often ineffectual attempts to "manage" effects. Ineffective management—reducing dangerous ingredients to levels claimed "acceptable" by self-interested industry or complicit regulatory agencies rather than banning them entirely—solves few real problems and creates many more.

The precautionary principle isn't just relevant to the cosmetics and personal-care products industry. It's also relevant in the case of genetically engineered food. Industry claims of safety regarding these foods are based on "trust us" assurances rather than published scientific data—claims that are called into question by the extensive scientific evidence on the veterinary and public health hazards cancer and called for carcinogenicity and mutagenicity testing of all dye ingredients.

More European Safety Regulations

The Seventh Amendment isn't the only example of ground-breaking regulations being enacted in Europe. Less well recognized by cosmetic companies are new regulations on the manufacturer of industrial chemicals in the original twenty-five member states of the EU. These regulations are referred to as REACH—Registration, Evaluation, and Authorization of Chemicals.[6] They passed their "first reading" in the European Parliament in 2004, were approved by the Environmental Committee of the Parliament in October 2006, and later were extended to the now twenty-seven-member bloc, including Romania and Bulgaria—a population larger than that of the U.S. Once REACH goes into effect, any new chemicals imported into Europe will need to be registered with a new European Chemicals Agency. Substances designated as toxic will be banned. Chemical registration is expected to begin by 2011. REACH's regulations are designed to phase out the production and use of approximately 30,000 common toxic industrial chemicals, some of which are often used in cosmetics and personal-care products, and to stimulate the manufacture and use of safe alternatives. Not surprisingly, U.S. industries remain strongly opposed.

The new EU regulations have had an impact on other European countries as well. In 2005, Switzerland enacted a new law that matched EU regulations for industrial chemicals, pesticides, and cosmetics, but went even further in banning toxic ingredients. Sweden has also improved upon the EU regulations by banning persistent organic pollutants and other persistent chemicals like lead, and by requiring the phasing out of chlorinated paraffins, a large class of toxic ingredients that includes plasticizers and flame retardants. Swedish companies were given five years, until 2010, to test the estimated 2,500 chemicals used in quantities over 1,000 tons per year for such effects. By 2010, chemicals used in lesser amounts will also have to be tested.

Safety Regulations in Other Countries

In China, the first regulations on cosmetics and personal-care products were issued in 2002, banning approximately 400 ingredients. In an effort to become more competitive in the global market, particularly in the U.S., China extended its ban to a total of 1,100 ingredients in 2007, and also developed more stringent regulations approaching those of the EU—showing that China intends to establish itself as a major player in the global industry.

ASEAN, an organization of ten southeastern Asian countries (Indonesia, Laos, Philippines, Thailand, Vietnam, Brunei, Cambodia, Myanmar, Malaysia, and Singapore), in August 2006 announced its intent to create a unified regulatory system to harmonize ASEAN cosmetic regulations. This initiative, like China's, is intended to attract major global players and investments, and allow ASEAN countries' products to compete internationally.

In Japan, prior to April 1, 2003, cosmetics were regulated under the Pharmaceutical Affairs Law (PAL) by the Pharmaceutical and Safety Bureau, under the authority of the Ministry of Health, Labor and Welfare. Beginning in 2003, however, cosmetics were effectively deregulated and responsibility shifted from the ministry to industry.

Abolition of the PAL has thus effectively harmonized the Japanese and U.S. markets. However, there are important differences between Japanese law and our own. Importing companies are now required to notify the ministry that they intend to sell a product in Japan. The industry must also assure the safety of all product ingredients and keep files supporting safety data. While testing of cosmetics is no longer required, safety data must be made available on request. The majority of ingredients remain controlled by two "Negative Lists." One list prohibits thirty ingredients, including formaldehyde. The other list sets restrictions on the use of many other ingredients, such as coal tar dyes, formaldehyde-releasing preservatives, and ultraviolet light absorbers. Words like "safe" and "no worries" are not allowed to appear on labels. Nor can superlatives (like "best in the world") be used without solid proof for such claims. Similarly, words claiming superiority of products (such as "number one," "available only from our company," and "first in Japan") are no longer allowed.

It's not just Asian countries that are changing their policies. Canada's Food and Drugs Act states that "no person shall sell a cosmetic product that has in it any substances that may injure the health of the user when the cosmetic is used according to its customary method." To help manufacturers meet this requirement, Health Canada, the government department responsible for public health, developed a periodically updated "Cosmetic Ingredient Hotlist" of restricted and prohibited ingredients. The list identifies about 420 of these ingredients, but until recently the law did not require products containing these ingredients to include warnings on the label, or even identify themselves as containing the ingredients.

Responding to mounting citizen protests, Health Canada reluctantly relented, and from January 2007 on, labeling requirements became law for all products except fragrances and perfumes. Health Canada now also requires that all ingredients be named by the worldwide standard Scientific International Nomenclature for Cosmetic Ingredients, in order to simplify the recognition of ingredient names by consumers. As a result of these actions, Canadian regulations now approach the high standards of the European Union. May our own soon follow.

12 | Two Healthy Trends in Your Future

There are two recent trends that should support attempts to bring sanity and safety to the personal-care industry. The first is the growth of "green chemistry," a philosophy that encourages the development of chemicals and industrial processes designed to have no toxic effects. The second and even more important trend is the growing availability, mainstream acceptance, and price competitiveness of organic ingredients and products.

Green Chemistry Means Safer Chemistry

The best way to ensure safer cosmetics and personal-care products is to design them at the outset using ingredients that pose no hazards to health. One way to do this is through green chemistry, a term that describes the development of sophisticated technologies for synthesizing non-toxic ingredients and products designed to degrade into wastes that won't hurt humans, wildlife, and the environment. Green chemistry is now being applied to the production of cosmetic and personal-care product ingredients from a variety of organic sources, particularly plant oils and vegetables, as well as to the synthesis of ingredients, including soy-based sunscreens, preservatives, and detergents.[1,2]

In one example of green chemistry's advances, several major food and other companies now use a process known as supercritical CO_2 to extract caffeine from raw coffee beans, carotenoids from tomatoes, and medicinal ingredients from herbs.[3] The process works by pumping carbon dioxide into a closed, temperature-controlled chamber under high pressure, which causes the gas to liquefy. The liquefied or supercritical gas then behaves as a very efficient solvent.

Another development is the discovery that almost completely removing dissolved air from water, a process known as de-gassing, converts water into a very efficient detergent, even more efficient than soap.[4] Not surprisingly, the multibillion dollar soap industry is hardly enthusiastic about these findings. They are, however, welcomed by ecologists, because traditional detergents promote the growth of environmentally damaging algae in rivers, streams, and lakes.

Green chemistry has also encouraged the phase-out of product packaging that relies on petrochemical plastic containers, particularly those containing Bisphenol-A and phthalates. These materials are being replaced with recycled, biodegradable, bio-based substitutes, including recycled paper. Such "green" packaging reduces energy use, greenhouse gases, and nondegradable or poorly degradable waste currently disposed of in landfills. Procter & Gamble, Estée Lauder and its Origins and Aveda companies, and the Australia-based packaging specialist Plantic are now taking the lead in the development and use of "green" packaging with 100 percent post-consumer recycled packaging. These and related initiatives have been supported by Green Blue, a non-profit organization that operates the Sustainable Packaging Coalition.

A report called "Green Chemistry in California," commissioned in 2004 by the California State Assembly and released by the University of California in 2006, was the first in the U.S. to recommend a framework for motivating industry to reduce all uses of toxic chemicals in favor of green alternatives.[5] The report emphasized that current U.S. federal laws regulating the use of industrial chemicals are very weak. For instance, the 1976 Toxic Substances Control Act does not require industry to generate information on the toxicity and environmental effects of 99 percent of the more than 83,000 synthetic chemicals in current use—less than 1,000 chemicals. In striking contrast, current European laws require such information for about 30,000 chemicals.

The "Green Chemistry in California" report emphasized that a growing number of California industries, including IBM, Intel, and Apple, are already developing and implementing policies to reduce the use of toxic chemicals. The report further identified a critical need to encourage research by progressive industry on the science and technology of green chemistry.

What must also be encouraged is an education campaign about the benefits of green chemistry, beginning in the universities where chemists are initially trained. "Astonishingly," wrote Stacy Malkan in her book *Not Just A Pretty Face*, "no university in the United States requires chemists to demonstrate knowledge about the health and environmental impacts of the chemicals they create— not one." Chemistry accreditation requirements at universities are set by major chemical, pharmaceutical, and product manufacturers, not the schools themselves, which does not exactly inspire trust and confidence about the curriculum's commitment to health and safety.

Investing in Green

An October 5, 2008, article by Jon Gertner in the *New York Times Magazine* stressed the role of leading venture capitalist firms, notably Kleiner Perkins and the Sequoia Fund, in investing in innovative green technology industries and businesses. The cosmetic and personal-care product industries are strong candidates, and well overdue, for such investment.

Twelve Principles of Green Chemistry

In 1998, while director of the EPA's green chemistry program, Paul Anastas, Ph.D., along with John Warner, Ph.D., director of green chemistry program at the University of Massachusetts, Lowell, came up with twelve principles for the design of chemicals and substances that will have no toxic effect on humans or the environment.

1. **Prevent waste:** Design chemical syntheses to prevent waste, leaving no waste to treat or clean up.
2. **Design safer chemicals and products:** Design chemical products to be fully effective, yet have little or no toxicity.
3. **Design less hazardous chemical syntheses:** Design syntheses to use and generate substances with little or no toxicity to humans and the environment.
4. **Use renewable feedstocks:** Use raw materials and feedstocks that are renewable rather than depleting. Renewable feedstocks are often made from agricultural products or are the wastes of other processes; depleting feedstocks are made from fossil fuels (petroleum, natural gas, or coal) or are mined.
5. **Use catalysts, not stoichiometric reagents:** Minimize waste by using catalytic reactions. Catalysts are used in small amounts and can carry out a single reaction many times. They are preferable to stoichiometric reagents, which are used in excess and work only once.
6. **Avoid chemical derivatives:** Avoid using blocking or protecting groups or any temporary modifications if possible. Derivatives use additional reagents and generate waste.
7. **Maximize atom economy:** Design syntheses so that the final product contains the maximum proportion

of the starting materials. There should be few, if any, wasted atoms.

8. **Use safer solvents and reaction conditions:** Avoid using solvents, separation agents, or other auxiliary chemicals. If these chemicals are necessary, use innocuous chemicals.

9. **Increase energy efficiency:** Run chemical reactions at ambient temperature and pressure whenever possible.

10. **Design chemicals and products to degrade after use:** Design chemical products to break down to innocuous substances after use so that they do not accumulate in the environment.

11. **Analyze in real time to prevent pollution:** Include in-process real-time monitoring and control during syntheses to minimize or eliminate the formation of by-products.

12. **Minimize the potential for accidents:** Design chemicals and their forms (solid, liquid, or gas) to minimize the potential for chemical accidents including explosions, fires, and releases to the environment.

Originally published by Paul Anastas and John Warner in *Green Chemistry: Theory and Practice* (Oxford University Press: New York, 1998).

Organics Emerge as Safe, Price-Competitive Alternatives

Since the early 1990s, there has been steady global growth in the sales of certified organic ingredients and products, with particular growth in organic dairy, soy, and grain food products.[6] This environmental- and consumer-driven growth now includes certified organic cosmetics and personal-care products both in the United States and globally.

From 2002 to 2004, new organic products in the world marketplace more than doubled, from 350 to 840, while all-natural products nearly tripled, from 615 to 1,475.[7] Cosmeceuticals, make-up, skin care, shampoos, and deodorants have dominated this growth, a trend that has prevailed for the last decade.[8] Sales of certified organic products in Europe have been increasing by over 20 percent annually; the German and Italian natural and certified organic markets are the largest, comprising almost 70 percent of total revenues.[9] However, the U.S. is still leading the way for the moment, with annual sales exceeding $5 billion, followed by the U.K., France, Canada, and Japan. Part of the reason for this may be that, in the U.S., natural and organic products are becoming mainstreamed, appearing in mass-market outlets including Wal-Mart and Target. Clearly what was once known as the "organic class divide" is rapidly disappearing.

Many of the new organic personal-care products are proving equal in effectiveness to more mainstream synthetic products. After several organic deodorants hit the U.S. market in 2005, *Health* magazine published an article noting how "natural sweat stoppers can leave much to be desired." But a test by magazine staffers found that some of the new organics—specifically Nature's Gate Organics Fruit Blend and Erbaviva Organic—"really do sop up wetness and leave you smelling sweet." (The journalists reached this favorable conclusion by applying the organic deodorants to themselves, working out on exercise machines, and then doing a "smell" test.)[10]

Japan is another of the fastest growing markets for organic products. As early as 1936, the company Kaneibo pioneered the use of organic ingredients when they used oils extracted from silkworm chrysalis in high-quality soaps. More recently, there has been an extensive and growing use of predominantly food-based, certified organic ingredients in cosmetics and personal-care products. These include tangerine, papaya, Mediterranean olives, olive oil, wine, grape seeds, potato juice, white and green tea, soy milk, fermented soybeans, and rice bran. Less common ingredients include high-quality, expensive, natural, certified organic essential oils, based on non-allergenic ingredients such as clove, lavender, vanilla, and ylang-ylang (note that non-allergenic does not mean non-toxic or non-irritating).

Rice, rice bran, and the lees left over from brewing are also becoming an important source for organic cosmetics in Japan. With sake sales sliding dramatically in recent years, brewers have found surprising new uses for their age-old drink. Some brewers are hoping sake skin-products will eventually account for 50 percent of their total sales. The trailblazer in these cosmetics is Komenuka Bijin, a product line manufactured by a leading brewer, Nihonsakari Company. This cleanser is also sold to the U.S., and the brewer is considering expanding into the Russian and Chinese markets as well. Other sake brands, including Gekkeikan and Hakutsuru, have launched lines of cleansers, toners, creams, and lotions. All of these products are free of fragrances, mineral oils, colorants, and other synthetic ingredients.[11] Following Japan's example, in 2006 the Malaysian Agriculture Development Authority (MADA) announced an initiative encouraging the development of cosmetic ingredients by rice farmers.

India is another hot market for organics. Amsar Private Limited, founded in 1963, was India's first manufacturer of standardized natural botanical colors and vegetable dyes, based in part on Ayurvedic medicinal traditions, which are used in a variety of shampoos, skin creams, lotions, and hair oils. Amsar also provides evidence of the safety and purity of their ingredients by the use of highly sophisticated scientific testing techniques. Unfortunately, AmsarVeda, Amsar's U.S. subsidiary established in 2006, introduced a variety of herbal supplements for which highly questionable medical claims have been made (including rejuvenation, treatment of hypertension, and "kidney health"), jeopardizing the reputation of its parent company.

Brazil has also emerged as one of the world's major indigenous sources of certified organic ingredients for cosmetics and personal-care products, particularly moisturizing oils. Emerging suppliers include S.O.S. (Save Our Seaweed), which seeks to ensure sustainable sourcing of seaweed, and Beraca Ingredients, which produces ingredients (including an oil from the seeds of Andiroba trees found in an island in the Amazon basin) in compliance with Forest Stewardship Council standards.

A related initiative is the collaboration between food giant Nestlé and cosmetic company L'Oreal to create the "beauty from the inside" nutricosmetic product line. Caleel + Hayden skin-care company and the giant international Whole Foods Market have embarked on a similar joint venture, announcing in 2006 the launching of their Mineral Fusion range of organic and natural products, to be sold through U.S. Whole Foods stores.

The strong trend toward the development and marketing of certified organic products in the U.S. and worldwide is being monitored by a London watchdog consumer group, Organic Monitor.

Principal Categories of Organic Cosmetics and Personal-Care Products

While organics have been making inroads throughout the cosmetic and personal-care products industry, the following categories have embraced organic ingredients more than the rest:

- **Cosmeceuticals.** Cosmeceuticals are the largest and most rapidly expanding group of products containing organic ingredients. Natural antioxidants used in cosmeceuticals in particular are more and more often being obtained from organic sources.
- **Natural baby and children's products.** The organic children's personal-care market continues to grow, which is of particular importance given the high permeability of children's skin.
- **Natural whiteners.** Organic whitening ingredients include arbutin, azaleic acid, burner root extract, kojic acid, licorice root extract, mulberry root extract, and the antioxidant vitamin C.
- **Natural soaps.** Certified organic vegetable oils are being used to replace synthetic detergents in many soaps.
- **Natural sunscreens and sunblocks.** Several "green" sunblocks have been discovered recently, including a combination of plant-products ferulic acid and vegetable oil, and

gamma oryzanol, from rice bran, and their ingredients can be obtained organically. (See chapter 8 for more natural sunscreens and sunblocks.)

• **Natural hair colorants.** Conventional hair dyes can be replaced by a variety of organic botanical or natural plant dyes, such as henna, indigo, and madder root. *Emblica officinalis* (amla/amlaki) is a botanical used thousands of years ago by Ayurvedic elders to blacken gray hair. This dye is an intensely colored multi-herb mixture which contains a group of anthocyanin antioxidants. The ingredients, when isolated, are notoriously unstable, but together are safe and effective. Another effective multi-herb mixture, *Eclipta alba,* is based on a host of sulfur-containing ingredients. Other Ayurvedic dyes include sterculia platanfolia, zizyphus spina-christi, mooncake, and lotus tree leaves. Unfortunately, there is little published information on the practical potential of these plant-based dyes and their ingredients.

In addition to substituting organic substances for their active ingredients, many products have also begun to use organic preservatives. A range of essential oils, notably chitosan-Inula helenium,[12] eucalyptus and salvia combinations,[13] lemongrass, and lemon tree complexes can be used as natural preservatives. The effectiveness of these ingredients can also be improved by increasing the product's acidity with ascorbic or sorbic acids. Other organic preservatives include grain or grape alcohol, salt, and vinegar.

As well, organic botanicals have become very popular. Well over sixty natural botanicals are currently included, in chemically pure or concentrated forms, in an increasing range of products. Many have been shown to be efficacious in clinical trials. Some of the most popular include: allatoin, aloe vera, comfrey, curcumin, date, grape seed oil, German chamomile, horse chestnut, olive oil, pomegranate, soya, and black, green, red, and white teas. The French company Zelda Gavison even uses organic chocolate in its Chocolatherapie line as a skin stimulant and anti-aging ingredient

What Does Organic Certification Mean?

Sensing profits to be made, mainstream corporate players have been buying up natural and organic producers of cosmetics and personal-care products over the past decade. Clorox Company, a manufacturer of bleach and other consumer products, purchased Burt's Bees, a product line of natural soaps, lotions, and shampoos, for $913 million in November 2007. In previous years, Colgate-Palmolive bought Tom's of Maine, the natural toothpaste and deodorant manufacturer, for $100 million, and L'Oreal paid $1.4 billion for The Body Shop chain of natural product stores.

Unfortunately, this has meant that these companies' previously safe products are in danger of being laced with problematic chemical ingredients as the companies' new corporate parents cut manufacturing corners or try to maximize company profits. As large corporations made similar inroads into organic foods, they lobbied the U.S. Congress to dilute organic standards so they could use more synthetic ingredients and still call their products organic or natural. The only insurance consumers have against these changes is the maintenance of rigid and dependable standards that determine what is and is not organic, along with product labeling that accurately and completely identifies product ingredients.

Organic product certification by a third party audit company has been the strength of, but also one of the greatest challenges for, the growing organic industry. Early on, it became apparent that a program was needed to verify that only approved natural processes were used to grow crops and to make sure these processes were monitored. To that end, organic programs such as the USDA's were created. Their function is to decide if the organic processors and growers have held true to the intent of organic philosophy as well as to organic regulations.

The system is a fairly good one when it comes to food. You can't, however, easily apply an agriculture-based organic system to personal-care products, because most of the ingredients these products use are so processed that it is difficult to recognize them as food at all. This difficulty has led certifiers such as the Soil Association and ECOCERT to develop alternate cosmetic organic standards to account for the difference.

Caution about Products Labeled Organic

When you see a personal-care product labeled or described as "natural" and "organic," even when it has been "certified" as such by a certifying agency, don't make the mistake of automatically assuming it contains nothing but safe ingredients. Exercise some healthy skepticism and study the label carefully. Here is a good reason why that is important.

In a study initiated by consumer activist David Steinman and the Organic Consumers' Association and released in March 2008, a laboratory analysis of ninety-nine personal-care products branded as natural and organic found that forty-five contained detectable levels of the carcinogen 1,4-dioxane. These included products made by some of the biggest names in the organics field (though not every product that was tested from these companies was contaminated): Nature's Gate, Jason, Giovanni, and Kiss My Face. "The labeling and formulation practices of these companies are so unsupportable," declared Organic Consumers Association executive director Ronnie Cummins, "that we wonder sometimes if the garbage manager is in charge of the products development."[15]

1,4-dioxane, recall, does not appear on product labels, as it is not intentionally added to products; it is created as an accidental byproduct of ethoxylation. But it can largely be removed simply by spending a little extra money on a vacuum-stripping process.

Among companies found in the study to be free of dioxane were Dr. Bronner's, Sensibility Soaps, Terressentials, Aubrey Organics, and Dr. Hauschka. The first three of these companies were certified organic by the USDA, while the other two received certification from BDIH in Germany. All of the products examined in this study certified by the USDA National

continued on the next page

> **Caution about Products Labeled Organic,** *continued*
>
> Organic Program were free of any detectable levels of the carcinogen. The reason is that USDA regulations for organic disallow the use of ethoxylation or any synthetic petrochemical modification of a product's ingredients. (For a complete list of "organic" products and their contamination ratings, go to: www.organicconsumers.org/bodycare/)

The standard guarantee here in the U.S. that a product is truly organic is the "USDA Organic" green seal, which indicates that the product contains at least 70 percent certified organic ingredients. This is very different from the "Contains/Made With Organic Ingredients" label, which means that the product is likely to contain varying amounts of non-organic ingredients. Even more misleading is the presence of the word "Organic" or "Non-Toxic" on the label, as there are no set definitions or standards for these words' use. Companies can also mislead the consumer by having "Organic" in their brand name, but few or minimal certified organic ingredients in the actual product. Often, in these last two cases, varying amounts of natural or organic ingredients are added to a predominant mix of synthetic ingredients specifically to mislead the customer. This kind of willful misrepresentation is known as "greenwashing."

Organic Certification Standards

Significant differences exist from country to country in organic certification standards, as well as in the consequences for noncompliance. Many global certified organic producers, regulators, and consumers are working toward an acceptable international certified organic standard, but there are huge barriers to establishing such unified standards. To begin with, the non-governmental organizations setting the standards and forcing compliance are often supported financially by companies that resist such changes.

Here are a few of the most prominent standards:

U.S. DEPARTMENT OF AGRICULTURE STANDARDS

USDA organic certification is a reliable way of ensuring a product is truly organic. This is the result of the U.S. Department of Agriculture's response to a 2005 federal court complaint filed by the activist Organic Consumers Association (OCA), in which it announced that its National Organic Program food standards also applied to cosmetics and personal-care products.[14] The USDA stated that it did not matter what type of product was certified and labeled as long as it followed the NOP rules. Based on this ruling, personal-care products and cosmetics, by virtue of their certified organic agricultural content, may be labeled as "100 percent organic," or "organic," and carry the USDA Organic green seal. Products may also carry the organic green seal if they contain 95 percent organics ingredients, so long as the remaining 5 percent includes only non-toxic synthetic ingredients.

Several months after this ruling, the industry's Organic Trade Association, together with newly emerging "organic" industry groups including Whole Foods, Wild Oats, Kraft, and General Mills, mounted a powerful opposition to certified organic standards. The industry introduced a "Sneak Attack" provision into Congressional legislation on the 2006 Agricultural Appropriations Bill that would have authorized the USDA National Organic Standards Board to allow the inclusion of numerous synthetic ingredients in products claimed to be certified organic. Fortunately, due to opposition from a coalition of activist citizen groups headed by the OCA, the bill did not go through.

The OCA and other consumer groups are still trying to formulate regulations for "organic" and "made with organic" product labels. In 2006, the OCA, together with Dr. Bronner's Magic Soaps, sued the USDA in federal court to require that no company could use the USDA's organic seal unless its products were 100 percent derived from certified organic ingredients. Yet the USDA still refuses to crack down on companies deceptively using the word "organic" or "organics" on their products, and there are still no comprehensive U.S. organic standards nor any regulations specifically for certified organic personal-care products. In March 2008, the OCA and Dr. Bronner's Magic Soaps issued "Cease and Desist" letters to organic cheaters that had misbranded their products as "organic" on labels, intended as a shot

Organic Certifying Organizations

There are numerous established, reputable certifying organizations. These include:

- USDA National Organic Program (NOP) 100% Certified Organic
- USDA NOP 95% (or more) Certified Organic
- USDA NOP 70% "Made with Organic Ingredients"
- USDA "Made with Organic XXX" (where XXX is the specific ingredient used)
- Soil Association Cosmetic Standard 95% (U.K.)
- Soil Association Cosmetic Standard 70% (U.K.)
- ECOCERT Association Cosmetic Standard (France)
- BDIH "Natural" Standard (Germany)
- AIAB Organic Standard (Italy)

Additionally, other standards have recently emerged. However, these do not meet the requirements of the USDA or of other reputable certifying organizations. These include:

- U.S. "Natural" Standard (released spring 2008)
- OASIS Standard (released spring 2008)
- New European "Harmonized" Standards (released summer 2008)

Note that the certifying organization or agency is not the same as the organic standard itself, and that certifying organizations often certify according to widely different standards.

across the bow to warn these companies of a crackdown by consumer groups on the reckless and misleading use of the word "organic."

INTERNATIONAL ECOCERT STANDARDS

France-based certification association ECOCERT's "International ECOCERT Standards for Ecological and Organic Cosmetics" were developed in 1995, and have since been expanded and formalized.

ECOCERT requires that "Certified Organic" products contain 95 percent or more organic ingredients, excluding added water. The certified standard also restricts the 5 percent or less of non-organic ingredients to synthetic ingredients, unless those ingredients are based on petroleum fractions, in which case the product cannot quality for certification at all. Organic certification further requires that all ingredients be identified on the product label by their standard scientific names to avoid the use of false or deceptive trade names.

At ECOCERT's initiative, a working group was put together in Europe to develop a single set of European standards. This group included ECOCERT (France); the prestigious Soil Association (England); AIAB (Italy); and BDIH (Germany). ECOCERT was also the driving force behind the September 2005 BioFach Tokyo trade fair's concentration on satisfying the growing demand for natural body care and cosmetic products. BioFach is now the international hub for certified organic products and the meeting place for all players interested in Asian organic markets.

DEMETER INTERNATIONAL STANDARDS

Demeter International's certification standards require that at least 90 percent of the product consist of organically certified ingredients. They also require, as far as possible, that names of the ingredients be in the language of the nation the product is sold in, or else a translation should also be listed. Their standards are less stringent than the USDA's.

QUALITY ASSURANCE INTERNATIONAL (QAI) STANDARDS

Quality Assurance International is a U.S.-based international third-party organic certification firm. Their standards are less stringent than the USDA's.

The Organic Trade Association Deceives Consumers

The Organic Trade Association (OTA) is a business association focusing on the North American organic business community. Despite its

Table 15: Certified Organic Product Companies

COMPANY	WEB SITE	CERTIFYING ORGANIZATION
Allo' Nature´	www.allonature.com	Soil Association
Anika Cosmetics	www.anika-cosmetics.de	BDIH
Balm Balm Ltd.	www.balmbalm.com	Soil Association
Bradford Personal Care	www.bradfordpersonalcare.com	Soil Association
CARE by Stella McCartney	www.stellamccartneycare.com	ECOCERT
Cemon Homeopathics Ltd.	www.cemon.eu	Soil Association
Diamond Lotus	www.diamondorganics.com	QAI
Dr. Bronner's Magic Soaps[1]	www.drbronner.com	USDA
Dr. Hauschka Skin Care	www.drhauschka.co.uk	BDIH
Druide	www.druide.ca	BDIH
Eco-Beauty Organics[2]	www.eco-beauty.com	BDIH
Eco Cosmetics	www.eco-cosmeticsuk.com	ECOCERT
Erbaorganics	www.erbaorganics.com	USDA
Erbaviva	www.erbaviva.com	USDA
Eselle Organics	www.eselle.co.uk	Soil Association
Essential Care (Organic) Ltd.	www.essential-care.co.uk	Soil Association
Gaia Skin Naturals	www.gaiaskinnaturals.com	AO
Ikove by Florestas	www.ikove.com	ECOCERT
Intelligent Nutrients	www.intelligentnutrients.com	USDA
Italchile	www.italchile.it/azienda-lang-en.html	ECOCERT
Jason Natural Products	www.jason-natural.com	QAI

Juice Beauty	www.juicebeauty.com	USDA
lavera GmbH	www.lavera.de	BDIH
L'Occitane	http://usa.loccitane.com	ECOCERT
Logona Herbal Hair Colors	www.logona.co.uk	BDIH
Miessence Organics[3]	http://organicgrp.mionegroup.com	QAI, AO
Mother Nature	www.mothernature.com	QAI
Nature's Best	www.naturesbest.com	QAI
Nature's Gate	www.natures-gate.com	USDA
Organic Apoteke	www.organicapoteke.com	ECOCERT
Organic Skincare Ltd.	www.circaroma.com	Soil Association
Pangea Organics	www.pangeaorganics.com	QAI, OPAM, GOC
Provida Cosmetik	www.provida.de	BDIH
Sante Naturkosmetik GmbH	www.sante.de	BDIH
Schupp GmbH & Co.	www.schupp-gmbh.de	BDIH
Sensibility Soaps	www.sensibilitysoaps.com	USDA
Sophyto	www.sophyto.com	Soil Association
Spiezia Organics	www.spieziaorganics.com	Soil Association
Suzanne aux Bains	www.suzanneauxbains.com	ECOCERT
Weleda	www.weleda.com	BDIH

[1]Made with 100% organic ingredients. Liquid soap is in 100% post-consumer recycled packaging (PCRP).
[2]Some products.
[3]Also Japan Agricultural Standard, and International Federation of Organic Agriculture Movement (IFOAM).

OPAM = Organic Producers Association of Manitoba, Canada
GOC = Guaranteed Organic Certification

name, the OTA has historically taken a weak, if not frankly deceptive, stand regarding organic products. There are no U.S. federal regulations overseeing the labeling of organic personal-care products, and the OTA refuses to take a position that would call on industry to truthfully advertise and help consumers distinguish true organic products from those that are misleadingly labeled as such. Store shelves are littered with personal-care products that claim to be organic but actually contain many of the same synthetic ingredients as their mainstream counterparts. As is the case with most industry trade associations, the OTA's position is closely allied with that of its large corporate members.

Even more disturbingly, the OTA is now spearheading the development of a new "organic personal-care standard" which will create allowances for products that contain just a few organic ingredients in a cocktail of synthetic ingredients. Accordingly, this initiative has been strongly challenged by the Organic Consumers Association.

13 | A Guide to Protecting You and Your Family

"The fear of hanging concentrates the mind wonderfully."

–Samuel Johnson

W e can't depend on the FDA to protect us from the dangers found in conventional cosmetics and personal-care products, and we certainly cannot trust industry to do so. But we can take steps to protect ourselves.

The biggest step is one you've already taken by reading this book: educating yourself about the toxic dangers these products present, and how to avoid them. Protecting yourself and those you care about requires nothing more than a modest degree of self-education, a heightened state of vigilance, and the willingness to exercise some self-discipline.

Safe alternatives to toxic ingredients and products do exist, and exercising choice in buying these safer products over conventional ones does have repercussions in the marketplace. The example you set for others, and your conversations with friends and family about the various risks and benefits of specific items, advances public awareness while placing competitive pressures on manufacturers. Disciplined buying choices *can* affect corporate decisions about product formulation and marketing, just as your voting choices in the political realm can influence whether government agencies will choose to enforce laws and regulations designed to safeguard your health and well-being.

Since we cannot yet rely upon the FDA or other federal regulatory agencies to act in the best interests of our health and safety, we must accept responsibility for doing so ourselves. This chapter is designed to help you do just that.

Four Deadly but Avoidable Killers

The details in this book are a lot to remember, especially when they involve so many long, unfamiliar chemical names. That's why I've created a compact tear-out sheet in Appendix One that you can take with you and consult when making purchasing decisions.

But if you only avoid four ingredients or categories of ingredients described in this book, make it these four: talc, powdered titanium dioxide, sunscreens, and certain dark hair dyes.

Talc, or talcum powder, has been strongly linked to ovarian cancer, which has become the fourth most common fatal cancer in women (after breast, colon, and lung). Yet one out of five premenopausal women continues to use it as a dusting powder or on tampons. (See chapter 6.)

Titanium dioxide powder, which often appears as a whitening agent in women's cosmetics powders, has been shown in rodent testing to be a source of respiratory tract cancer if inhaled. Numerous studies have demonstrated this effect, yet its use remains widespread, even in products otherwise billing themselves as safe and natural. (See chapter 6.)

Sunscreens, either alone or used in cosmetics or lotions, give users an illusion of safety that encourages them to stay out in the sun longer, exposing them to greater amounts of dangerous longwave ultraviolet radiation. Sunscreens also contain chemicals linked in laboratory experiments to hormone disruption . (See chapter 8.)

Hair dyes, specifically black and dark brown permanent and semi-permanent dyes, contain many frank and hidden carcinogens. Frequent and prolonged use of these dyes has been linked to leukemia, multiple myeloma, Hodgkin's lymphoma, non-Hodgkin's lymphoma, and bladder and breast cancers. While the European Union has banned many hair dye ingredients, United States manufacturers and regulatory agencies remain stubbornly blind to the dangers. (See chapter 7.)

Deciphering Product Labels

Simply knowing what ingredients to avoid sometimes isn't enough. How can you avoid ingredients if the manufacturer doesn't reliably list them on the label? Learning to decipher product labels is another key step in protecting yourself from toxic ingredients.

Federal law requires that product ingredients be listed on labels in descending order of concentration, beginning with the largest down to the smallest. The first ingredient listed will often be water or an oil used as the product's base, and fragrances and color additives usually appear last.

Even so, the identity of ingredients is often disguised or hidden in a variety of ways. Ingredients can be listed under different names, rendering familiar ingredients unrecognizable. Trade secrecy laws enable manufacturers to protect their formulas to some extent by grouping specific ingredients under generic terms like "fragrances" or "natural colorings."

You should also exercise healthy skepticism when it comes to claims on the label that a product is "hypoallergenic," "allergy tested," or "safe for sensitive skin." Since product manufacturers are not required to validate such claims with the FDA, they could be entirely meaningless.

A few other terms to be skeptical of when you see them on labels:

- **Natural ingredients.** The word "natural" on a label can mean very little. Arsenic is natural, for instance, but that doesn't mean it's safe to put in toothpaste. Having "natural" on the label should not automatically make you think the product is safe. Manufacturers are also not required to prove these claims, as with "hypoallergenic" and its ilk. Truly natural products should not include synthetics of any sort, which means no ingredients derived from petrochemicals. A label that announces that a product is "organic" or "all-natural" without any further ingredient identification or clarification should be a red flag.

- **"Ultra-fine" or "micro-fine" ingredients.** There are no labeling requirements in the U.S. for nanoparticle ingredients. If a manufacturers uses the terminology "ultra-fine" or "micro-fine" in connection with specific chemical ingredients, that usually means nanoparticles are being used. The safety of nanoparticles remains a huge question mark; you're better off avoiding products that include them.
- **"Inactive" ingredients.** If you see the term "inactive" listed under an ingredient on a label, think twice about buying that product. This is a term commonly used to mask the identity of potentially harmful chemicals.

Tips for Choosing Safe Products and Alternatives

Generally, when choosing cosmetics and personal-care products, choose those that contain the fewest ingredients; these will be the safest. As the list of a product's ingredients grows, so does the possibility that the product will cause adverse reactions, including allergy, irritation, and cancer. As well, the more ingredients a product contains, the greater the chance those ingredients will interact with each other in unpredictable ways.

There are two types of ingredients—safe synthetics produced by green chemistry, and certified organics—that have proven records of safety that you can trust. Chapter 12 explained these trends, and what to watch out for—especially regarding products labeled "organic"—in detail. Certified organic products are increasingly price competitive, particularly in major urban areas where demand has stimulated supply. But as we saw in chapter 12, vigilance about product quality and ingredient safety and purity remains largely the responsibility of consumers.

Strategies to Protect Your Health

If, after reading this book, you want to do something about the health threat posed by cosmetics and personal-care products, here are seven common-sense steps you can take that will have a positive impact.

First, learn to decipher product labels, and always exercise skepticism about ingredients that are unfamiliar to you.

Second, actively avoid all dangerous ingredients listed in the tables found in this book.

Third, boycott companies known to be indifferent to health and safety concerns.

Fourth, buy only certified organic cosmetic and personal-care products. Be active in helping to keep organic and natural products manufacturers resolute in their commitment to product ingredient purity and open disclosure.

Fifth, spread the word to your family and friends about the need to avoid toxic products and the companies that manufacture and promote them. Be a vocal public advocate.

Sixth, ask your local retail outlets to stock cosmetics and personal-care products that contain only safe ingredients, or at the very least, to post warnings about products that fail to meet minimum safety standards.

Seventh, become active in consumer and environmental groups that have made product safety a priority and are pressuring manufacturers, regulatory agencies, and political candidates to take actions that will benefit the public health.

Common Questions about Product Safety

As you change your buying habits to avoid the toxic ingredients you've read about in this book, you may find that your friends and family want to know why. Here are some common questions they might ask, along with simple and direct answers you may find useful to provide them.

continued on the next page

Common Questions about Product Safety, *continued*

Q. Aren't cosmetics and personal-care products regulated for dangerous chemicals?

Believe it or not, cosmetics and personal-care products are the least regulated products under the Federal Food, Drug, and Cosmetic Act (FFDCA). The FFDCA does not require pre-market safety testing, review, or approval for either cosmetics or personal-care products, and the U. S. Food and Drug Administration can pursue enforcement action only after a cosmetic and personal-care product enters the marketplace.

Q. Doesn't the cosmetic and personal-care products industry regulate itself to make sure products are safe?

On numerous occasions FDA officials have found that many cosmetic manufacturers lack adequate data from safety tests and have generally refused to disclose the results of the tests they have done. The FDA estimates that only 3 percent of the 4,000 to 5,000 cosmetic and personal-care product distributors have filed reports with the government on injuries to consumers. Additionally, it is estimated that less than 40 percent of the nation's 2,000 to 2,500 cosmetic manufacturers are even registered, meaning there's no way for the industry to even know what these rogue companies are doing.

Q. What can I do to protect myself against hazardous cosmetics and personal-care products?

The best way to protect yourself against hazardous cosmetics and personal-care products is to educate yourself on the toxic ingredients they can contain, and to try your best to avoid them. Look for the USDA organic seal—the only way to ensure a product is truly organic. And choose products with as few ingredients as possible; the fewer the ingredients, the less likely those ingredients are to react dangerously in the product or in your body.

The Bottom Line

Avoiding toxic cosmetics and personal-care products doesn't mean giving up any of the conveniences of modern life, it just means exercising some judgment. We have little to lose, and much to gain, from taking the time to be vigilant about what we put on our skin.

It is my hope that this book contributes to your understanding of the invisible price tags attached to our cosmetics and personal-care products. If the way you think about the shampoo you buy, the deodorant you choose, and the lipstick you apply has changed, even a little bit, for the safer and healthier, then this book will have fulfilled its promise.

APPENDICES

Tear these two pages out of the book and take them with you when shopping for cosmetics and personal-care products.

INGREDIENT	TOXIC EFFECT
1,4-dioxane	Carcinogen
2,5-Toluene diamine	Allergen
3,4-Toluene diamine	Allergen
4-methyl-benzylidene camphor (4-MBC)	Hormone disrupter
Acesulfame	Carcinogen
Acid Blue 9	Allergen
Acid Orange 3	Allergen
Acid Yellow 10	Allergen
Acid Yellow 17	Allergen
Acid Yellow 23	Allergen
Acid Yellow 6	Allergen
Acrylamide	Carcinogen
Acrylate polymer	Contains hidden carcinogens
Alpha isomethyl ionone	Allergen
Alpha-hydroxycaprylic acid	Penetration enhancer
Alpha-hydroxyethanoic acid	Penetration enhancer
Alpha-hydroxyoctanoic acid	Penetration enhancer
Aluminum	Hormone disrupter
Ammonium thioglycolate	Allergen
Amyl cinnamal	Allergen
Amyl cinnamyl alcohol	Allergen
Anise alcohol	Allergen
Arnica	Allergen
Arsenic	Carcinogen
Aryl sulfonamide	Allergen
Aspartame (NutraSweet)	Carcinogen
Auramine	Carcinogen

INGREDIENT	TOXIC EFFECT
Avobenzone (Parsol), or Butyl-methoxy-dibenzoylmethane (B-MDM)	Hormone disrupter
Balsam of Peru	Allergen
Benzalkonium chloride	Allergen
Benzophenone-3 (Bp-3), or Oxybenzone	Hormone disrupter, penetration enhancer, allergen
Benzyl alcohol	Allergen
Benzyl benzoate	Allergen
Benzyl cinnamate	Allergen
Benzyl salicylate	Allergen
Benzylparaben	Hormone disrupter
Beta-hydroxybutanoic acid	Penetration enhancer
Bisabolol	Penetration enhancer
Bisphenol-A (BPA)	Carcinogen, hormone disrupter
Brononitrodioxane (nitrite donor)	Nitrosamine precursor
Bronopol (nitrite donor)	Nitrosamine precursor
Butadiene	Carcinogen
Butane	Contains hidden carcinogens
Butylated hydroxyanisole (BHA)	Carcinogen, allergen
Butylbenzene phthalate (BBP)	Hormone disrupter
Butyl benzyl phthalate	Carcinogen
Butyl-methoxydibenzoylmethane (B-MDM), or Avobenzone (Parsol)	Hormone disrupter
Butylparaben	Hormone disrupter
Butylphenyl/methylpropional	Allergen
Cadmium	Hormone disrupter
Castor oil	Allergen

INGREDIENT	TOXIC EFFECT
Cetearaths	Carcinogens, contain hidden carcinogens
Cetyl alcohol	Allergen
Chromium trioxide	Carcinogen
CI Disperse Blue 1	Carcinogen
Cinnamal	Allergen
Cinnamic aldehyde	Allergen
Cinnamic salicylate	Allergen
Cinnamyl alcohol	Allergen
Citral	Allergen
Citric acid	Penetration enhancer
Citronellol	Allergen
Clove oil	Allergen
Cobalt chloride	Carcinogen
Cocamidopropyl betaine	Nitrosamine precursor
Colophony	Allergen
Copper	Hormone disrupter
Coumarin	Allergen
Crystalline silica	Carcinogen
Cyclamates	Carcinogen
D&C dyes	Contain hidden carcinogens
D&C Green 5	Carcinogen
D&C Orange 17	Carcinogen
D&C Red 3,4,8,9,17,19,33	Carcinogen
DEA cocamide condensate	Carcinogen, formaldehyde releaser
DEA oleamide condensate	Carcinogen, formaldehyde releaser
DEA sodium lauryl sulfate	Carcinogen, formaldehyde releaser
Diaminophenol	Carcinogen
Diazolidinyl urea	Formaldehyde releaser, allergen
Dibutyl phthalate (DBP)	Hormone disrupter, allergen

INGREDIENT	TOXIC EFFECT
Diethanolamine (DEA)	Carcinogen, formaldehyde releaser, nitrosamine precursor, penetration enhancer
Diethyl phthalate (DEP)	Hormone disrupter
Diethylhexyl phthalate (DEHP), or Dioctyl phthalate	Carcinogen, hormone disrupter, allergen
Dimethyl phthalate (DMP)	Hormone disrupter
Dioctyl adipate	Carcinogen
Disodium EDTA	Penetration enhancer and hormone disrupter
Disperse blue 1	Carcinogen
Disperse yellow 3	Carcinogen
DMDM-hydantoin	Formaldehyde releaser and allergen
Ethyl methacrylate	Neurotoxin and allergen
Ethylene oxide	Carcinogen
Ethylenediamine	Allergen
Ethylenediamine tetra-acetic acid (EDTA)	Hormone disrupter, penetration enhancer
Ethylhexyl acrylate	Carcinogen
Ethylparaben	Hormone disrupter
Eugenol	Allergen
Evernia furfuracea (treemoss extract)	Allergen
Evernia prunastri (oakmoss extract)	Allergen
Farnesol	Allergen
FD&C dyes	Contain hidden carcinogens
FD&C Blue 2	Carcinogen, allergen
FD&C Green 3	Carcinogen
FD&C Red 2	Allergen
FD&C Red 4, 40	Carcinogen
FD&C Yellow 6	Carcinogen and Allergen

From *Toxic Beauty*, by Samuel S. Epstein, MD, with Randall Fitzgerald

INGREDIENT	TOXIC EFFECT
Fennel oil	Allergen
Formaldehyde	Carcinogen and Allergen
Geraniol	Allergen
Glutaral	Carcinogen
Glyceryl	Allergen
Glyceryl laurate	Penetration enhancer
Glyceryl thioglycolate	Allergen
Glycolic acid	Penetration enhancer
Glyoxal	Contains hidden carcinogens
HC Blue No. 1	Carcinogen
Henna	Allergen
Hexyl cinnamal	Allergen
Homosalate (HMS)	Hormone disrupter
Hydroquinone	Carcinogen
Hydroxycaprylic acid	Penetration enhancer
Hydroxycitronellol	Allergen
Imidazolidinyl urea	Formaldehyde releaser, allergen
Isoeugenol	Allergen
Isomethyl ionone	Allergen
Jasmine	Allergen
Lactic acid	Penetration enhancer
L-alpha-Hydroxy acid	Penetration enhancer
Lanolin and lanolin alcohols	Contains hidden carcinogens, allergen
Laureths	Contains hidden carcinogens
Lavender oil	Hormone disruper, allergen
Lead	Carcinogen, hormone disrupter
Lead acetate	Carcinogen
Lemongrass oil	Allergen
Limonene	Carcinogen, allergen
Linalool	Allergen

INGREDIENT	TOXIC EFFECT
Malic acid	Penetration enhancer
Methacrylate polymer	Contains hidden carcinogens
Metheneamine	Carcinogen, formaldehyde releaser, allergen
Methyl anisate	Allergen
Methyl coumarin	Allergen
Methyl methacrylate	Neurotoxin
Methyl-2 octynoate	Allergen
Methyldibromoglutaronitrile	Allergen
Methylene chloride	Carcinogen
Methylparaben	Hormone disrupter
Mineral oils	Carcinogen
Mixed fruit acid	Penetration enhancer
Monoethanolamine	Penetration enhancer
Morpholine	Nitrosamine precursor
Nanoparticles ("micro-fine," "ultra-fine")	Penetration enhancers
Narcissus absolute	Allergen
Nitro musks	Allergen
Nitrofurazone	Carcinogen
Nonoxynols	Contains hidden carcinogens, hormone disrupter
Nonylphenol	Hormone disrupter
Oakmoss	Allergen
Octinoxate, or Octyl-methoxycinnamate (OMC)	Hormone disrupter, penetration enhancer
Octoxynols	Contains hidden carcinogens, hormone disrupter
Octyl-dimethyl-paba (OD-PABA)	Hormone disrupter
Octyl-methoxycinnamate (OMC), or Octinoxate	Hormone disrupter, penetration enhancer

INGREDIENT	TOXIC EFFECT
Oleths	Contains hidden carcinogens
Organochlorine pesticides	Carcinogen
Oxybenzone, or Benzophenone-3 (Bp-3)	Hormone disrupter, penetration enhancer, allergen
Padimate-O	Nitrosamine precursor
Palmitic acid	Penetration enhancer
Para-aminobenzoic acid (PABA)	Allergen
Parabens	Hormone disrupters
PCBs	Carcinogen
Petroleum	Contains hidden carcinogens
Phenol ethoxylates	Hormone disrupters
Phenol formaldehyde resin	Allergen
Polyacrylamide	Contains hidden carcinogens
Poly-alpha-hydroxy acid	Penetration enhancer
Polycyclic aromatic hydrocarbons	Carcinogen
Polyethylene glycol (PEG)	Contains hidden carcinogens
Polyoxyethylene	Formaldehyde releaser
Polyoxymethylene	Formaldehyde releaser
Polyoxymethylene urea	Contains hidden carcinogens
Polyquaternium	Contains hidden carcinogens
Polysorbates	Contains hidden carcinogens
p-Phenylenediamine (ppd)	Carcinogen (following oxidation), allergen
Propylene glycol	Allergen
Propyl gallate	Allergen
Propylparaben	Hormone disrupter
p-Toluenediamine	Allergen
Pyrocatechol	Carcinogen
Quaternium	Nitrosamine precursor, formaldehyde releaser

INGREDIENT	TOXIC EFFECT
Quaternium-15	Formaldehyde releaser, allergen
Red 22	Allergen
Red 2G	Formaldehyde releaser, allergen
Resorcinol	Hormone disrupter, allergen
Saccharin (Sweet'N Low)	Carcinogen
Salicylic acid	Penetration enhancer
Sarcosine	Nitrosamine precursor
Silica (when crystalline)	Carcinogen
Sodium hydroxymethylglycinate	Formaldehyde releaser
Sodium lauryl sarcosinate	Penetration enhancer
Sodium lauryl sulfate	Penetration enhancer
Stearic acid	Allergen
Sugar cane extract	Penetration enhancer
Talc (in powder form)	Carcinogen, lung irritant
Tea tree oil	Hormone disrupter
Thimerosal	Allergen
Thioglycolate	Allergen
Tin	Hormone disrupter
Titanium dioxide (in powder form)	Carcinogen
Trethocanic acid	Penetration enhancer
Tri-alpha-Hydroxy acid	Penetration enhancer
Triclocarban	Hormone disrupter
Triclosan	Hormone disrupter
Triethanolamine (TEA)	Nitrosamine precursor, penetration enhancer
Triple fruit acid	Penetration enhancer
Tropic acid	Penetration enhancer
Vanillin	Allergen
Ylang-ylang	Allergen

APPENDIX TWO
Resources for Your Health

Want to educate yourself about safe or dangerous cosmetics and personal-care products and their ingredients, or get actively involved in campaigns to rid the marketplace of hidden toxins and unsafe products? These groups and resources may be helpful.

CANCER PREVENTION COALITION (CPC)
A non-profit organization of worldwide experts in cancer prevention, founded in 1992. The CPC Web site provides extensive information (including press releases) on carcinogenic and other toxic ingredients, particularly talc and DEA, in cosmetics and personal-care products, and also Citizen's Petitions to the FDA requesting the banning of toxic products. (I am the chairman.)
www.preventcancer.com

CHEMICALS POLICY INITIATIVE
A project at the Lowell Center for Sustainable Production at the University of Massachusetts, Lowell, that proposes model solutions to achieve green chemistry innovation and to change state policies to support the creation of safer chemical alternatives to toxic products.
www.chemicalspolicy.org

BIG GREEN PURSE
A consumer activist site that keeps a list of companies that primarily use safe, certified organic ingredients in their cosmetics and personal-care products.
www.biggreenpurse.com

THE NAKED TRUTH PROJECT

A site that bills itself as a resource for non-toxic living. It maintains a consumer products guide that reveals toxins in everyday products, along with lists of safe and natural alternatives.
www.thenakedtruthproject.org

THE CAMPAIGN FOR SAFE COSMETICS

A coalition calling for the elimination of ingredients in cosmetics that are linked to cancer, birth defects, and other health problems. The Web site includes an A-to-Z list of companies that have pledged not to use toxic ingredients in their products.
www.safecosmetics.org

THE ENVIRONMENTAL WORKING GROUP'S SKIN DEEP DATABASE

A cosmetic safety database, based on fifty toxicity databases, listing ingredients in 25,000 beauty products.
www.cosmeticsdatabase.com

OSOECO

A "green" social shopping Web site and online community, founded in 2007, where you can research green products, including safe cosmetics and personal-care products, or make recommendations.
www.osoeco.com

ENVIRONMENTAL HEALTH ASSOCIATION OF NOVA SCOTIA'S GUIDE TO LESS TOXIC PRODUCTS

A Web guide to less toxic products, including cosmetics and personal-care products.
www.lesstoxicguide.ca

DRUGSTORE.COM

A Web site that features cosmetics and personal-care products with full lists of product ingredients along with any relevant warning labels.
www.drugstore.com

APPENDIX THREE
Industry Trade Associations and What They Conceal from You

There are four major worldwide trade groups: the Personal Care Products Council in the U.S. (formerly known as the Cosmetic, Toiletry and Fragrance Association, CTFA); the European Trade Association (COLIPA); the Japanese Cosmetic Industry Association (JCIA); and the International Fragrance Association (IFRA). These associations work in close cooperation on a range of issues, particularly:

- Commenting on proposed regulatory changes.
- Developing an international database of products and ingredients, and their benefits and effectiveness.
- Organizing "Mutual Understanding Conferences."
- Dealing with global trade issues and barriers.
- Harmonizing international marketing and policies reacting to negative publicity.

The Personal Care Products Council

Founded in 1894, the Personal Care Products Council is the leading U.S. trade association for the multibillion dollar cosmetics and personal-care product industry.[1] The Council advances the industry's interests at the local, state, national, and international levels on behalf of its more than 600 member companies. Those companies include manufacturers, distributors, and suppliers of the vast majority of cosmetics, personal-care, and fragrance products marketed in the U.S., and include major companies such as Estée Lauder, Procter & Gamble and its Clairol acquisition L'Oreal, and Unilever.

There are unresolved questions as to the extent to which the Council represents the entire industry. The FDA has speculated that nearly 40 percent of all U.S. cosmetic manufacturers, an estimated 1,500 companies, have chosen to remain unregistered.[2] This is contested by the Council, which claims that the "not registered" companies are no longer in business.

The Council's mission is "to protect the freedom of the industry to compete in a fair marketplace." It also claims that it assures the safety of industry's products "by voluntary self-regulation and reasonable governmental requirements." The Council pursues a highly aggressive political agenda at both the national and state levels, with an emphasis on fighting what it considers to be "unreasonable or unnecessary labeling or warning requirements." Examples include blocking an "unneeded New York State bill—to require cancer warning labels on cosmetic talc powder," and attempting to block the 2005 California State Cosmetics Act. One of its broader initiatives is to defeat other State bills requiring "new and unnecessary warnings" for cosmetics and personal-care products.[1]

TESTING GUIDELINES

The guidelines the industry uses in testing products for safety aren't the creation of a neutral scientific body, but the Personal Care Products Council, and are instructive as to what the industry looks for when testing for safety—and more important, what it does not.

The Council first began publishing testing guidelines for cosmetic products in its 1969 *Cosmetic Journal*; the latest version was published in 2006.[3] These guidelines emphasize that:

> responsibility for ensuring the safety of cosmetic products rests with the manufacturer and/or distributor. Product manufacturers should first consider the need for safety testing, taking into account various factors, including available toxicological and other data on individual ingredients in the product (and on

products similar in composition to the product being evaluated) before undertaking any testing program.

According to the guidelines, these ingredients, either individually or compositely, should be tested for primary skin, eye, and mucous membrane irritation; sensitizing potential; sensitization to light; oral toxicity; and inhalation toxicity. However, all these are short-term tests (the longest duration is only ninety days), and exclude testing for the effects of chronic use and for carcinogenicity. The word "carcinogenicity" is conspicuous in its absence from the guidelines. However, a section on "Evaluation of Cosmetic Products" admits that the "potential for chronic toxicity should be considered in the evaluation of safety."[3]

The FDA was so impressed by the Council's guidelines that it decided to rely on them rather than formalize good manufacturing practice regulations on its own. In 1983, FDA Commissioner Arthur Hayes, Jr. publicly enthused about the guidelines' publication in advance of the FDA requesting them, and about the guidelines' excellent quality. Unbelievably, the FDA's position and reliance on these guidelines remains unchanged despite a wealth of evidence showing their inadequacies.

LABELING MANUAL

The Council's Labeling Manual, last updated in 1997, is also revealing of the association's lack of safety concern. This manual provided information on FDA's labeling requirements under the Fair Packaging and Labeling Act (FPLA) and the Food, Drug, and Cosmetic Act (FD&C) Act. The manual states that the "industry takes pride in its reputation for providing safe products while requiring the minimum use of government resources."[4]

Conspicuous in the manual, however, is the absence of any reference to the carcinogenicity of product ingredients. A meaningless exception is the reference to two carcinogenic coal tar dyes, which had already been banned in 1978. For other "coal tar" dyes, the manual relies on the Hair Dye Exemption clause of the FD&C Act, which allows these dyes' use provided there is a trivializing warning to the effect that these dyes may "cause skin irritation in certain individuals."

Most major industrialized nations now require ingredient labeling, even though this is minimally, if at all, informative in the absence of appropriate warnings. (Disturbingly, the Council noted that "disclosure of ingredients is still not required on the package of cosmetic products" in Canada, and also that "there is no requirement for full ingredient labeling" in Korea.[5]) Products that appear in hotels, restaurants, condominiums, public washrooms, and schools are still generally unlabeled. Additionally, unlabeled products manufactured by small, unregistered "rogue" industries are commonplace.

COSMETIC INGREDIENT REVIEW COMPENDIUM

The Council does have a publication reporting on ingredient safety, but this report, like its testing guidelines and labeling manual, is deeply flawed. The Cosmetic Ingredient Review (CIR) was established by the Council in 1976, and approved by the Council's member companies before being published annually. The Cosmetic Ingredient Review Compendium is claimed to be a "unique endeavor by the [U.S.] industry to have the safety of ingredients used in cosmetics thoroughly reviewed in an unbiased and expert manner." The Compendium is published in the Council's trade journal front, the *International Journal of Toxicology*, published by the American College of Toxicology.

The 2007 Compendium provided information on more than 1,300 individual and groups of closely related ingredients in cosmetics, with the notable exception of perfumes and fragrances.[6] Based on a review of the listed ingredients, the Compendium concluded:

- Nine ingredients were admittedly "Unsafe."
- Data on 119 ingredients was "Insufficient to support safety."
- Another 408 ingredients were claimed "Safe for use with qualifications."
- 784 ingredients were claimed "Safe in current practices of use."

It is important to emphasize that the expert committee behind the Compendium itself admits that 128 of its ingredients, about 10 percent, are unsafe or else there is "Insufficient data to support safety." Additionally, and even more disturbing, among the 408 ingredients which are claimed to be "Safe with qualifications" are several frank carcinogens, such as formaldehyde and diethanolamine. The category also includes numerous hidden carcinogens, including formaldehyde, released by quaternium 15 and diazolidinyl urea; 1,4-dioxane and ethylene oxide, contaminating a wide range of ethoxylated detergents; and nitrosamine precursors, including bronopol and diethanolamine (DEA).

The Council continues to challenge evidence on the carcinogenicity of such ingredients and contaminants. Responding to the U.S. National Toxicology Program 1997 draft report on the carcinogenicity of DEA following skin painting of mice, the Council alleged several problems with the studies. These included the use of an ethanol solvent as a potential confounding factor; the potential for the mice to have orally ingested the DEA; claims of undefined "serious limitations in analytical chemistry"; and "inadequate time available for proper review of the studies." While these objections—all highly contrived—were considered by the National Toxicology Program, its conclusions remained unchanged in the final 1999 report.

The Compendium still endorses the use of carcinogenic ingredients or contaminants, provided their concentrations in any finished product are below arbitrarily defined "limitations."[6] This reflects unawareness, or self-interested denial, of the overwhelming scientific consensus that there is no basis for assigning safe limits or thresholds for carcinogens. It also reflects inconsistency with the position of the mainstream chemical industry, which agrees that there are no safe limits for carcinogens.

Furthermore, the Compendium makes confusing exceptions to its allowable use of carcinogens below "concentration limitations." One illustration is nonoxynol (nonylphenol), an ethoxylate detergent commonly used in hair dyes and colors that is contaminated with the potent carcinogen ethylene oxide at levels up to 35 parts per million. The Compendium warns of the need to ensure that the use of nonoxynol-containing cosmetic products not result in ethylene oxide exposures that approach 0.1 milligrams daily. However, the Compendium's summary table states that nonoxynols are "safe as used in rinse-offs [and] safe at less than 5 percent in leave-ons." The Compendium also reassuringly claims that the small amounts of ethylene oxide in cosmetics "were not considered sufficient to pose a carcinogenesis risk."

The Compendium also authorizes the use of amines and amides under conditions supposedly preventing nitrosation and the formation of nitrosamine carcinogens. This is unrealistic, as nitrosation can occur in the absence of nitrite ingredients, from the interaction between amines or amides and nitrite contaminants in the finished product, or even atmospheric nitrogen oxides on the skin.

Apart from the risks of any individual carcinogenic ingredient, the Compendium appears unaware of the additive, let alone multiplicative, risks from lifelong—including prenatal—exposures of multiple carcinogenic ingredients in multiple cosmetics and personal-care products.

The Compliance Code

Reacting to mounting pressure from citizen activist groups and the Cancer Prevention Coalition, and to the 2005 California State Cosmetics Act, the Council held a conference on a new "compliance code" in 2006. The code requires that Council members provide the FDA with all product and ingredient safety data, and that they also report any "serious or unexpected" toxic effects to the FDA. The code also required that all member companies agree to comply by January 2007.

Dr. John Bailey is the Council's Executive Vice President for Science, and the former director of the FDA's Office of Cosmetics and Colors. In a July 20, 2007, interview with the Web site CosmeticsDesign.com, Bailey announced that "it is time to fight back . . . against the increasing number of attacks by lobby groups on the U.S. cosmetics and personal-care industry."[7] Bailey claimed that "[t]hese campaigns often do a great disservice to consumers by using inflammatory and alarmist rhetoric to create scientifically unsubstantiated health scares." To bolster his claims, the Council announced the formation of a Cosmetic Ingredient Review Web site which would help consumers "make informed decisions for themselves." While this sounds like a positive move in theory, given the Council's past behavior and emphasis on profit, it is unlikely that the site's information could be trusted.

The European Trade Association

The European Trade Association (COLIPA) is the world's most influential cosmetic trade association due largely to the size of the European Union's cosmetic industry. With retail sales of approximately $50 billion, the EU industry's manufacturing output is one-third greater than that of the U.S., and twice that of Japan.

Responding to growing concerns about the high frequency of allergic reactions to fragrances and perfumes, the European Parliament proposed that twenty-six allergenic ingredients (see Table 7 in chapter 6) should be labeled in all cosmetics (as well as all perfumes and fragrances), when their concentrations exceed 0.01 percent in rinse-off products or 0.001 percent in leave-on products.[8] The proposal affirms the EU's Seventh Amendment, which bans the use of ingredients known or suspected to be "Carcinogens, Mutagens, or Reproductive toxicants."[9]

The Japanese Cosmetic Industry Association

The Japanese Cosmetic Industry Association (JCIA) is Japan's equivalent to COLIPA. The JCIA was instrumental in influencing the Japanese government to deregulate its previously restrictive pre-market approval system, bringing it more in line with that of the U.S. As of 2001, the new system opened the Japanese market up to new cosmetic products, as long as they did not contain ingredients on Japan's prohibited or negative lists.

Prior to 2001, Japan's Ministry of Health had been responsible for regulating cosmetics under the Pharmaceutical Affairs Law. But in response to pressure by the Japanese Cosmetic Industry Association, the Ministry largely abdicated its authority and deregulated the industry, with the exception of limited ingredient categories that are restricted above defined concentrations. (It should be stressed that there is little if any practical difference between the regulatory abdication of the Japanese Ministry of Health in favor of industry interests, and the failure of the U.S. FDA to regulate in spite of its unarguable authority to do so.) The government has gone still further by allowing companies to market products without any labeling if they make claims of "medical benefits."

Concerns about the dangers of cosmetic products remain unrecognized by the Japan Cosmetic Industry Association, and also by major international companies selling to Japan such as Shiseido Co., Ltd., Kose Corporation, Mandom Corporation, Noevia Co., Ltd., Avon Products Co., Ltd., Parfums Christian Dior Japan S.A., Chanel K.K., and Estée Lauder. According to an Estée Lauder Japan August 2005 internal memorandum, "There is no concern in the Japanese public about Japanese cosmetics safety (and), Japanese and non-Japanese companies have not made any special effort at improving safety of products."[10]

However, the Japanese industry has no option but to comply with the 2005 European regulations on ingredient safety in order to market its cosmetics in Europe. The Japanese industry must now decide whether to comply with these standards in Japan as well or to adopt European safety standards only for the products it sells in the EU.

The International Fragrance Association

Founded in 1973, the International Fragrance Association (IFRA) is an organization of more than 100 perfume and fragrance manufacturers representing fifteen regions, including the Far East, Australia, U.S., South America, and Europe. Perfumes are very big business, and represent nearly 50 percent of all prestige beauty dollars now spent in the U.S. Fragrances are also extensively used in a wide range of other products.

The primary objectives of IFRA are to protect the self-regulatory practices, policies, and status of the industry by the development of a Code of Practices and safety guidelines. These objectives include:

- Maintaining a self-policing system based on its own Code of Practices.
- Establishing international usage guidelines.
- Maintaining the "trade secret" status of fragrances.
- Monitoring legislative trends worldwide, and assuring their consistency to avoid the development of trade barriers.
- Most importantly for this book, preempting national and international legislative labeling and safety initiatives.

A fragrance may be restricted by IFRA on a variety of grounds, including use in products at higher-than-recommended concentrations, sensitization, photosensitization, phototoxicity, allergenicity, neurotoxicity, carcinogenicity, undefined biological effects, and inadequate data. This restriction, though, works better in theory than in practice. There is no pre-approval process for ingredient safety. Instead, there is the Research Institute for Fragrance Materials.

THE RESEARCH INSTITUTE FOR FRAGRANCE MATERIALS

The Research Institute for Fragrance Materials is an international "non-profit organization," created by IFRA in 1966 to conduct research and testing of fragrance ingredients. However, testing is minimal, and restricted to effects on human skin and short-term toxicity tests in rodents. Evaluation of ingredient safety is made by an "independent" board of toxicologists, pharmacologists, and dermatologists, without disclosure of their qualifications and potential conflicts of interest. Their findings are presented to IFRA's Scientific Advisory Board, and then published in its trade journal, *Food and Chemical Toxicology*. The information reported in this journal forms the basis on which IFRA formulates safety guidelines.

Of the more than 5,000 ingredients used in the fragrance industry, approximately 1,300 have so far been evaluated by the Research

Institute. However, due to the "trade secret" status of fragrances, manufacturers are not required to include product ingredients on the label, or disclose ingredients in any other way, rendering even the tests the industry does do largely useless.

When the Environmental Health Network of California hired two testing laboratories to undertake chemical analyses on Calvin Klein's Eternity perfume following repeated complains of respiratory, neurological, and other toxic effects, a review of the laboratories' reports by the Cancer Prevention Coalition revealed the following:

- 26 ingredients in which "Toxicological properties have not been investigated," or "toxicology properties have not been thoroughly investigated."
- 25 ingredients that are "Irritants."
- 5 ingredients that are "Skin sensitizers," or allergens.
- 3 ingredients that show "Fetal, hormonal, and reproductive toxicity."
- 2 ingredients that "May cause cancer."[11]

In an effort at damage control, IFRA agreed that information on allergenic cosmetic ingredients in perfumes like Eternity should be made available—but only on request, and only to dermatologists, for diagnostic purposes.[12] This "Fragrance On-Call List" action continues to deny the public its right to know. IFRA has failed to respond to repeated requests that "all fragrance products be labeled to the effect that, apart from the absence of known skin and respiratory allergens, they contain no known carcinogens, gene damaging, hormonal, or otherwise toxic ingredients."[13]

Corporate Social Responsibility

An October 25, 2007, *New York Times* four-page supplement, "Corporate Social Responsibility" (CSR), reported on an international meeting in San Francisco of more than 1,000 business leaders from a range of corporations and industries. Their goal was to create a sustainable and environmentally sensitive global economy, based on safe technologies, and energy and public health concerns. Attendees included Nike, McDonald's, Wal-Mart, and representatives of other major food and safe household cleaning product companies and industries. Notably absent from the meeting were representatives of major cosmetic and personal-care product industries, which by continuing to market toxic products reject CSR principles.

APPENDIX FOUR
Badges of Honor

The following deserve badges of honor for their efforts toward promoting safe products:

COMPANIES
(for innovative products and technologies)

Acquarella Nail Products (water-based nail products)
www.aquarellapolish.com

Burt's Bees (natural sunscreen and sunblock)
www.burtsbees.com

iSoy Technology Corporation (soy-based sunscreen)
http://isoytech.com/

Logona (organic hair dyes)
www.logona.co.uk

ORLY (safe nail polish)
www.orlybeauty.com

Q-Med (restylane anti-wrinkling agent)
www.q-med.com

Solumbra (protective clothing)
www.solumbra.com

(for USDA Certified Organic products)
Aubrey Organics
www.aubrey-organics.com

Dr. Bronner's Magic Soaps
www.drbronner.com

Erbaorganics
www.erbaorganics.com

Erbaviva
www.erbaviva.com

Intelligent Nutrients
www.intelligentnutrients.com

Mercola Healthy Skin
www.mercolahealthyskin.com

Nature's Best
www.naturesbest.com

Nature's Gate
www.natures-gate.com

Neways International
www.neways.com

Organic and Natural Enterprise Group (ONE Group)
www.mionegroup.com

Sensibility Soaps
www.sensibilitysoaps.com

Terressentials
www.terressentials.com

NON-PROFIT ORGANIZATIONS
(for warning consumers of toxic ingredients and products)

Breast Cancer Action
www.bcaction.org

Breast Cancer Fund
www.breastcancerfund.org

Environmental Health Network of California
www.ehnca.org

Campaign for Safe Cosmetics
www.safecosmetics.org

Cancer Prevention Coalition
www.preventcancer.com

Environmental Defense Fund
www.edf.org

Environmental Working Group
www.ewg.org

Friends of the Earth
www.foe.org

Health Care Without Harm
www.noharm.org

Intelligent Nutrients
www.intelligentnutrients.com

National Congress of Black Women, Inc.
www.nationalcongressbw.org

National Organization for Women
www.now.org

Organic Consumers Association
www.organicconsumers.org

Public Citizen
www.citizen.org

REFERENCES

Chapter One: History's Beauty Industry Influences

For detailed historical information on the development of cosmetics and personal-care products, you might find the following sources to be illuminating:

Ackerman, Diane. *A Natural History of the Senses*. Vintage Books, 1991.

Beyer, Lyssa. "The History of . . . Deodorant." *The Spectator*, www.spectatornews.com, February 8, 2007.

"Cosmetics In The Ancient World." Cosmeticsinfo.org.

Genders, Roy. *A History of Scent*. London: Hamish Hamilton, Ltd., 1972.

Laden, Karl. *Antiperspirants and Deodorants*. Marcel Dekker, 1988.

Riordan, Teresa. *Inventing Beauty: A History of the Innovations that Have Made Us Beautiful*. Broadway Books, 2004.

Robinson, Julian. *The Quest for Human Beauty: An Illustrated History.* W.W. Norton, 1998.

Chapter Two: The Chemical Threat to Your Health

1. Cancer Prevention Coalition. Citizen Petition Seeking Labeling of Nitrite-Preserved Hot Dogs for Childhood Cancer Risk. April 25, 1995.

2. Steinman, D. and Epstein, S. S. *The Safe Shopper's Bible.* Macmillan, 1995.

3. Davis, D. and Hoel, D. (eds). *Trends in Cancer Mortality in Industrial Countries.* New York Academy of Sciences 609: November 21, 1990.

4. National Cancer Institute. U.S. National Institutes of Health. SEER (Surveillance, Epidemiology, and End Results) Cancer Statistics Review, 1975–2005.

5. Natural Resources Defense Council. "Intolerable risk: pesticides in our children's food." February 27, 1989.

6. Environmental Working Group. Skin Deep Report, Carcinogens in Personal Care Products, June 2004.

7. Cancer Prevention Coalition. Citizen Petition Seeking Cancer Warning on Cosmetics Containing DEA. October 22, 1996.

8. National Toxicology Program. "Toxicological and Carcinogenicity Studies on Diethanolamine." TR 478, December 1997.

Chapter Three: Losing the Winnable Cancer War

1. Kolata, Gina. "Environment and Cancer: The Links Are Elusive." *The New York Times,* December 13, 2005.

2. Montague, Peter. "Why We Cannot Prevent Cancer." *Rachel's Democracy & Health News.* Issue #829, October 27, 2005.

3. Davis, D. and Hoel, D. (eds.) *Trends in Cancer Mortality in Industrial Countries.* New York Academy of Sciences, November 21, 1990.

4. Epstein, S. S., et al. "The Crisis in U.S. and International Cancer Policy." *International Journal of Health Services* 32(4):669–707, 2002. Endorsed by more than 30 leading scientists.

5. Lichtenstein, P., et al. "Environmental and Heritable Factors in the Causation of Cancer: Analysis of Cohorts of Twins from Sweden, Denmark and Finland." *New England Journal of Medicine* 343(2):78–85, 2000.

6. Epstein, S. S. "American Cancer Society: The World's Wealthiest 'Non-Profit' Institution." *International Journal of Health Services* 29:565–78, 1999.

7. Hall H., and Williams G. "Professor vs. Cancer Society." *The Chronicle of Philanthropy.* January 28, 1992, pg. 6.

8. Epstein, S. S. The Stop Cancer Before It Starts Campaign. How to Win the Losing War Against Cancer. February 2003. Endorsed by approximately 140 leading cancer experts, and representatives of national consumer groups.

9. Doll, R. and Peto, R. *The Causes of Cancer: Quantitative Estimates of Avoidable Risks of Cancer in the United States Today.* Oxford University Press, 1981.

10. Joint Conference of the International Union of Cancer and the International Agency for Research on Cancer. Remarks by Richard Doll. June 2002.

11. Davis, D. L., et al. "International Trends in Cancer Mortality in France, West Germany, Italy, Japan, England and Wales, and the USA." *Lancet* 336(8713):474–81, 1990.

Chapter Four: You Lost Your "Right to Know"

1. Epstein, S. S. and Grundy, R. D. "The Regulation of the Safety of Cosmetics." Chapter Two, Volume Two. *The Legislation of Product Safety: Consumer Health and Product Hazards.* Cambridge: Massachusetts Institute of Technology Press, 1974.

2. Agency for Toxic Substances and Disease Registry. Toxicological Profile for 1,4-Dioxane. July 2006.

3. Parisian, S. *FDA: Inside and Out.* Front Royal, VA: Fast Horse Press, 2001.

4. Environmental Working Group. www.cosmeticdatabase.com/research/fdapetition.php. 2004.

Chapter Five: Products Targeting Infants and Children

1. Greenpeace International and WWF-UK. "A Present for Life: Hazardous Chemicals in Umbilical Cord Blood." September 2005.

2. Gray, T. J. and Butterworth, K. R. "Testicular Atrophy Produced by Phthalate Esters." *Archives of Toxicology Supplement* 4:452–5, 1980.

3. A Present for Life, pg. 35.

4. Environmental Working Group. "Body Burden—The Pollution in Newborns." www.ewg.org. July 2005.

5. Diskin, Colleen. "Slew of Pollutants Found in Babies." *North Jersey Record*, July 13, 2005.

6. Vandenberg, L. N., et al. "The Human Exposure to bisphenol a (BPA)." *Reproductive Toxicology* 24(2):139–77, 2007.

7. Richter, C. A., et al. "In Vivo Effects of Bisphenol A in Laboratory Rodent Studies." *Reproductive Toxicolology* 24(2):199–224, 2007.

8. Darbre, P. D., et al. "Estrogenic Activity of Benzylparaben." *Journal of Applied Toxicology* 23:43–51, 2003.

9. Routledge, E. J., et al. "Some Alkyl Hydroxy Benzoate Preservatives (Parabens) Are Estrogenic." *Toxicology & Applied Pharmacology* 153:12–19, 1998.

10. Oishi, S. "Effects of Propyl Paraben on the Male Reproductive System." *Food and Chemical Toxicology* 40(12):1807–13, 2002.

11. Darbre, P. D., et al. "Concentrations of Parabens in Human Breast Tumors." *Journal of Applied Toxicology* 24:5–13, 2004.

12, Office of Cosmetics and Colors, FDA. www.cfsan.fda.gov/~dms/cos-para.html. March 20, 2006.

13. Pitman, S. "Ageing Claims Put Parabens Back Under the Spotlight." www.cosmeticsdesign.com. August 29, 2005.

14. Veldhoen, N., et al. "The Bacterial Agent Triclosan Modulates Thyroid Hormone-Associated Gene Expression and Disrupts Postembryonic Anuran Development." *Aquatic Toxicology* 80:217–27, 2006.

15. Levy, S. B. "Anti-Bacterial Household Products: Cause for Concern." *Emerging Infectious Diseases* 7:512–515, 2001.

16. Foran, C. M., et al. "Developmental Evaluation of a Potential Non-Steroidal Estrogen: Triclosan." *Marine Environmental Research* 50:153–6, 2000.

17. Lynch, B. S., et al. "Toxicology Review and Risk Assessment of Resorcinol: Thyroid Effects." *Regulatory Toxicology and Pharmacology* 36:198–220, 2002.

18. Jobling, S., et al. "Inhibition of Testicular Growth in Rainbow Trout Exposed to Alkylphenolic Chemicals." *Environmental Toxicology and Chemistry* 15:194–202, 1996.

19. White, R. S., et al. "Environmentally Persistent Alkylphenolic Compounds Are Estrogenic." *Endocrinology* 135:175–82, 1994.

20. Acevedo, R., et al. "The Contribution of Hepatic Steroid Metabolism to Serum Estradiol and Estriol Concentrations in Nonylphenol Treated MMTVneu Mice and Its Potential Effects on Breast Cancer Incidence and Latency." *Journal of Applied Toxicology* 25:339–53, 2005.

21. Mylchreest, E., et al. "Disruption of Androgen-Regulated Male Reproductive Development by di(n-butyl) Phthalate During Late Gestation in Rats Is Different from Flutamide." *Toxicology and Applied Pharmacology* 156:81–95, 1999.

22. Blount, B. C., et al. "Levels of Seven Urinary Phthalate Metabolites as a Human Reference Population." *Environmental Health Perspectives* 108(10):979–82, October 2000.

23. Centers for Disease Control and Prevention. Second National Report on Human Exposure to Environmental Chemicals, 2003.

24. Duty, S. M., et al. "The Relationship Between Environmental Exposures to Phthalates and DNA Damage in Human Sperm Using the Natural Comet Assay." *Environmental Health Perspectives* 111(9):1164–9, July 2003.

25. Swan, S., et al. "Decrease in Anogenital Distance Among Male Infants with Prenatal Phthalate Exposure." *Environmental Health Perspectives* 113(8):1056–61, 2005.

26. Cone, Marla. "Study Finds Genital Abnormalities in Boys." *Los Angeles Times*, May 27, 2005.

27. Houlihan, J., et al. "Not Too Pretty: Phthalates, Beauty Products and the FDA." Environmental Working Group, July 8, 2002.

28. Eriksson, E., et al. "Household Chemicals and Personal Care Products as Sources for Xenobiotic Organic Compounds in Grey Wastewater." *Water SA* 29(2):135–46, 2003.

29. Duty, S. M., et al. "Personal Care Product Use Predicts Urinary Concentrations of Some Phthalate Monoesters." *Environmental Health Perspectives* 113:1530–5, 2005.

30. Hauser, R., et al. "Altered Semen Quality in Relation to Concentrations of Phthalate Monoester and Oxidative Metabolites." *Epidemiology* 17:682–91, 2006.

31. Cosmetic Ingredient Review Compendium, 2007.

32. Markey, C. M., et al. "Long Term Effects of Fetal Exposure to Low Doses of the Xenoestrogen Bisphenol-A in the Female Mouse Genital Tract." *Biology of Reproduction* 72:1344–51, 2005.

33. Vom Saal, F. S. and Hughes, C. "An Extensive New Literature Concerning Low-Dose Effects of Bisphenol-A Shows the Need for a New Risk Assessment." *Environmental Health Perspectives* 113:926–33, 2005.

34. Ho S-M., et al. "Developmental Exposure to Estradiol and Bisphenol A Increases Susceptibility to Prostate Carcinogenesis and Epigenetically Regulates Phosphodiesterase Type 4 Variant 4." *Cancer Research* 66:5624–32, 2006.

35. Durando, M., et al. "Prenatal Bisphenol A Exposure Induces Preneoplastic Lesions in the Mammary Gland in Wistar Rats." *Environmental Health Perspectives* 115(1):80–6, 2007.

36. Henley, D. V., et al. "Prepubertal Gynecomastia Linked to Lavender and Tea Tree Oils." *New England Journal of Medicine* 356(5):479–85, 2007.

37. Darbre, P. D. "Aluminum, Antiperspirants and Breast Cancer." *Journal of Inorganic Biochemistry* 99(9):1912–9, September 2005.

38. Martin, M. B. "Estrogen-Like Activity of Metals in Mcf-7 Breast Cancer Cells." *Endocrinology* 144(6):2425–36, 2003.

39. Graves, A. B., et al. "The Association Between Aluminum-Containing Products and Alzheimer's Disease." *Journal of Clinical Epidemiology* 43:35–44, 1990.

40. Food and Drug Administration. Antiperspirant Drug Products for Over-the-Counter Human Use; Final Monograph. Federal Register 68, No. 110, June 9, 2003/Rules and Regulations.

Chapter Six: Products Targeting Women

1. Environmental Health Network. "Phthalates Found in Perfume—Analysis of One Perfume—Calvin Klein's Eternity." http://users.lmi.net/wilworks/FDApetition/analysis.htm. 1998.

2. Cancer Prevention Coalition and Environmental Health Network. Press Release. "Cupid's Arrow or Poison Dart." February 7, 2000.

3. FDA correspondence to Cancer Prevention Coalition. www.preventcancer.com.

4. Environmental Working Group. "Investigation Finds More Than 400 Cosmetic Products on U.S. Shelves Unsafe When Used as Directed Based on Industry Ingredient Assessments." Ewg.org. Sept. 25, 2007.

5. Steinman, D. and Epstein, S. S. *The Safe Shopper's Bible*. Macmillan, 1995.

6. Nielsen, N., and Menne, T. "The Glostrup Allergy Study, Denmark." *Acta Dermato-Venereologica* 72:456–60, 1992.

7. Marks, J. G., et al. "North American Contact Dermatitis Group." *American Journal of Contact Dermatitis* 38:911–8, 1998.

8. Kennedy, Edward M. The Food Allergen Consumer Protection Act, S. 2499, 2002.

9. Bridges, B. "Fragrance: Emerging Health and Environmental Concerns." *Flavour and Fragrance Journal* 17:361–71, 2002.

10. Harlow BL., et al. "Perineal Exposure to Talc and Ovarian Cancer Risk." *Obstet Gynecol* 80(1): 19-26, 1992.

11. Westerhof, W., and Kooyers, T. J. "Hydroquinone and Its Analogues in Dermatology—A Potential Health Risk." *The Journal of Cosmetic Dermatology*. 4(2):55–9, June 2005.

12. Campaign for Safe Cosmetics. "A Poison Kiss: The Problem of Lead in Lipstick." www.safecosmetics.org. October 2007.

13. Malkan, Stacy. *Not Just a Pretty Face*. New Society Publishers, 2007, pg. 10.

14. Geehr, Edward C. "Is Your Lipstick Leaded?" www.lifescript. com. November 11, 2007.

15. National Environmental Trust. Toxic Chemicals Widespread in Consumer Products. www.net.org. July 2004.

Chapter Seven: Products Targeting Beauty and Nail Salons

1. Georgia State Board of Cosmetology. Cosmetology School Curriculum. www.rules.sos.state.ga.us/cgi-bin/page. cgi?g=Georgia_State_Board_of_Cosmetology.

2. "Common Dreams. The Beauty Industry's Ugly Secret." www. commondreams.org. September 20, 2006.

3. "Hairspray Linked to Birth Defect." BBC News. November 21, 2008.

4. Kronoveter, K. J. Health Hazard Evaluation Determination Report No. HHE-76-82-361, Hair Zoo, Penfield, New York, National Institute of Occupational Safety and Health (NIOSH), 1977.

5. The Danish Case on Injury Following the Use of Hair Dyes. http://www.forbrugerradet.dk. December 4, 2005.

6. National Cancer Institute. SEER Cancer Statistics Review, 1975–2005.

7. IARC Monograph. Occupational Exposures of Hairdressers and Barbers and Personal Use of Hair Colourants; Some Hair Dyes, Cosmetic Colourants, Industrial Dyestuffs and Aromatic Amines. 57:43–118, 1993.

8. European Commission, Health and Consumer Protection. Scientific Committee on Consumer Products. Memorandum on Hair Dye Substances and Their Skin Sensitizing Properties. December 19, 2006.

9. Mikami, K. "New York Hairstylist Takes Technique Straight to the Bank." *The Japan Times*, April 14, 2007.

10. Kolar, G. G. and Miller, A. "Hair Straighteners," in *Cosmetics Science and Technology*, Vol. 2, 2nd ed., ed. MS Balsam and E Sagarin. New York: Wiley Interscience, 1972, p. 251.

11. Gorman A, et al. "Glossed Over: Health Hazards Associated with Toxic Exposures in Nail Salons." A Report by Women's Voices for the Earth. www.womenandenvironment.org. February 2007.

12. Savitz, J., et al. "Spontaneous Abortions Among Cosmetologists." *Epidemiology*. 5(2):147–55, 1994.

13. Sole-Smith, Virginia. "The High Price of Beauty." *The Nation*, October 8, 2007.

14. Cosmetic Ingredient Review (CIR) Compendium, 2007.

15. Blount, B. C., et al. "Levels of Seven Urinary Phthalate Metabolites in a Human Reference Population." *Environmental Health Perspectives* 108(10):979–82, October 2000.

16. Personal communication with George Schaeffer, President & CEO, OPI Products, Inc.

17. Campaign for Safe Cosmetics. "Nail Polishes to Become a Little Safer." Press Release. www.safecosmetics.org. August 30, 2006.

18. Women's Voice for the Earth. "Leading Nail Polish Manufacturer Removes Toxic Ingredients." www.womenandenvironment. org, March 29, 2007.

19. Environmental Working Group. Skin Deep Report. Ewg.org/reports/skindeep/. June 2004.

20. Steinman, D. and Epstein, S. S. *The Safe Shopper's Bible*. Macmillan, 1995.

Chapter Eight: Products Targeting Sun Worshippers

1. Taylor, Steve. *Two Fingers To Sunscreen? An Essential Guide for the Effective Use of Sunscreens*. www.sunblaster.co.nz/downloads/Full_txt_c.pdf. 2002.

2. Garland, C. F., et al. "Could Sunscreens Increase Melanoma Risk?" *American Journal of Public Health* 82(4):614–5, 1992.

3. National Cancer Institute. SEER Cancer Statistics Review, 1975–2005.

4. Environmental Working Group. Skin Deep Report. June 2004.

5. Hanson, K. M., et al. "Sunscreen Enhancement of UV-Induced Reactive Oxygen Species in the Skin." *Free Radical Biology and Medicine* 41:1205–12, 2006.

6. Schlumpf, M., et al. "In Vitro and in Vivo Estrogenicity of UV Screens." *Environmental Health Perspectives* 109(3):239–44, 2001.

7. Kadry, A. M., et al. "Pharmacokinetics of Benzophenone-3 After Oral Exposure in Male Rats." *Journal of Applied Toxicology* 15:97–102, 1995.

8. Cosmetic Ingredient Review Compendium, 2007.

9. Bowles, Jennifer. "UCR Scientist Finds Key to Sex Alterations in Fish." *San Bernardino Press-Enterprise*, November 15, 2005.

10. Hany, J. and Nage,l R. "Nachweis von UV-Filtersubtanzen in Muttermilch. (Detection of Sunscreen Agents in Human Breast Milk)." *Deutche Lebensmittel-Rundschau* 91(11):341–5, 1995.

11. Calafat, A. M., et al. "Concentrations of the Sunscreen Agent, Benzophenone-3, in Residents of the U.S.: National Health and Nutrition Examination Survey 2003–2004." *Environmental Health Perspectives* (available online March 21, 2008).

12. Environmental Working Group. EWG Statement on Latest FDA Proposed Sunscreen Safety Standards. www.ewg.org. August 23, 2007. (Cites skin penetration studies: Cross 2007; Garner 2006; Gottbrath 2003; Mavon 2007.)

13. International Center for Technology Assessment (CTA). "Consumer, Health, and Environmental Groups Launch First-Ever Legal Challenge on Risks of Nanotechnology." May 16, 2006.

14. Howard, C. V. "Nanoparticles and Toxicity." Press Releases April 12, 2003, and May 11, 2003.

15. Inoue, K. "Effects of Airway Exposure to Nanoparticles on Lung Inflammation by Bacterial Endotoxin in Mice." *Environmental Health Perspectives* 114(9):1325–30, 2006.

16. "Nanoparticles in Sun Creams Can Stress Brain Cells." Nature.com. June 16, 2006.

17. Friends of the Earth. "Nanomaterials, Sunscreens and Cosmetics: Small Ingredients, Big Risks." May 16, 2006.

18. The Royal Society & The Royal Academy of Engineering. "Nanoscience and Nanotechnologies: Opportunities and Uncertainties." www.nanotec.org.uk. July 2004.

19. Lu, Y-P, et al. "Topical Applications of Caffeine or (-)-Epigallocatechin Gallate (EGCG) Inhibit Carcinogenesis and Selectively Increase Apoptosis in UVB-Induced Skin Tumors in Mice." *Proceedings, National Academy of Sciences* 99(19):12455–60, 2002.

20. Laszlo, J. A., Compton, D. L., Willis, R. A. "Sunscreen Active Derived from Soybean Oil and Ferulic Acid: Synthesis and Applications." Proceedings of the 6th International Symposium on the Role of Soy in Preventing and Treating Chronic Disease, Chicago, IL. 2005. Page 51.

21. Juliano, Claudia, et al. "Antioxidant Activity of Gamma-oryzanol: Mechanism of Action and its Effect on Oxidative Stability of Pharmaceutical Oils." *International Journal of Pharmaceutics.* 299(1–2):146–54. 2005.

Chapter Nine: Products Targeting Youth Seekers

1. "The Future of Cosmeceuticals: An Interview with Albert Kligman." *Dermatologic Surgery* 31(7, part 2):890–1, July 1005.

2. Thornfeldt, C. "Cosmeceuticals Containing Herbs: Fact, Fiction and Future." *Dermatologic Surgery* 31:873–881, 2005.

3. Hilton, L. "An Update on Latest in Cosmeceuticals: Biologically Active Skincare." *Cosmetic Surgery Times* November–December 2004.

4. Lupo, Mary. "Cosmeceutical Peptides." *Dermatologic Surgery* 31:832–6, 2005.

5. Bailly, J. "Is This Any Way to Treat a Face?" *O, The Oprah Magazine,* March 2007.

6. Cosmetic Ingredient Review Compendium, 2007.

7. Food and Drug Administration. "Skin Peelers." Human Health Services News. May 21, 1992.

8. Food and Drug Administration. "AHAs and UV Sensitivity. Results of New FDA Sponsored Studies." Office of Cosmetics and Color Fact Sheet. March 2, 2000.

9. Food and Drug Administration. Guidance for Industry: Labeling for Topically Applied Cosmetic Products Containing AHAs as Ingredients. December 2, 2002.

10. Centurion, S. A., et al. "Cosmeceuticals." www.emedicine.com. February 4, 2004.

11. "Skin Whitening Agents." Medidermlab.com.

12. Seigel, J. "Fat Chance." Op-Ed. *The New York Times*. August 15, 2005.

13. Draelos, Z. D. "Cosmeceutical Peptides: Generic vs. Brand." *Dermatology Times*. February 1, 2005.

14. Pitman, S. "Janson Beckett Unveils Peptide-Based Anti-Wrinkle Product." www.cosmeticsdesign.com. December 7, 2005.

15. Q-Med. Uppsala, Sweden. May 6, 2002.

16. 11th Congress of the EADV, Prague, Czech Republic. October 4, 2002.

17. PR Leap. "*Allure* Magazine Awards L'Oreal Paris Skin Genesis as a Best Beauty Breakthrough for 2007." September 26, 2007.

18. *Consumer Reports*. www.consumerreports.org.

19. Chiu, A. E., et al. "Double-Blinded Placebo-Controlled Trial of Green Tea Extracts in the Clinical and Histologic Appearance of Photoaging Skin." *Dermatologic Surgery* 31(7, Part 2):855–60, 2005.

20. Bauza, E., et al. "Date Palm Kernel Extract Exhibits Anti-aging Properties and Significantly Reduces Skin Wrinkles." *International Journal of Tissue Reactions* 24(4):131–6, 2002.

21. Stinchfield, Kate. "Skip the Botox." *Time*, November 13, 2007.

Chapter Ten: Products Targeting Everyone

1. Natural Resources Defense Council. "Protect Your Family from the Hidden Hazards in Air Fresheners." www.nrdc.org/health/home/airfresheners.asp. September 2007.

2. Blount, B. C., et al. "Levels of Seven Urinary Phthalate Metabolites as Human Reference Population." *Environmental Health Perspectives* 108(10):979–82, October 2000.

3. Houlihan, J., et al. Environmental Working Group. Not Too Pretty Report, 2002.

4. DiGangi, J., et al. "Pretty Nasty: Phthalates in European Cosmetic Products." Health Care Without Harm, Swedish Society for Nature Conservation, Women's Environmental Network. November 2002.

5. Eui-Sun Yoo, et al. "Phthalates in Cosmetics in Korea." Citizens' Institute for Environmental Studies and Seoul Branch of the Korean Federation for Environmental Movement. April 2003.

6. Swan, S., et al. "Decrease in Anogenital Distance Among Male Infants with Prenatal Phthalate Exposure." *Environmental Health Perspectives* 113(8):1056–61, August 2005.

7. Duty, S.M., et al. "Phthalate Exposure and Human Semen Parameters." *Epidemiology* 14(3):269–77, May 2003.

8. Duty, S. M., et al. "The Relationship Between Environmental Exposures to Phthalates and DNA Damage in Human Sperm Using the Natural Comet Assay." *Environmental Health Perspectives* 111(9):1164–9, July 2003.

9. National Toxicology Program. 11th Report. Pp. 118–22. 2004.

10. Cone, Marla. "Testing Finds Traces of Carcinogen in Bath Products." *Los Angeles Times*, February 9, 2007.

11. National Toxicology Program 11th Report. Pp. 40–1. 2004.

12. Williams, A. C. and Barry, B. W. "Penetration Enhancers." *Advanced Drug Delivery Reviews* 56:603–18, 2004.

13. Cosmetic Ingredient Review Compendium, 2007.

14. Nielsen, G. D., et al. "Effects of Industrial Detergents on the Barrier Function of Human Skin." *International Journal of Occupational and Environmental Health* 6(2):138–42, April–June 2000.

15. Nielsen, J. B. "Effects of Four Detergents on the in-vitro Barrier Function of Human Skin." *International Journal of Occupational and Environmental Health* 6(2):143–7, April–June 2000.

16. Darbre, P. D. "Metalloestrogens: An Emerging Class of Inorganic Xenoestrogens with Potential to Add to the Oestrogenic Burden of the Human Breast." *Journal of Applied Toxicology* 26(3):191–7, 2006.

17. Smith, Michael. "Antiperspirants Linked to Breast Cancer." MedPage Today, March 1, 2006.

18. Routledge, E. J., et al. "Some Alkyl Hydroxy Benzoate Preservatives (Parabens) Are Estrogenic." *Toxicology and Applied Pharmacology* 153:12–19, 1998.

19. Jacob, S., et al. "Focus on T.R.U.E. Test Allergen #8: Parabens." *Skin & Aging* 15(3):31–6, March 2007.

20. El Hussein, S., et al. "Assessment of Principal Parabens Used in Cosmetics After Their Passage Through Human Epidermis-Dermis Layers (*ex-vivo* study)." *Experimental Dermatology* 16(10):830–6, October 2007.

21. Nakazawa, H., et al. "Analysis of Chlorobenzenes, Parahydroxybenzoic Acid Esters and Herbicide in Human Subjects." A report of the Research Fund of Health and Welfare of Japan. Tokyo: Ministry of Health and Welfare, 1999.

22. American Environmental Safety Institute. "Judge Enters Institute's Settlement Regarding Lead in Crest Toothpaste." www.ems.org. August 17, 2005.

23. Associated Press. "FDA Says Avoid Toothpaste Made In China." June 1, 2007.

24. Glaser, A. "The Ubiquitous Triclosan: A Common Anti-Bacterial Agent Exposed." *Pesticides and You* 24(3):12–24, 2004.

25. Foran, C. M., et al. "Developmental Evaluation of a Potential Non-Steroidal Estrogen: Triclosan." *Marine Environmental Research* 50:153–6, 2000.

26. National Toxicology Program 11th Report. Pp. 111–54. 2004.

27. Lasley, B., et al. "Triclocarban Enhances Testosterone Action: A New Type of Endocrine Disrupter?" *Endocrinology* (online), November 29, 2007.

Chapter Eleven: Reforming the Cosmetics and Personal-Care Products Industry

1. Von Woedtke, T., et al. "Aspects of the Antimicrobial Efficacy of Grapefruit Seed Extract and Its Relation to Preservative Substances Contained." *Pharmazie* 54(6):452–6, June 1999.

2. Epstein, S. S. Testimony on Corporate Criminal Liability. Hearings Before the Subcommittee on Crime of the House Committee of the Judiciary (HR 4973). December 1979.

3. Seventh Amendment to the Cosmetics Directive of the European Union. October 31, 2001.

4. Epstein, S. S. *What's In Your Milk? An Exposé of Industry and Government Cover-Up on the Dangers of the Genetically Engineered (rBGH) Milk You're Drinking.* Trafford Publishing, 2006.

5. Reuters. "EU Bans 22 Hair Dye Substances to Ensure Safety." July 20, 2006.

6. Epstein, S. S. "REACH: An Unprecedented European Initiative for Regulating Industrial Chemicals." *International Journal of Health Services* 35(1):1–38, 2005.

Chapter Twelve: Two Healthy Trends in Your Future

1. Dweck, A. C. "Natural Ingredients for Coloring and Styling." *International Journal of Cosmetic Science* 24:287–302, 2002.

2. ECOCERT. Standards for Ecological and Organic Cosmetics. January 2003.

3. Poliakoff, M., et al. "Green Chemistry: Science and Politics of Change." *Science* 297:807–10, 2002.

4. Villa, C., et al. "Eco-friendly Methodologies for the Synthesis of Some Aromatic Esters, Well Known Cosmetic Ingredients." *International Journal of Cosmetic Science* 27:11–16, 2005.

5. Wilson, M. P., et al. "Green Chemistry in California: A Framework for Leadership in Chemicals Policy and Innovation." California Policy Research Center, University of California, Berkeley. March 14, 2006.

6. "Cosmetics Made from Food." http://web-japan.org/trends/fashion. January 18, 2005.

7. "Global Organic Cosmetic Market Booms." www.cosmeticsdesign.com. June 1, 2005.

8. Leading Cosmetic Players Make Gains in the Stagnant Market. www.cosmeticsdesign.com. August 25, 2005.

9. NPI Center. Natural Cosmetics Boom in EU, Though Debates Continue Over Which Brands are Actually Organic, Sept. 19, 2006.

10. *Health.* "Organic Deodorant: Does it Work?" May 2005.

11. Lloyd, T. "Blueprint for a Cosmetic Empire: NSBrands Enter a Hot Japanese Market." www.japaninc.com. September 2004.

12. Laszlo, J., et al. "Sunscreen Active Derived from Soybean Oil and Ferulic Acid: Synthesis and Applications." Proceedings of the 6th International Symposium on the Role of Soy in Preventing and Treating Chronic Disease, Chicago, Illinois, p. 51, November 2, 2005.

13. Laszlo, J, et al. "Pack-bed Reactor Synthesis of Feruloylated Monoacyl- and Diacyl Glycerols: Clean Production of a "Green" Sunscreen." *Green Chemistry* 5:382–6, 2003.

14. Robinson, B. C. Deputy Administration Agricultural Marketing Service. USDA Memorandum. "Certification of Agricultural Products That Meet NOP Standards." August 23, 2005.

15. Organic Consumers Association. "Carcinogenic 1,4-Dioxane Found in Leading 'Organic' Brand Personal Care Products." www.organicconsumers.org, March 14, 2008.

Appendix Three: Industry Trade Associations and What They Conceal from You

1. CTFA. Annual Report, 2007.

2. Parisian, S. *FDA: Inside & Out.* Front Royal, VA: Fast Horse Press. 2001.

3. CTFA Technical Guidelines: Safety Testing Guidelines. 1991.

4. CTFA Labeling Manual. A Guide to Labeling and Advertising Cosmetics and OTC Drugs, Second Edition. 1997.

5. CTFA. International Regulatory Resource Manual. 2001.

6. CTFA. Cosmetic Ingredient Review Compendium 2007.

7. Pitman, S. "CTFA Targets Misinformation to Counteract Lobby Groups." www.cosmeticsdesign.com. July 20, 2007.

8. Directive (2003/15/EC) of the European Parliament and of the Council, Relating to Consumer Products, February 27, 2003.

9. The Scientific Committee on Cosmetic Products and Non-food Products Intended for Consumers (SCCNFP), September 25, 2001.

10. Kondo, A. Manager, Regulatory Affairs. Estée Lauder Japan, 2005.

11. Environmental Health Network, Petition 99P-1340, to the Food and Drug Administration requesting the Commissioner to take administrative action and declare "Eternity Eau de Parfum by Calvin Klein Cosmetics Company Misbranded." May 7, 1999.

12. Vey, M. (Scientific Director, International Fragrance Association). Letter to the Editor. *Contact Dermatitis* 48:56–8, 2003.

13. Epstein, S. S. E-mails, 8/26/03, 9/22/03, 9/30/03, and 10/1/03 to Dr. M. Vey, President of the IFRA.

ACKNOWLEDGMENTS

Warm commendations are due to Congressman David Obey and Senator Ron Wyden, for their long-standing concern about the dangers of cosmetic and personal-care product ingredients; Senator Edward Kennedy, for his 1997 endorsement of the General Accounting Office report on carcinogenic ingredients in cosmetics, and for his warning that "The cosmetics industry has borrowed a page from the playbook of the tobacco industry by putting profits ahead of public health"; Congressman John Conyers, Chairman of the House Judiciary Committee, for his long-standing legislative initiatives on white-collar industry crime; Congresswoman Jan Schakowsky for her 2001 bill (HR 1947) requiring warning labels on fragrances containing allergens and other toxic ingredients; and California State Senator Carole Migden for her 2005 California Safe Cosmetics Act requiring disclosure of toxic ingredients in cosmetics, authorized by Governor Arnold Schwarzenegger in January 2007.

As chairman of the non-profit Cancer Prevention Coalition, I am pleased to acknowledge the following for their support in our mission of winning the losing war against cancer and providing citizens with information on unknowing exposures to environmental carcinogens and a wide range of avoidable carcinogens in consumer products: the Goldsmith, Schneider, Oestreicher, Goodman, Helianthus, and Heinz Family foundations; and Horst M. Rechelbacher, past president of Aveda and current CEO of Intelligent Nutrients (IN).

I would like to thank: Ralph Nader, for his prescient chapter on cosmetics in the 1974 MIT Press book which I co-edited, and also for co-sponsoring my September 1995 Washington, D.C., press conference on the "Dirty Dozen" toxic cosmetics and other consumer products; the late, indomitable Studs Terkel, for frequent invitations to discuss cancer politics and avoidable causes of cancer on his highly celebrated radio program series; and Dr. Quentin Young, chairman of the Health and Medicine Policy Research Group and past president of the American Public Health Association, for his unflagging support, involvement in a wide range of CPC initiatives, and concerns relating to avoidable causes of cancer, including carcinogenic ingredients in cosmetics and personal-care products.

I would also like to thank George Schaeffer, CEO of OPI Products, Inc., for constructive comments on salon nail products; Robin Brown and Anna Cirronis of Erbaviva, for information on their certified organic baby products; Michael Wrightson, president of Natural Europe Enterprises, and Logona, a German company, for information on organic herbal hair dyes; Ronnie Cummins of the Organic Consumers Association, for his critical review and stellar contributions on certified organic ingredients; Melissa Christenson, president of Intelligent Nutrients, for assistance on evaluating organic products; and Horst Rechelbacher, CEO of Intelligent Nutrients, for his U.S. and international leadership role on safe organic products, well exemplified by his epic insistence, "Don't put anything on your skin which you would not put in your mouth."

It is also a pleasure to acknowledge the over 100 leading scientific experts in cancer prevention and public health and the representatives of activist citizen groups who endorsed the Cancer Prevention Coalition's February 2003 report, "Stop Cancer Before It Starts Campaign: How to Win the Losing War Against Cancer." This report deals with a wide range of avoidable causes of cancer, including unlabeled carcinogenic ingredients in consumer products, particularly cosmetics and personal-care products, and related public policy concerns.

Finally, writing this book has been dependent on the support of my assistant Julie Hlavaty.

INDEX

ABOUT THE AUTHORS

Samuel S. Epstein, M.D., Professor Emeritus of Environmental and Occupational Medicine at the School of Public Health, University of Illinois at Chicago, is an internationally recognized authority on the causes and prevention of cancer, the toxic and carcinogenic effects of pollutants in air, water, soil and the workplace, and ingredients and contaminants in consumer products—food, household products, and cosmetics and toiletries.

He has published some 270 articles in leading scientific journals, authored or co-authored fifteen books, and contributed numerous editorials and letters to regional and national newspapers.

Dr. Epstein's past committee involvements include serving as president of the Society of Occupational and Environmental Health and president of the Rachel Carson Council, Inc. In 1993, he founded the non-profit international Cancer Prevention Coalition which has since published approximately 100 press releases.

Dr. Epstein's public policy activities include his roles as the lead expert witness involved in the banning of DDT in 1969 and consultant to the U.S. Senate Committee on Public Works. He has drafted Congressional legislation, is frequently invited to give Congressional testimony, and holds membership in key federal agency advisory committees including the Environmental Protection Agency, the Health Effects Advisory Committee, and the 1973 Department of Labor Advisory Committee on Regulating Occupational Carcinogens. From 1974 to 1993, he was the nation's lead expert in criminal litigation against over 30 petrochemical industries.

He is the leading international expert on the dangers of the genetically engineered bovine growth hormone (rBGH), used for increasing milk production, and of sex hormones used for fattening cattle in feedlots, on which he consulted for the European Commission and presented testimony to the EU Parliament in May 1997. In December 1998 he presented draft "Legislative Proposals for Reserving the Cancer Epidemic" to the Swedish Parliament. In March 2006 he presented an analysis of "The Role of Socially Responsible Corporations in Winning the Losing Cancer War" at the United Nations in New York.

Dr. Epstein's honors include the 1969 Society of Toxicology Achievement Award; the 1977 National Conservancy Award of the National Wildlife Federation; the 1981 Yale University Henry Kaiser Award; the 1989 Environmental Justice Award; the 1990 Rachel Carson Legacy Award, for "Significantly Advancing Medical Research in Toxic Chemicals and Bringing His Knowledge Forcefully to World Attention"; the 1993 University of Tasmania Richard Jones Memorial Award Lecture; the 1998 Right Livelihood Award (the Alternative Nobel Prize) for International Contributions to Cancer Prevention and for his leadership role in warning of the dangers of genetically engineered milk; the 1999 Bioneers Award; the 2000 Humanitarian Award from the National Silver Haired Congress; the 2000 Project Censored Award; the 2005 Albert Schweitzer Golden Grand Medal for Humanitarianism, for International Contributions to Cancer Prevention; and the 2007 Dragonfly Award from the non-profit Beyond Pesticides. In 2003 he was also named an Honorary Member of the World Innovation Foundation.

Dr. Epstein has extensive media experience, with numerous appearances on major national TV networks including *60 Minutes, Face the Nation, Meet the Press, McNeil/Lehrer NewsHour, Donahue, Good Morning America,* the *Today* show, and documentaries including the 2004 prize-winning *The Corporation.* He has also made frequent appearances on Canadian, European, Australian, and Japanese TV.

Randall Fitzgerald has been an investigative newspaper and magazine reporter and book author for thirty-seven years. He has written investigative features for *Reader's Digest, The Washington Post,* and *The Wall Street Journal.*

His most recent book is *The Hundred Year Lie: How Food And Medicine Are Destroying Your Health,* published in hardcover in 2006 by Penguin/Dutton and in paperback in 2007 by Plume.